THE SPANISH PLAYS OF NEOCLASSICAL ENGLAND

Books by John Loftis

As author:
Steele at Drury Lane
Comedy and Society from Congreve to Fielding
The Politics of Drama in Augustan England
The Spanish Plays of Neoclassical England

As editor:
Richard Steele, *The Theatre*
The Works of John Dryden, vol. 9 (with V. A. Dearing)
Nathaniel Lee, *Lucius Junius Brutus*

As general editor:
The Regents Restoration Drama Series
(twenty-nine volumes)

THE SPANISH PLAYS OF NEOCLASSICAL ENGLAND

BY JOHN LOFTIS

NEW HAVEN AND LONDON
YALE UNIVERSITY PRESS, 1973

Library of Congress catalog card number: 73-77158
International standard book number: 0-300-01301-9

Designed by Sally Sullivan
and set in Baskerville type.
Printed in the United States of America by
Vail-Ballou Press, Inc., Binghamton, N.Y.

Published in Great Britain, Europe, and Africa by
Yale University Press, Ltd., London.
Distributed in Latin America by Kaiman & Polon,
Inc., New York City; in Australasia and Southeast
Asia by John Wiley & Sons Australasia Pty. Ltd.,
Sydney; in India by UBS Publishers' Distributors Pvt.,
Ltd., Delhi; in Japan by John Weatherhill, Inc., Tokyo.

This book is dedicated to A.N.L.,
who shared the travels that made it possible

CONTENTS

PREFACE

Among the advantages Englishmen have over Americans is an inherited esteem for the literature of Spain. Even though this esteem has never been unqualified, it is of long duration and is broadly based. For reasons that may have something to do with the proximity of the United States to the Latin American countries, Americans have found it difficult to evaluate Spanish literature justly. Even William Prescott was not immune to the national prejudice. Forced by the weakness of his eyes to give up the study of German, he turned to Spanish, assuming that it was easier to learn, but not without misgivings: "I doubt whether there are many valuable things," he wrote, "that the key of knowledge will unlock in that language!" [1] He was soon disabused, as were other American writers before and after him. Yet the national prejudice he articulated has persisted. Prescott's doubts are not unlike those of many modern American students of English literature.

This book is about a specialized subject in dramatic history, but even so it may help to dispel the notion that Spanish has only marginal importance for the study of English literature. In their parallel developments, the English and Spanish dramas have more in common than either has with any other of the national dramas of Europe. The evolution of Renaissance drama from an earlier religious drama is much alike in the two countries. Yet in Shakespeare's time, so far as we can determine, dramatists knew little about the plays that Lope de Vega and his countrymen were writing. In Dryden's time, for reasons I shall explain, matters were otherwise: in the whole range of English history, there is no other period when

1. Quoted from R. A. Humphreys, *William Hickling Prescott: The Man and the Historian* (London, 1959), p. 8.

dramatists turned more frequently to Spain for sources and formal models. And because the beginnings of systematic criticism of the drama—in the work of Dryden—coincide with the Restoration, we can approach the adaptations from the Spanish with some knowledge of what contemporaries thought about them.

Even so, the task of arriving at a just estimate of the Spanish strain in Restoration drama is intimidating. I approach the subject with diffidence—and with good reason. So distinguished a historian of the drama as Allardyce Nicoll has warned of its difficulty:

> The question of Spanish influence on English drama at this time has . . . never fully been worked out, and perhaps the immensity of the task might well dissuade any student from attempting it. From what already has been done on this line, however, we know that the influence was no slight one.[2]

The task is indeed immense, and yet many, including Nicoll himself, have provided help with it.

At every stage of my work, as my notes reveal, I have drawn on the discoveries of my predecessors. My debt to several of them requires a statement here. In my conception of the "Spanish plot" and its history on the Restoration stage, I am particularly indebted to Allison Gaw, "Sir Samuel Tuke's *Adventures of Five Hours* in relation to the 'Spanish Plot' and to Dryden," in *Studies in English Drama,* University of Pennsylvania, 1917; and to David W. Maurer, "The Spanish Intrigue Play on the Restoration Stage" (Ph.D. dissertation, Ohio State University, 1935), published in part in *Ohio State University Abstracts of Doctors' Dissertations,* no. 18, pp. 275–82. I am indebted to James U. Rundle for his important discoveries of sources in Spanish drama for Restoration plays—discoveries presented in his unpublished dissertation, "The Influence of the Spanish *Comedia* on Restoration Comedy: A First Essay" (University of Cincinnati, 1947), and in published articles. I have learned much about William Wycherley's Spanish borrowings from my former student, David Stuart Rodes, who has edited *Love in a Wood* and *The Gentleman Dancing-Master* (Ph.D. dissertation, Stanford University, 1968). I have made profitable use of Floriana T. Hogan's

2. Nicoll, *A History of English Drama, 1660–1900,* vol. 1, *Restoration Drama* (Cambridge, 1955), pp. 191–92.

"Notes on Thirty-One English Plays and Their Spanish Sources," *Theatre Notebook* 6 (1967): 56–59; I have found Dr. Hogan's analysis of Aphra Behn's sources particularly helpful. I have frequently consulted Hilda U. Stubbings, *Renaissance Spain in Its Literary Relations with England and France: A Critical Bibliography* (Vanderbilt University Press, 1969), a work to which I can refer my readers who may wish a comprehensive bibliographical account of modern scholarship on the subject.

Even with the assistance provided by my twentieth-century predecessors, as well as by that most accomplished of seventeenth-century source-hunters Gerard Langbaine, I cannot feel confidence that I have not overlooked plays relevant to my subject. I do not think that I have missed many of them, but occasional discoveries of Spanish sources will no doubt continue to be made. I can merely say that I have not knowingly failed to comment on any English play, written and first performed between 1660 and 1702, that includes an important episode or a plot taken over, directly or through intermediate works, from Spanish drama. I am selective, however, in my discussion of plays derived from Spanish prose fiction and of plays that are formal imitations of what Dryden called "Spanish plots." I believe that I consider most of the important ones, but—except in the instances of substantive borrowings from Spanish drama—I have not attempted an exhaustive account. Only in the case of Dryden, the central figure in my study, do I examine the use made in the drama of Spanish (and Portuguese) history. My terminal date, that of the accession of Queen Anne, is one of expediency; the quality of drama declines in the eighteenth century and so does the English interest in the *comedia*.

If the relations of eighteenth-century drama to the comedia provide a subject of sharply reduced importance, the same cannot be said about Renaissance drama. As I have already suggested, it is difficult, in the absence of comment by informed contemporaries, to assess the Renaissance dramatists' knowledge of Spanish drama. Yet the special interest of the Renaissance phase of the subject derives, not from English importations of Spanish literary materials, but from the fact that the Spanish and English stages and the plays performed on them are in important respects strikingly similar. The parallel and largely independent development of the two national dramas deserves closer study. In this book I refer to the subject in summary fashion; in a later book I shall examine it more comprehensively.

Several literary terms, two of them Spanish words without English equivalents, require comment. *Comedia* does not mean "comedy" but rather is the inclusive term for the form of secular drama, tragedy as well as comedy, established by Lope de Vega and written by Calderón de la Barca and the other dramatists with whom I am concerned. A *gracioso* is a type of comical character of inferior social station, often a servant who provides a contrast for his master, much as Sancho Panza does for Don Quijote. The Restoration term for the English adaptations of the cape and sword plays, and the term I customarily use, is "Spanish plot." For some of the later plays that follow the Spanish conventions more loosely, I use the term (employed by the editors of *The London Stage*) "comedy of 'Spanish romance,'" without attempting, however, a firm differentiation of those plays from the "Spanish plots."

The adjective *neoclassical* has recently become controversial. Yet if, as has been demonstrated, it has limited usefulness in describing a body of literature as varied as that produced in England from 1660 to 1800, I may nevertheless feel confidence in using it in a book that from first to last makes reference to Dryden's critical essays. The organizing principle of Dryden's *Of Dramatick Poesie* is a comparison of modern drama—English, French, and to some extent Spanish—with Greek and Roman drama. Dryden and his younger contemporaries Thomas Rymer and John Dennis studied the French criticism written by such men as Pierre Corneille and René Rapin, who in turn made frequent reference to the drama and criticism of antiquity. Throughout the later seventeenth century English drama critics were preoccupied with conceptions of genre, plot construction, and didactic strategy that were assumed to have Ancient precedent. As will become apparent in this book, their attitudes toward Spanish drama were conditioned by assumptions about the nature of drama derived, or allegedly derived, from antiquity.

Brief portions of this book have previously appeared, in different form, in several publications: *The Augustan Milieu: Essays Presented to Louis A. Landa* (Clarendon Press, 1970); *Comparative*

Literature (1959); *The Emory University Quarterly* (1964); *England in the Restoration and Early Eighteenth Century* (University of California Press, 1972); *Modern Language Review* (1970); and *On Stage and Off* (Washington State University Press, 1968). I thank the editors and publishers for allowing me to incorporate my earlier work into this more comprehensive study.

I have worked on this book, in the intervals of other tasks, longer than I care to acknowledge, and in doing so I have incurred many obligations: to the Fund for the Advancement of Education for a fellowship that enabled me to spend a year at the University of California at Berkeley, studying Spanish literature; to the Fulbright Commission for a lectureship in Peru; to Stanford University for—in addition to much else—assignments to teach in France; to the John Simon Guggenheim Memorial Foundation and the Folger Shakespeare Library for fellowships that provided the time during which most of the book was written. My obligations to individuals are too numerous to list at length, but three persons require acknowledgment. Mrs. Willard F. King and David M. Vieth read earlier versions of the book with meticulous care and gave me assistance of the most useful kind. Mrs. Carol B. Pearson provided skillful research and editorial assistance at all stages of my work and also prepared the index.

J. L.

Stanford University
January, 1973

I: INTRODUCTION

Spanish Drama in Neoclassical England

AN assessment of Restoration attitudes toward Spain requires a conscious effort to avoid anachronism, to remember that in 1660 Spain was a great power. If Spain's political and economic strength had been declining, the consequences were not fully apparent, and in any event had not yet reached the arts. The *siglo del oro* was a continuing reality: Velázquez died in the year of the English Restoration; Calderón lived until 1681. Spain controlled and for a long time would continue to control Mexico, the West Indies, Florida, and most of South America, and it remained a major force in European politics. Even in the first half of the eighteenth century, England fought two wars in which the disposition of the Spanish empire was a principal issue.

The political circumstances of Restoration England have obscured the prominence of Spanish culture in the life of the nation even as they have emphasized the prominence of French culture. Charles II's mother was the daughter, sister, and aunt of kings of France, and in time his younger sister married the brother of Louis XIV. Charles himself spent long periods of his young manhood in France. He could write and speak French correctly, and he knew French literature well, far better than he knew Spanish literature. Yet he spent most of four years in the Spanish Netherlands and he made a trip into Spain; he could speak Spanish well enough to communicate with his Portuguese wife in the early years of their marriage; he could read Spanish; and he knew enough about the literature to recommend, on at least two occasions, that English dramatists write adaptations of Spanish plays. In his literary taste, as in much else, he was typical of the thinking part of the nation. Englishmen generally did not know Spanish as well as they knew French literature, and they may not have known it as well as they knew Italian literature; but they knew it better than most of us know it today, and better than we usually assume they did. Sale catalogs of Restoration libraries provide firm evidence that many Englishmen owned—and presumably read—Spanish books.

The chronologies of Spanish and French literatures provide one of the explanations for the strength of the interest in Spanish writers early in the Restoration. Alongside the undoubted accomplishments of the French, the English in 1660 would have encountered the work of Cervantes and Mateo Alemán in prose fiction, of Gracián and Quevedo in critical and moral writing, of Fray Luis de León and Góngora in poetry, and of Lope, Tirso, and Calderón in the drama. The next century was to shift the balance of accomplishment in the direction of the French; but at the time of the Restoration, before the French of the later seventeenth and eighteenth centuries had written, an evaluative critic unprejudiced by neoclassicism might have found reason to prefer the Spanish over them. And in no literary form would he have found the advantage of the Spanish more impressive than in drama. Their greatest dramatists had completed their best plays, whereas on the French side only Corneille had done so. Molière had begun to write comedies, but his chief successes were ahead; Racine, at the age of twenty-one, was not to produce his first tragedy for four years. English critics would find it steadily more difficult to understand and appreciate the Spanish accomplishment as literary taste came to be more strongly controlled by neoclassicism; [1] but they approached neoclassicism with some knowledge of a brilliant Spanish Renaissance literature which, like their native literature of Shakespeare's age, had been written with limited attention to neoclassical precept.

All this is clarified by the writings of John Dryden, the first major critic in England and, after Milton, the great literary figure of the later seventeenth century. It is Dryden above all who makes the Spanish strain in Restoration drama worth studying—Dryden who turned repeatedly to Spanish history for the themes of his serious plays, who used the conventions of the "Spanish plot" with the orig-

1. Thomas Rymer, John Dennis, Charles Gildon, and Lewis Theobald, among others, were all severely critical of the comedia.

inality of genius, who drew on Spanish drama, directly or through intermediate dramatic or narrative works, for at least two of his comedies, and who wrote the first important English criticism of Spanish drama. Because he wrote so extensively, and so specifically, about the principles that shaped his plays, often using references to foreign drama to elucidate his points, we may understand his attitudes toward the comedia more fully than those of any earlier English dramatist. Having Dryden's dedicatory epistles and prefaces, as well as those written by his contemporaries who followed his example in criticism, we may study the Spanish strain in the drama with confidence in our ability to reach the truth of the matter, not in all details—some of them important details—but at least in the larger patterns. Certainly we are in a far better position to study the Spanish sources and themes of Restoration drama, having contemporary discussions of the subject available, than we are to study the Spanish sources and themes of Renaissance drama, in which we must proceed almost entirely without external evidence.

Dryden and the Neoclassical Criticism of Spanish Drama

Dryden's *Of Dramatick Poesie* is an essay in comparative literature, a learned and wide-ranging attempt to evaluate English drama of the first few years after the Restoration by comparing it with Greek and Roman drama of antiquity, Spanish and English drama of the late sixteenth and early seventeenth centuries, and French drama of the mid-seventeenth century. It is an essay about dramatic theory, a speculative effort to arrive at an understanding of the nature of drama, and about its relation alike to the external world and to the world of the spectators' imaginations. The series of comparisons that comprise the essay are controlled by Dryden's desire to explicate problems confronting him as a dramatist, especially those having to do with dramatic language and with the construction of plots. Not unnaturally, the plays he had already written or was then writing determined some of the emphases and preoccupations in the essay, which shows throughout a speculative concern for first principles tempered by the experience of a very busy and successful dramatist.

If we look at his current and earlier work in drama, we can understand well enough why Dryden should give attention in the essay to Spanish and French drama. He wrote *Of Dramatick Poesie* in its original form, it would appear, during 1665 and 1666, while he was at his father-in-law's estate at Charlton in Wiltshire, where with his wife he had taken refuge from the plague.[2] At about the same time he wrote *Secret Love,* his first tragicomedy with two separate plots, and hence the prominence in the essay of considerations of tragicomedy, notably discussions of the rapid alternation of scenes with contrasting emotional impact. He revised the essay and published it in 1668, the year in which his *An Evening's Love; Or, The Mock Astrologer* was acted, a play based in some measure on Calderón's *El astrólogo fingido.*[3]

Looking back to the beginning of his dramatic career, we find other plays with components from Spanish literature, though it is invariably difficult to assess the nature of his Spanish borrowings. His second play, *The Rival Ladies* of 1664, is Spanish in locale and characters and has a plot that approximates a conventional one of the comedia. Whatever the immediate source of the plot, it derives ultimately from Cervantes's novel *Las dos doncellas.*[4] His third play, *The Indian Queen,* a collaborative effort with Sir Robert Howard, has the complex background common to the heroic play, in which the French romances are conspicuous; [5] and yet the Peruvian setting and Incan exoticism are reminiscent of the conquistadores' own narratives of their adventures. So also his unaided *The Indian Emperour,* which much more than the earlier play draws on the historical accounts of the Spaniards, and indeed presents in telescoped form a dramatic version of Cortes's conquest of Mexico.[6] This much is certain. Dryden may also owe a more specific debt for the play to Calderón's *El príncipe constante,* to which *The Indian Emperour* bears a resemblance in several episodes and situations.[7] For *Secret*

2. For the chronology of his literary activities from 1664 to 1667 see Edward Niles Hooker, H. T. Swedenberg, Jr., et al., eds., *The Works of John Dryden* (Berkeley and Los Angeles, 1956–), 1 : 260 (hereafter cited as Dryden, *Works*).

3. Dryden's sources for *An Evening's Love* are complex, and it is not certain that he borrowed directly from Calderón rather than merely through French intermediaries. In his preface to the play he implies that he had read *El astrólogo fingido.* See below, pp. 107–13.

4. Dryden, *Works,* 8 : 265–67.

5. Ibid., pp. 284–92.

6. Dryden, *Works,* 9 : 306–14.

7. N. D. Shergold and Peter Ure, "Dryden and Calderón: A New Spanish Source for *The Indian Emperour,*" *Modern Language Review* 61 (1966) : 369–83.

Love the sources and the more obvious literary relationships are French, not Spanish; [8] and yet the tragicomical form of the play has more in common with the comedia than with the neoclassical plays of the French.

Dryden's critical remarks imply that he had considered the dramatic theory embodied in the comedia, as when he writes in his preface to *Albion and Albanius* (1685) in defense of that opera's three-act structure: "For even Aristotle himself is contented to say simply, that in all actions there is a beginning, a middle, and an end; after which model all the Spanish plays are built." [9] Yet notwithstanding the prominence of Spanish themes in his plays, the tone of Dryden's references to Spanish drama, in *Of Dramatick Poesie* and elsewhere in his writings, is ambivalent or depreciatory. He frequently criticizes the Spaniards for violation of neoclassical rules, as he does late in his life in his preface to *A Parallel betwixt Painting and Poetry* (1695), where he warns others "not to make new rules of the drama, as Lopez de Vega has attempted unsuccessfully to do, but to be content to follow our masters, who understood Nature better than we." [10] He had made a similar point more fully in *The Grounds of Criticism in Tragedy* (1679):

> As the action ought to be one, it ought, as such, to have order in it; that is, to have a natural beginning, a middle, and an end. A natural beginning, says Aristotle, is that which could not necessarily have been placed after another thing; and so of the rest. This consideration will arraign all plays after the new model of Spanish plots, where accident is heaped upon accident, and that which is first might as reasonably be last; an inconvenience not to be remedied, but by making one accident naturally produce another, otherwise it is a farce and not a play.[11]

This may reflect the greater rigidity of Dryden's neoclassicism in the years after Thomas Rymer had written. Yet even his spokesman Neander in *Of Dramatick Poesie* (1668) is critical of the "irregularity" of Spanish plots, praising the French for improving them in

8. Dryden, *Works,* 9 : 334–44.
9. *Essays of John Dryden,* ed. W. P. Ker (Oxford, 1926), 1 : 279 (hereafter cited as *Essays*).
10. Ibid., 2 : 139.
11. Ibid., 1 : 208–09.

their adaptations of the comedia. In discussions of rhyme in drama he several times alludes to the Spanish precedent, and on one occasion at least, in his letter to Sir Robert Howard prefixed to *Annus Mirabilis* (1667), he implies that he had looked closely at the versification of the Spanish plays. This would mean that he had studied the comedia in the original language, and there is every reason to believe that he had indeed done so.[12]

The argument that Dryden made use of Calderón's *El príncipe constante* in writing *The Indian Emperour* is of central importance to an assessment of Dryden's knowledge of Spanish drama.[13] He wrote the play early in his career, presumably during the winter of 1664–65, and when it was produced in the spring of 1665 it had a success beyond that of any of his previous plays. So far as we know, Calderón's play had not been translated into either English or French by 1665; if Dryden used it he must have read it in the original Spanish, in one of the several editions of Calderón's *Primera parte*.[14] To assume that Dryden made use of *El príncipe constante* is also to assume that even before he wrote *Of Dramatick Poesie* he had studied intensively one of Calderón's masterpieces in the original language—in fact, had studied it in a volume containing a number of Calderón's best plays. There is nothing impossible in the assumption: Dryden could read Spanish, and in at least two other plays, *An Evening's Love* and *The Assignation*,[15] he seems to have borrowed from Calderón. Nevertheless, I am not convinced that in *The Indian Emperour* he did so,[16] partly because of the difficulty of

12. Several of Dryden's contemporaries accused him of plagiarizing Spanish authors: cf. the introductory epistle in the anonymous *The Medal of John Bayes* (1682); Gerard Langbaine, *An Account of the English Dramatick Poets* (Oxford, 1691), pp. 149, 158; Samuel Wesley, *An Epistle to a Friend concerning Poetry* (London, 1700), p. 18. Their charge seems to have been well founded factually if not in the interpretation they placed on it.

Dryden implies that he could read Spanish when, in his Epistle to the Reader prefixed to *The Hind and the Panther*, he identifies the Spanish original from which an English treatise had been translated: *The Works of John Dryden*, ed. Sir Walter Scott and George Saintsbury (Edinburgh, 1882–93), 10 : 114–15; cf. also ibid., 17 : 253–54 n.

13. Cf. Shergold and Ure, "Dryden and Calderón."

14. On the publication of Calderón's plays see Edward M. Wilson, "The Two Editions of Calderón's *Primera Parte* of 1640," *The Library*, 5th ser., 14 (1959) : 175–91; and Shergold and Ure, "Dryden and Calderón."

15. Cf. James Urvin Rundle, "The Source of Dryden's 'Comic Plot' in *The Assignation*," *Modern Philology* 45 (1947) :104–11.

16. Cf. Dryden, *Works*, 9 : 306–07. See below, pp. 181–88.

reconciling what he said about that dramatist in *Of Dramatick Poesie* (which he wrote in first draft soon after finishing the play) with a close knowledge of *El príncipe constante.*

His several references in the essay to Calderón and the Spanish drama suggest that his conception of the comedia, at that time at least, was largely bounded by the form of intrigue comedy then best known in England from Sir Samuel Tuke's *The Adventures of Five Hours,* an adaptation of *Los empeños de seis horas* (probably by Antonio Coello, but then thought to be by Calderón).[17] It is scarcely necessary to add that this conception is inadequate to the variety and profundity of Spanish drama. Of the four interlocutors in *Of Dramatick Poesie,* it is Neander whose opinions coincide most closely with the opinions then held by Dryden, and making all allowances for the tentative and conversational nature of the essay, we must think of Neander's criticism of the comedia as in some measure representing a judgment by Dryden. The following would seem to be the crucial passage:

> But of late years Molière, the younger Corneille, Quinault, and some others, have been imitating afar off the quick turns and graces of the English stage. They have mixed their serious plays with mirth, like our tragi-comedies, since the death of Cardinal Richelieu; which Lisideius and many others not observing, have commended that in them for a virtue which they themselves no longer practice. Most of their new plays are, like some of ours, derived from the Spanish novels. There is scarce one of them without a veil, and a trusty Diego, who drolls much after the rate of the *Adventures.* But their humours, if I may grace them with that name, are so thin-sown, that never above one of them comes up in any play. . . .
>
> I grant the French have performed what was possible on the ground-work of the Spanish plays; what was pleasant before, they have made regular: but there is not above one good play to be writ on all those plots; they are too much alike to please often; which we need not the experience of our own stage to justify. As for their new way of mingling mirth with serious

17. Allison Gaw, "Sir Samuel Tuke's *Adventures of Five Hours* in Relation to the 'Spanish Plot' and to John Dryden," in *Studies in English Drama,* 1st ser., ed. Allison Gaw (University of Pennsylvania, 1917), p. 23.

plot, I do not, with Lisideius, condemn the thing, though I cannot approve their manner of doing it.[18]

Although this sounds as though Dryden had studied the comedia appreciatively, it would nevertheless suggest that he shared the common Restoration notion of "Spanish plots" as plays of love intrigue and sword play; and indeed nothing in *Of Dramatick Poesie,* spoken by Neander or anyone else, suggests that he had reached a more comprehensive estimate of the Spanish achievement in drama.

How much did Dryden know about the comedia, we may reasonably ask. The most important—and the most subtle—evidence turns on the use he made of it in his own plays (above all, his possible use of Calderón in *The Indian Emperour*), and this we must consider at length below. But his remarks in his critical essays warrant the conclusion that he failed to perceive the magnificence of the Spanish artistic achievement, although he had studied Spanish drama in a comparatist's spirit of examining alternative approaches to the perennial problems of dramatic form, and had studied it, at least in his earlier years, with a mind not fully convinced of the rightness of French neoclassical formalism. Dryden's criticism and dramatic practice alike prove that he had no doubt of Corneille's greatness.[19] The stature of Calderón—it would seem to me, the equal of Corneille's—receives no just critical acknowledgment from Dryden, whatever the facts about the sources of *The Indian Emperour.* His failing is, of course, explicable with reference to the assumptions of the age in which he lived. To chide him for not writing a just appreciation of Calderón—and Lope and other Spanish dramatists—is to criticize him for not possessing a literary discernment shown by no other Englishman of the seventeenth century.

If he failed to give the dramatists their due, he seems to have given the Spanish critics rather more than theirs. "Dryden has assured me," Lord Bolingbroke told Joseph Spence many years after Dry-

18. *Essays,* 1 : 68–69. In 1665 Thomas Sprat had written of the French dramatists "that the greatest part of their most excellent pieces have been taken from the Spaniard": *Observations on Monsieur de Sorbier's Voyage into England* (London, 1665), pp. 247–48.

19. Pierre Legouis, "Corneille and Dryden as Dramatic Critics," in *Seventeenth Century Studies Presented to Sir Herbert Grierson* (Oxford, 1938), pp. 269–91; Frank Livingstone Huntley, *On Dryden's "Essay of Dramatic Poesy"* (Ann Arbor, Mich., 1951), pp. 6–8; John M. Aden, "Dryden, Corneille, and the *Essay of Dramatic Poesy,*" *Review of English Studies,* n.s., 6 (1955) : 147–56.

den's death, "that he got more from the Spanish critics alone than from the Italian and French and all other critics put together." [20] Presumably Dryden had in mind Lope's *Arte nuevo de hazer comedias en este tiempo,* to which he apparently refers in the preface to *A Parallel betwixt Painting and Poetry,* in a passage already quoted. In Lope's verse epistle he would have found an expression of restiveness with the dogmas of neoclassicism more intense than his own, even though Lope, like Dryden, was neoclassical in many assumptions.[21] Neander in *Of Dramatick Poesie* quotes Corneille's remark: " 'Tis easy for speculative persons to judge severely; but if they would produce to public view ten or twelve pieces of this nature, they would perhaps give more latitude to the rules than I have done, when, by experience, they had known how much we are bound up and constrained by them, and how many beauties of the stage they banished from it." [22] Corneille's remark is in the spirit of Lope's essay, a successful dramatist's pragmatic appeal to theatrical experience; and indeed Lope says much the same thing at greater length.[23] All this is consonant with one of the strains of Dryden's essay: a neoclassicism tempered by an appeal to experience in the theater.

Lope published his verse epistle, the most systematic exposition of his theory of drama, in 1609. The poem is conversationally organized and argued, and it includes few perceptions that cannot be traced to earlier critics; yet it is important because it articulates the critical theory of the dramatist who more than any other shaped the dramatic form of the comedia. In overt statement Lope is deferential to the neoclassicists; he accepts many of their precepts and is apologetic about his departures from others, using the prudential defense that as a professional dramatist he had to please his audiences. But the tone of the essay undercuts the modesty of its explicit argument (and it has been well suggested that Lope in oral presentation might have accentuated his irony by facial gestures),[24] with the result that

20. Joseph Spence, *Observations, Anecdotes, and Characters of Books and Men,* ed. James M. Osborn (Oxford, 1966), 1 : 317. For discussion of the background for this remark, see Huntley, *"Essay of Dramatic Poesy,"* pp. 3–6.

21. Duncan Moir, "Spanish Dramatic Theory and Practice," in *Classical Drama and its Influence,* ed., M. J. Anderson (New York, 1965), p. 196.

22. *Essays,* 1 : 75–76.

23. In Henry John Chaytor, ed., *Dramatic Theory in Spain* (Cambridge, 1925), p. 16.

24. Otis H. Green, *Spain and the Western Tradition* (Madison, Wisc., 1963–66), 3 : 274.

his note of apology can scarcely be taken seriously. He was writing from a position of acknowledged eminence as Spain's leading dramatist, and, as Tirso de Molina later suggested, his deferential tone is perhaps to be attributed to a tactful modesty rather than to conviction.[25]

Lope's conception of the comedia as embracing characters and situations divided by the neoclassicists between tragedy and comedy would seem to be relevant to Dryden's critical thought. As already noted, Dryden alludes in *Of Dramatick Poesie* to the comedia's mixed nature. It is a complex dramatic form of great variety, sometimes taking the form of comedy and sometimes that of tragedy, and generalizations about it are difficult; but it consistently avoids the rigid distinctions of character, situation, and emotion considered appropriate to the separate genres by the more severe neoclassicists. The comedia differs in form from English tragicomedy—and even from Shakespearian drama with its frequent intermingling of characters and episodes of differing emotional impact—but it embodies some similar critical assumptions.

The tragic and the comic should be mixed, writes Lope, who refers to his experience in the theater as well as to the conditions of human life. Lope does not have in mind, however, a two-plot drama such as the form of tragicomedy praised by Neander, but drama with interwoven plot lines.[26] That Dryden did not accept Lope's argument on this point we may be sure from the example provided by his two-plot tragicomedies as well as from his remarks in *Of Dramatick Poesie*. More than Lope, Dryden was influenced by neoclassical conceptions of decorum and, paradoxically as it may seem to us, found in the double plot of tragicomedy a means of avoiding unseemly groupings of characters, while yet attaining pleasing contrasts and diversity.[27] On this, as on most other topics, Dryden is more systematic than Lope, and a more severe neoclassicist; but he may well have welcomed Lope's support against such English critics as he represents fictionally in *Of Dramatick Poesie* in the character of Lisideius.

Did Dryden, in his tribute to the Spanish critics, have others than

25. *Los cigarrales de Toledo*, in Chaytor, *Dramatic Theory*, p. 63.
26. *Arte nuevo*, in Chaytor, *Dramatic Theory*, p. 21.
27. Frank Harper Moore, *The Nobler Pleasure* (Chapel Hill, N. C., 1963), pp. 43–45; Dryden, *Works*, 9 : 334–36.

Lope in mind? Perhaps not. His essays do not include references to others by name or passages that can easily be traced to works other than the *Arte nuevo*.[28] Spain had not, before Dryden wrote, produced critical work of sophistication comparable to his own.[29] (Nor for that matter had England; we recall Samuel Johnson's denomination of him as the father of English criticism.)[30] Other critics than Lope had anticipated Dryden's pragmatic appeal to theatrical effectiveness in opposition to neoclassical theory, and they had, more specifically, anticipated his reservations about the unities and some of his arguments in praise of tragicomedy. But such opinions were commonplace in the criticism of the Renaissance, and I would guess that Dryden at most gained from the Spaniards reinforcement of opinions that he already held.

W. P. Ker believed that Tirso de Molina's *Los cigarrales de Toledo* might have provided suggestions for *Of Dramatick Poesie*,[31] and the weight of Ker's learning compels us to consider the possibility. *Los cigarrales,* a miscellany of prose and drama published in 1624, includes a conversation piece in which gentlemen who have seen a performance of Tirso's own *El vergonzoso en palacio* discuss the comedia with reference to the drama of antiquity. Tirso establishes an antithesis between a traditionalist, who criticizes the moderns for departing from the rules of the ancients, and a defender of Lope and his followers—an antithesis similar to that between Dryden's Crites and Neander.

Tirso's defense of the moderns is more emphatic than Dryden's, and it is not so fully qualified by the suspension of judgment which in *Of Dramatick Poesie* results from the vigorous presentation of divergent opinion. Dryden's Neander has the final and strongest ar-

28. It is suggestive of the limited knowledge in England of Spanish criticism that Gerard Langbaine, in the preface to *A New Catalogue of English Plays* (London, 1688), mentions Lope de Vega alone among the Spaniards in a list of foreign dramatic critics.

29. For accounts of dramatic criticism in Renaissance Spain, see Alfred Morel-Fatio, "Les Défenseurs de la comedia," *Bulletin Hispanique* 4 (1902) : 30–62; and Moir, "Spanish Dramatic Theory and Practice," in *Classical Drama and its Influence*. Chaytor, *Dramatic Theory,* and Federico Sánchez Escribano and Alberto Porqueras Mayo, eds., *Preceptiva dramática española del renacimiento y el barroco* (Madrid, 1965), provide valuable selections of the critical texts. E. C. Riley, *Cervantes's Theory of the Novel* (Oxford, 1962), includes much that is relevant to the comedia, even though it is primarily concerned with prose fiction.

30. "Dryden," *Lives of the English Poets,* ed. G. Birkbeck Hill (Oxford, 1905), 1 : 410.

31. *Essays,* 1 : xxxv–xxxvi.

gument, to be sure, but he does not rout the opposition so completely as does Tirso's spokesman for the moderns, nor is his praise of Shakespeare and other English dramatists so free of neoclassical bias as is Tirso's spokesman's praise of Lope. Neander's admiration for Shakespeare is extravagant enough, but it is limited by a statement of his faults; and furthermore Neander isolates for extended praise Ben Jonson's *The Silent Woman,* a comedy that is neoclassical in form and spirit. On the other hand, Tirso's modern praises Lope as possessing sufficient authority to establish new rules for drama.[32] If less eloquent than Dryden's praise of Shakespeare as "the man who of all modern, and perhaps ancient poets, had the largest and most comprehensive soul," [33] his praise of Lope is nevertheless bolder in its theoretical implications.

Despite the similarities between his own and Tirso's arguments and their common use of the dialogue structure, I see no reason to assume that Dryden had read the earlier work. The dialogue structure was as old as Plato and Cicero, and Tirso's literary opinions were common property.[34] Tirso, as I have said, was less systematic a neoclassicist than Dryden. In texture their arguments rarely resemble one another. The resemblance is most apparent in their separate defenses of tragicomedy, and yet even on this subject there are significant differences, Dryden thinking of the form as having a double plot, and Tirso as incorporating in a single plot elements traditional to both comedy and tragedy. The strongest objection to Dryden's indebtedness is perhaps the simplest: the defense of the *nueva comedia* in *Los cigarrales* in comparison with *Of Dramatick Poesie* is casual and slight, having none of the comprehensiveness or logical and aesthetic rigor of Dryden's essay, which Samuel Johnson justly considered "the first regular and valuable treatise [in English] on the art of writing." [35]

At the time he wrote *Of Dramatick Poesie,* Dryden had reason enough for interest in Lope, his criticism, and Spanish drama—in particular for an interest in the contrast between the busy and complex plots of the Spaniards and the simpler and more neatly ordered plots of the French. This contrast, and a parallel to it in English

32. In Chaytor, *Dramatic Theory,* pp. 62–63.
33. *Of Dramatick Poesie* (London, 1668), in *Essays,* 1 : 79.
34. Cf. Chaytor, and Morel-Fatio, "Les Défenseurs de la comedia," passim.
35. "Dryden," *Lives of the Poets,* 1 : 411. Cf. Morel-Fatio.

drama (for there is an implied comparison of the Spanish to Renaissance English drama and the French to Restoration drama), provides a major theme in the essay. Which is preferable, Dryden asks through his interlocutors, a drama with a strong narrative line, with excitement, suspense, and bustle; or a quieter drama, largely dispensing with these qualities, which has in compensation emotional intensity and extended analysis of the characters' minds?

Lisideius presents the case for the French:

> Another thing in which the French differ from us and from the Spaniards, is, that they do not embarrass, or cumber themselves with too much plot; they only represent so much of a story as will constitute one whole and great action sufficient for a play; we, who undertake more, do but multiply adventures; which, not being produced from one another, as effects from causes, but barely following, constitute many actions in the drama, and consequently make it many plays.
>
> But by pursuing close one argument, which is not cloyed with many turns, the French have gained more liberty for verse, in which they write; they have leisure to dwell on a subject which deserves it; and to represent the passions (which we have acknowledged to be the poet's work), without being hurried from one thing to another, as we are in the plays of Calderon, which we have seen lately upon our theatres, under the name of Spanish plots.[36]

From the nature of Lisideius's criticism of Spanish plots and praise of the French, his endorsement of the unities follows as a logical correlative. Here, indeed, may be found a rationale for the unities of French drama more convincing to the modern mind than the argument on grounds of versimilitude; the simplicity of action and restricted time-scheme and locale of, say, *Cinna, Horace,* and *Polyeucte* provide aids to the depiction of passions and, conversely, barriers against the dispersal of the spectators' interest in a complex action. The pace of French classical drama, the time-scheme in which

36. *Essays,* 1 : 59–60. In 1665 Sir Robert Howard had written in a similar vein about the comedia: *"The* Spanish *Plays pretend to more* [than the Italian], *but indeed are not much, being nothing but so many Novels put into Acts and Scenes, without the least attempt or design of making the Reader more concern'd than a well-told Tale might do":* Epistle "To the Reader," *Four New Plays* (London, 1665).

dramatic time approximates elapsed time in the theater, enforces extended analysis of characters' motives for action, and makes more difficult the substitution of interest in the resolution of suspense for that in the characters' response to the problems confronting them. If not the usual grounds for the defense of the unities in the seventeenth century, this argument for them as a means to a concentration on the essentials of drama has a certain continuing force, unlike the argument exploded by Samuel Johnson that the unities of time and place aid the spectator in his imaginative acceptance of dramatic action.[37]

Although in *Of Dramatick Poesie* Dryden does not relate the debate on the unities to the contrast between Spanish and French dramas, it is steadily relevant to that contrast. Strict observance of the unities is difficult in a drama having a strong narrative line (though, as Neander notes, Tuke's *The Adventures of Five Hours,* the Spanish plot par excellence, does conform to them); [38] it leads to the French emphasis on character and motive rather than the Spanish emphasis on action.[39] And it also leads to a concentration on a single emotional state—of varying intensities to be sure—rather than on a succession of contrasting states. Thus it is incompatible with many Spanish and English plays of the Renaissance.

As with most important subjects in the essay, Dryden is ambivalent about tragicomedy, damning it in the person of Lisideius and praising it in that of Neander. "There is no theatre in the world had any thing so absurd as the English tragi-comedy;" says Lisideius, " 'tis a drama of our own invention, and the fashion of it is enough to proclaim it so; here a course of mirth, there another of sadness and passion, a third of honour, and a fourth a duel." [40] And a moment later

37. Preface to Shakespeare in *Johnson on Shakespeare,* ed. Arthur Sherbo (New Haven, 1968), in *Works,* 7 : 75–80.

38. *Essays,* 1 : 83.

39. Cf. A. A. Parker, *The Approach to the Spanish Drama of the Golden Age* (London, 1957), pp. 3–4: "The generic characteristic of the Spanish drama is, of course, the fact that it is essentially a drama of action and not of characterization. It does not set out to portray rounded and complete characters, though certain plays may do so incidentally. Some of the misunderstanding from which the Spanish drama has suffered, more particularly the plays of Calderón, has been due to the regret critics have felt at the absence of fully developed lifelike characterization. We must, however, waive any preconceptions and accept the fact that the Spanish drama works on the assumption—which after all has the authority of Aristotle behind it—that the plot and not the characters is the primary thing."

40. *Essays,* 1 : 57–58.

he explains the grounds of his objection: "The end of tragedies or serious plays, says Aristotle, is to beget admiration, compassion, or concernment; but are not mirth and compassion things incompatible? and is it not evident that the poet must of necessity destroy the former by intermingling of the latter? that is, he must ruin the sole end and object of his tragedy, to introduce somewhat that is forced in, and is not of the body of it." [41]

English drama, not Spanish, is the target of this censure; and yet the criticism has an obvious relevance to the comedia, which does intermingle "mirth and compassion"; and in the implied antitheses of the essay this arraignment of tragicomedy becomes relevant to Spanish drama. At the outset of his defense of the English, in a passage quoted above, Neander takes into account a movement in French drama in the direction of Spanish practice, showing in doing so that Dryden was a remarkably well-informed reader of recent plays; and Neander expresses what we may take to be Dryden's own opinion on the subject, since it coincides with his current dramatic practice in *Secret Love*. His defense of tragicomedy, which has been described as the first important defense of it in English,[42] glances at Spanish drama, but with a certain note of depreciation; and he praises the French for their improvements on the Spanish plots:

> As for their new way of mingling mirth with serious plot, I do not, with Lisideius, condemn the thing, though I cannot approve their manner of doing it. He tells us, we cannot so speedily recollect ourselves after a scene of great passion and concernment, as to pass to another of mirth and humour, and to enjoy it with any relish: but why should he imagine the soul of man more heavy than his senses? Does not the eye pass from an unpleasant object to a pleasant in a much shorter time than is required to this? and does not the unpleasantness of the first commend the beauty of the latter? The old rule of logic might have convinced him, that contraries, when placed near, set off each other. A continued gravity keeps the spirit too much bent; we must refresh it sometimes, as we bait in a journey, that we

41. *Essays*, 1 : 58.

42. Frank Humphrey Ristine, *English Tragicomedy, Its Origin and History* (New York, 1910), p. 169.

> may go on with greater ease. A scene of mirth, mixed with tragedy, has the same effect upon us which our music has betwixt the acts; and that we find a relief to us from the best plots and language of the stage, if the discourses have been long. I must therefore have stronger arguments, ere I am convinced that compassion and mirth in the same subject destroy each other; and in the mean time cannot but conclude, to the honour of our nation, that we have invented, increased, and perfected a more pleasant way of writing for the stage, than was ever known to the ancients or moderns of any nation, which is tragi-comedy.[43]

And thus at the same time that he defends qualities in Spanish drama that were controversial, in qualified measure taking the Spanish side against at least the earlier French practice, Dryden insists on the originality of the English invention of tragicomedy, denying its origin in any other country. This is an intelligible attitude if we distinguish between two qualities in Dryden's own tragicomedy: the double plot on the one hand, and the alternation of moods on the other. The former of these qualities was not present in Spanish drama, not at least in the manner of Dryden's plays; the latter was. Although some of the specifics of Dryden's praise of tragicomedy are irrelevant to his attitude toward the comedia, much of what he says about it is relevant, just as it is also relevant to his attitude toward the English drama of the Renaissance.

Constantly in the background of Dryden's criticism of the comedia is a comparison of it to English Renaissance drama, which also ignored the unities, had busy plots, and combined qualities of tragedy and comedy, and a differentiation of the comedia from French classical drama, which with less incident gained more intensity—either of tragic or comic emotion—and more leisure for the detailed analysis of character and motive. Spanish and French drama sometimes represent in Dryden's writings a schematic antithesis: drama of action, exciting perhaps, but diffuse; and drama of character, sometimes tedious, but orderly and at best concentrated and moving. And this antithesis is broadly analogous to his conception of the contrast between the drama "of the last age" and that of his own.

43. *Essays,* 1 : 69–70.

The Spanish Inheritance from Renaissance England

In the chronology of its development, Spanish drama has far more in common with English than with French drama. "Les Anglais," Voltaire wrote in *Lettres sur les Anglais* (1733), "avaient déjà un théâtre aussi bien que les Espagnols, quand les Français n'avaient encore que des tréteaux. Shakespeare que les Anglais prennent pour un Sophocle, florissait à peu près dans le temps de Lope de Véga: il créa le théâtre." [44] Oversimplification, but only that. So striking are the parallels in the evolutionary development of the two national dramas that a specialist in English, long familiar with the works of E. K. Chambers and G. E. Bentley, may well read N. D. Shergold's *A History of the Spanish Stage from Medieval Times Until the End of the Seventeenth Century* with a feeling that he has encountered the subject before in a different key. In Spain, as in England, Renaissance drama developed from an earlier liturgical drama, retaining an important residue from its religious origins. The three categories of theatrical performance, the religious, the popular, and the court, are broadly analogous in Spain and England, though with the difference that religious drama in Spain came to maturity later and in the work of men who were also the most able writers for the secular stage, Lope and Calderón.[45] The evolution of the stage itself is much alike in the two countries, and so is, as a corollary, theatrical tradition as expressed in habits of dramatic representation.

The timing in the development of the two dramas becomes especially important when we take account of neoclassicism as a force in drama. Unlike the French, both the Spanish and the English dramas reached maturity before neoclassical principles of dramatic construction were almost universally accepted. Lope's *Arte nuevo,* as we have seen, rejects several important critical prescriptions grounded on the practice of the ancients and asserts the dramatist's duty to please his audience by the best means available. Shakespeare left no such statement, but the example of his plays and the nature of Ben Jon-

44. Voltaire, "Letter XVII," in *Oeuvres complètes,* ed. Louis Moland (Paris, 1877–85), 22 : 148–49 (hereafter cited as Voltaire, *Oeuvres*).

45. Alexander A. Parker, "Notes on the Religious Drama in Mediæval Spain and the Origins of the 'Auto Sacramental,'" *Modern Language Review* 30 (1935) : 170–82. See also Clifford Leech, *Shakespeare's Tragedies and Other Studies in Seventeenth Century Drama* (London, 1950), p. 226.

son's criticism of them assure us that, though he presumably knew nothing about Lope, he was in fundamental agreement with him on the subject of the rules. Rapin, in a work translated by Rymer, criticized Lope for "following rather a capricious genius than nature," and his remarks can be applied to Shakespeare.[46] Certainly Boileau's formalistic criticism of Lope in his *L'Art poétique* could be extended to some of Shakespeare's plays as well:

> Un rimeur, sans péril, delà les Pyrénées,
> Sur la scène en un jour renferme des années:
> Là souvent le héros d'un spectacle grossier,
> Enfant au premier acte, est barbon au dernier
> Mais nous, que la raison à ses règles engage,
> Nous voulons qu'avec art l'action se ménage;
> Qu'en un lieu, qu'en un jour, un seul fait accompli
> Tienne jusqu'à la fin le théâtre rempli.[47]

Boileau's older contemporary Corneille, whatever his private sentiments on the matter, had to write his plays from the outset of his career with attention to the formulations of the neoclassicists. The production of *Le Cid* occasioned a celebrated controversy over his alleged violations of decorum; and through the French Academy and its patron Richelieu the power of government was brought to the support of the neoclassicists.[48] Corneille learned his lesson, and subsequently produced a series of remarkable plays in which dramatic power was reconciled with a dramatic form acceptable to the Academy. French dramatists writing later than Corneille found their most impressive models in neoclassical plays, whereas Spanish and English dramatists, writing after the first great period of their own national dramas, found it difficult, in view of the achievements of Lope and Shakespeare, to accept neoclassicism unreservedly.

The similarities in the development of Spanish and English drama, and their mutual differences from French drama, did not escape scholars and critics of the eighteenth century. Charles Gildon in 1721 complains that most of the English dramatists of the Renais-

46. Rapin, trans. Rymer, *Reflections on Aristotle's Treatise of Poesy in General,* in *The Continental Model,* ed. Scott Elledge and Donald Schier (Minneapolis, 1960), p. 292.
47. Boileau, *L'Art poétique,* song 3, ll. 39–46.
48. Paul Bénichou, *Morales du grand siècle* (Paris, 1948), pp. 83–87.

sance were as indifferent as the Spanish to the rules.[49] James Ralph in 1743 refers to the English liking for Spanish drama (presumably he means during the reign of Charles II):

> We were formerly very fond of the *Spanish* Taste, and *Spanish* Plays, and to say the Truth, they come very near our own. We need not therefore be surprized, that the Critics are very angry at their Irregularity, which is excused by some of the best *Spanish* Writers, in the same Manner that we excuse *Shakespear,* that is to say, by alledging that ordinary Writers, are bound by Rules, but that great Wits are above them.[50]

The complexity of Spanish plots and their violation of the rules, this is a commonplace of neoclassical criticism, in which the cautionary example of Elizabethan and the exemplary one of French drama are sometimes cited.

All this appears with the clarity of caricature in a letter Voltaire wrote in 1776 to the French Academy. It merits quotation at length:

> La vérité, qu'on ne peut déguiser devant vous, m'ordonne de vous avouer que ce Shakespeare, si sauvage, si bas, si effréné, et si absurde, avait des étincelles de génie. Oui, messieurs, dans ce chaos obscur, composé de meurtres et de bouffonneries, d'héroïsme et de turpitude, de discours des halles et de grands intérêts, il y a des traits naturels et frappants. C'était ainsi à peu près que la tragédie était traitée en Espagne sous Philippe II, du vivant de Shakespeare. Vous savez qu'alors l'esprit de l'Espagne dominait en Europe, et jusque dans l'Italie. Lope de Vega en est un grand exemple.
>
> Il était précisément ce que fut Shakespeare en Angleterre, un composé de grandeur et d'extravagance, quelquefois digne modèle de Corneille, quelquefois travaillant pour les petites-maisons, et s'abandonnant à la folie la plus brutale, le sachant très-bien, et l'avouant publiquement dans des vers qu'il nous a laissés, et qui sont peut-être parvenus jusqu'à vous. Ses contemporains, et encore plus ses prédécesseurs, firent de la scène espagnole un monstre qui plaisait à la populace. Ce monstre fut

49. Gildon, *The Laws of Poetry . . . Explain'd and Illustrated* (London, 1721), p. 174.

50. *Case of our Present Theatrical Disputes* (London, 1743), p. 36.

> promené sur les théâtres de Milan et de Naples. Il était impossible que cette contagion n'infectât pas l'Angleterre; elle corrompit le génie de tous ceux qui travaillèrent pour le théâtre longtemps avant Shakespeare.[51]

This is oversimplified literary history, it is fiercely partisan, and in important respects it is wrong; yet even in its prejudices and errors it illustrates the neoclassical mind.[52] Voltaire implies, of course, that Shakespeare borrowed from the Spanish dramatists, probably an error; [53] but the fact that Voltaire should think so means that he saw similarities between the Spanish and English plays, which certainly do exist, though modern scholarship assumes that they are mainly the result of parallel and independent development from the religious drama of the Middle Ages.[54]

The religious and political differences between England and Spain, reflected in the two national dramas, provide a complicating dimension in the literary relations between them. The one country was Protestant and the other Catholic, even reactionary Catholic. But these differences did not prevent English and Spanish religious poetry from sharing stylistic and thematic qualities, perhaps the result of English imitation of Spanish models (for Donne, Herbert, and Crashaw, among others, may have read Spanish), though more likely the result of a common medieval heritage and the employment of common practices of devotion.[55] P. E. Russell thus explains the matter: "It was . . . almost certainly the survival in England, as in Spain, of intellectual formulae identical with, or directly derived

51. Voltaire, *Oeuvres,* 30 : 364.

52. For discussion of Voltaire on the Spanish dramatists, see Alejandro Cioranescu, "Calderón y el teatro clásico francés," in *Estudios de literatura española y comparada* (Laguna, Canary Islands, 1954), pp. 140–47.

53. Henry Thomas, writing about "Shakespeare and Spain," uses Shakespeare's own words "Much Ado About Nothing" as an epitome of his subject, or more precisely as an account of earlier investigations of the subject: The Taylorian Lecture, 1922, in *Studies in European Literature* (Oxford, 1930).

54. Cf. Ernst Robert Curtius, *European Literature and the Latin Middle Ages,* trans. Willard R. Trask (New York, 1953), p. 268.

55. Edward M. Wilson, "Spanish and English Religious Poetry of the Seventeenth Century," *Journal of Ecclesiastical History* 9 (1958) : 38–53. See also Louis L. Martz, *The Poetry of Meditation* (New Haven, 1954), pp. 5–7. Samuel Johnson wrote in the preface to his edition of Shakespeare (1765): "The English nation, in the time of Shakespeare, was yet struggling to emerge from barbarity . . . and those who united elegance with learning, read, with great diligence, the Italian and Spanish poets." *Johnson on Shakespeare,* ed. Sherbo, in *Works,* 7 : 81–82.

from, those of western Europe in the Middle Ages which made Spanish literature intelligible to and acceptable to seventeenth-century Englishmen."[56] The similarities of texture in Spanish and English poetry lead us to a better understanding of how Catholic themes in Spanish drama can resemble themes in English drama. Much recent investigation has had as its special accomplishment the elucidation of the medieval inheritance of Elizabethan drama, that is to say, the inheritance that it shares with the Spanish. As we study the two dramas, we discover more comprehensive similarities between them than Voltaire and other eighteenth-century critics noted.

One of the most conspicuous parallels in the development of the two dramas, and one to which Voltaire alluded, is the simultaneity of and resemblance between the careers of Lope and Shakespeare. Lope was born just two years before Shakespeare, and he began to write plays in Madrid at about the time Shakespeare began to write them in London, in the late 1580s. Both men had important predecessors, and in each country permanent theaters existed when they began to write. Yet each man brought a supreme genius to bear on a drama in which distinction had previously been of a different order, and with extraordinary rapidity produced plays in a variety of forms that constitute the core of their respective national repertories.

Shakespeare and Lope are alike in their copiousness, their eclecticism in the use of sources, their inventiveness of situation and metaphor, their mastery of the resources provided by their stages, their disdain for constricting academic formulations and easy triumph over them, their joyousness and lyricism. They were popular dramatists, writing for the people at large as well as sometimes for a coterie audience. They were patriotic dramatists, who captured central themes and preoccupations of their nations, contributing to their national mythologies, to the shared beliefs that produce a national identity. They are prized both by the learned and by the ignorant. They delight us with a tale well told and surprise us with a subtle parable.

Their plays are not all of a quality. We could apply to Lope,

56. P. E. Russell, "English Seventeenth-Century Interpretations of Spanish Literature," *Atlante* 1 (1953): 77.

Dryden's summary judgment of Shakespeare: "I cannot say he is every where alike; were he so, I should do him injury to compare him with the greatest of mankind." And curiously we may apply to Lope, Dryden's bill of charges against Shakespeare: "He is many times flat, insipid; his comic wit degenerating into clenches, his serious swelling into bombast." [57] Both of them shared the Renaissance delight in word play, the pleasure of exploring a metaphor to its limits. Though we may be more tolerant than Dryden of extravagance in conceits, we can agree with him that Shakespeare—and we could add Lope—sometimes suffers from his own ingeniousness.

Lope and Shakespeare each began his career in the decade after the establishment of the first permanent theater in his capital city, and some of the resemblances between their plays derive from similarities between the theaters for which they wrote. The Theatre opened in London in 1576 followed by The Curtain in 1577; the Corral de la Cruz opened in Madrid in 1579 followed by the Corral del Príncipe in 1583.[58] In both cities the permanent theaters were structural developments from earlier improvised sites, in courtyards and in open spaces between houses; and in fundamentals they shared a common design. They were outdoor theaters, and they were of a physical nature to discourage efforts at scenic illusion and to encourage mobility of imagined action. They could not use light and darkness effectively for representational deception, and they made only limited use of stage properties. They had a discovery space at the rear of the stage,[59] and they had balconies or windows by which to represent differences in scene and elevation. They could rapidly change locale without becoming specific. The conception of place was handled casually in both countries, and insofar as it became precise it was often made so by dialogue rather than by scenic representation. Even in their audiences Lope's and Shakespeare's outdoor theaters resembled one another. Not private or coterie theaters, they had a pit for the common folk and enclosed rooms and galleries for

57. *Of Dramatick Poesie,* in *Essays,* 1 : 80.

58. N. D. Shergold, *A History of the Spanish Stage from Mediaeval Times until the End of the Seventeenth Century* (Oxford, 1967), pp. 181–82, 185–86.

59. See Richard Hosley, "The Discovery-Space in Shakespeare's Globe," *Shakespeare Survey* 12 (1959) : 34–46; L. L. Barrett, "The Inner Recess on the Public Stage in Renaissance Spain," *Research Opportunities in Renaissance Drama* 10 (1967) : 25–31.

the quality; and they accommodated the people of all ranks who attended the plays.[60]

Dramatic conventions of their countries, however, separate Shakespeare and Lope. To an English-speaking student, the most striking difference lies, perhaps, in Shakespeare's limited use of the long speech and his approximation to the rhythms of conversation within the formal pattern of blank verse,[61] in contrast to Lope's use of the long speech[62] and a polymetric structure. Shakespeare's dramatic language can perhaps be associated with his preoccupation with character;[63] Lope's, with his stronger emphasis on narrative.

So far I have been concerned with parallels in the development of Spanish and English drama, parallels that are the result of independent development from medieval drama. Voltaire was surely wrong in assuming that the similarities between the dramas of the two nations derived from extensive English imitation of the comedia. It has been a mark of good scholarship in the twentieth century to be cautious and conservative in asserting direct borrowings from the comedia in the English Renaissance. And yet there may have been isolated instances in which English dramatists turned to the Spaniards. The subject is complex and obscure in the extreme; it has not yet been investigated comprehensively. Here I can merely call atten-

60. Leslie Hotson has used records of the Spanish stage in support of his argument that the Renaissance English stage, so like its Spanish counterpart, was an amphitheater or coliseum, surrounded on all sides by the spectators. His argument is controversial. Yet he is surely justified in reminding us, as H. A. Rennert did early in this century, of the affinities between the physical stages as well as the plays produced upon them. Hotson, *Shakespeare's Wooden O* (London, 1959), pp. 70–79, 89–90, 105–15, 216–24, 233–35. See also H. A. Rennert, *The Spanish Stage in the Time of Lope de Vega* (New York, 1909), passim.

61. On the history of the "set speech" before Shakespeare, see Wolfgang Clemen, *English Tragedy before Shakespeare,* trans. T. S. Dorsch (London, 1961).

62. The later Spanish dramatists, unlike the English, retained the long set speech. Albert E. Sloman has in fact demonstrated that Calderón, in his reworkings of earlier plays, habitually lengthened the monologues: *The Dramatic Craftsmanship of Calderón* (Oxford, 1958), pp. 303–04.

63. On the English dramatists' concern with character, cf. Clifford Leech's summary remark: "in the great decade near the beginning of the seventeenth century the minds of dramatists were directed much more to the exploration of the individual personality than to the enunciation of general truths." *John Webster* (London, 1951), p. 59.

The Spaniards, on the other hand, frequently used their plots for "the enunciation of general truths," often suggested in the titles of their plays and summarized in concluding speeches.

tion to such investigation as has already been conducted and suggest some of the tentative conclusions that have been reached, conclusions that are well summarized in G. E. Bentley's *Jacobean and Caroline Stage*.

A starting point for considering this vexing and elusive subject is provided by an essay published early in this century by Rudolph Schevill, "On the Influence of Spanish Literature upon English in the Early Seventeenth Century." [64] Schevill's essay is at once a comprehensive review of previous scholarship, an original contribution, and an anticipation of the skeptical attitude toward claims for English borrowings from the Spanish that has marked the scholarship of subsequent years. Severely critical in his insistence on hard evidence, Schevill nevertheless approaches the subject with a certain diffidence, acknowledging the methodological difficulties confronting anyone who attempts an assessment of the English dramatists' debt to the Spanish. The plays of both nations are numerous, and they have rarely if ever been studied at length by persons who are specialists in both literatures.

The number of Spanish plays makes it difficult for an investigator to be confident he is not overlooking a dramatic source for an English play. If he discovers a resemblance between an English and an earlier Spanish play, he knows that the two plays may have a common source in the voluminous prose fiction of the romance literatures, or even a common source in human nature. Schevill is skeptical that Spanish was widely known in early seventeenth-century England.[65] He argues that the ideological differences between the two nations would have made a lively cultural interchange impossible—an argument that now seems of dubious validity (see above, pp. 20–21). He is most convincing perhaps in his argument from the absence of evidence. Although English dramatists of James I's reign made use of Spanish prose fiction, they did not, so far as Schevill could determine, turn to the comedia. Shirley was, he believed, the

64. *Romanische Forschungen* 20 (1905–06) : 603–34.

65. Dale B. J. Randall provides a valuable study of "Those Who Learned Spanish" in *The Golden Tapestry: A Critical Survey of Non-chivalric Spanish Fiction in English Translation (1543–1657)* (Durham, N. C., 1963), pp. 231–33. His well-documented conclusions suggest that the language was more widely known in England than Schevill implies, though perhaps not so widely known as to invalidate Schevill's argument.

earliest to do so, in *The Young Admiral* (1633) and *The Opportunity* (1634).[66]

The intensive research of the sixty-five years since Schevill wrote has added complications and qualifications to his argument,[67] but it has not changed except in detail his conclusion that before the 1630s the English dramatists made little direct use of the comedia. Certainly G. E. Bentley is reluctant to admit borrowing. Yet an apparent instance of it has been discovered in Fletcher's *The Fair Maid of the Inn,* acted at the Blackfriars in 1622, which seems to be based on *La ilustre fregona,* sometimes attributed to Lope, rather than on Cervantes's novel of the same title, which was the source of the play.[68] Such a discovery should lead us to caution against overconfident generalization. There may be a number of unidentified sources in the comedia for English plays of the first third of the century. Yet it seems unlikely that there could be enough of them to warrant our assuming that many of the dramatists knew the comedia.[69]

John Fletcher was perhaps the earliest important dramatist to make extensive use of Spanish sources—Spanish sources certainly but not, at least not for the most part, dramatic ones and not necessarily in the original language.[70] The Hispanic strain in his plays is the more significant because the Restoration dramatists knew and at times imitated them. Dryden's first "Spanish plot," *The Rival Ladies,* resembles Fletcher's *Love's Pilgrimage,* which is based on Cervantes's novel *Las dos doncellas.* Dryden himself commented, in the preface to *An Evening's Love,* on Beaumont and Fletcher's predilection for Spanish sources, writing that they had most of their plots "from Spanish novels: witness *The Chances, The Spanish*

66. The Spanish sources for these plays were discovered by A. L. Stiefel, "Die Nachahmung spanisher Komödien in England unter den ersten Stuarts," *Romanische Forschungen* 5 (1890) : 193–220; 19 (1907) : 309–35.

67. A useful guide to research on this topic is provided by Hilda U. Stubbings, *Renaissance Spain in Its Literary Relations with England and France: A Critical Bibliography* (Nashville, Tenn., 1969).

68. A. E. Sloman, "The Spanish Source of *The Fair Maid of the Inn,*" in *Hispanic Studies in Honour of I. González Llubera,* ed. Frank Pierce (Oxford, 1959), pp. 331–41.

69. Sloman, ibid., p. 331, writes that "Spanish sources have been discovered for some part at least of more than twenty plays, and parallels in Spanish literature have been drawn with the situations of nearly a dozen more." But the sources and parallels are mainly in prose fiction.

70. For a comprehensive account of the English translations of Spanish prose fiction, see Randall, *The Golden Tapestry.*

Curate, Rule a Wife and have a Wife, The Little French Lawyer, and so many others of them as compose the greatest part of their volume in folio." [71]

Hyperbole perhaps, but only that. Early in this century Felix Schelling asserted that about seventeen of the more than fifty plays attributed to Beaumont and Fletcher had been traced, in part at least, to Spanish sources; [72] and this estimate has in the interval undergone revision, up and down. Formerly it was assumed that Fletcher depended on French or English translations, but the discoveries of E. M. Wilson and Albert E. Sloman would suggest that, though he undoubtedly used translations, he was not restricted to them. In *The Chances, The Island Princess, Rule a Wife and Have a Wife,* and *The Fair Maid of the Inn,* he apparently worked directly from the Spanish.[73] His knowledge of the language seems not to have been profound, but presumably he could read it fluently enough to dispense with a translation if none was available. Both the plays he wrote alone and those in collaboration with Beaumont and others show him assimilating novelistic materials from many sources, French and English as well as Spanish, and combining and reinterpreting them, with the result that it is often meaningless to differentiate what is borrowed from what is original.

In their frequent use of Spanish prose fiction, Fletcher, Beaumont, and their collaborators combined and recombined the Spanish plots, and they felt no scruple about modifying the moral structure of the materials borrowed.[74] Like Fletcher, Massinger could apparently read Spanish, though he too used translations as well as originals,[75] and he too ignored, largely or completely, the comedia. Why, we may ask, did the dramatists, in view of their obvious liking for Spanish stories, not make more use of the comedia? Perhaps the best explanation is the simplest one: that the verse of the plays was harder to read than the prose of the novels, many of which were in any event

71. *Essays,* 1 : 146.

72. *Foreign Influences in Elizabethan Plays* (New York, 1923), p. 119.

73. Wilson, "Did John Fletcher Read Spanish?" *Philological Quarterly* 27 (1948) : 187–90; Sloman, "The Spanish Sources of *The Fair Maid of the Inn,*" in *Hispanic Studies,* ed. Pierce.

74. Edward M. Wilson, "Cervantes and English Literature of the Seventeenth Century," *Bulletin Hispanique* 50 (1948) : 27–52.

75. Cf. *The Custom of the Country,* ed. R. Warwick Bond in *The Works of Francis Beaumont and John Fletcher* (London, 1904–12), 1 : 480–81.

available in French or English translation.[76] Apart from Fletcher in *The Fair Maid of the Inn,* Shirley would seem to be the earliest dramatist who drew from the comedia—from Lope's *Don Lope de Cardona* for *The Young Admiral* and from Tirso's *El castigo del penséque* for *The Opportunity.*[77]

The accelerating tempo of interest in Spanish literature in the seventeenth century, perceptible in the reigns of James I and Charles I though not marked until after the Restoration, is partly to be explained by the increasing frequency of travel between the two countries.[78] J. W. Stoye has described the "Return of the English to Spain" in 1605, when an era of closer relations between the countries was symbolically marked by the earl of Nottingham's embassy to Valladolid, with five hundred persons in his train, to see King Philip III ratify a peace treaty that terminated a war then a generation old.[79] The embassy was conducted with pomp on both sides, and the Spanish entertained the English with the production of *autos sacramentales* in a Corpus Christi festival.[80] Nottingham soon returned home with most of his followers (some of whom wrote about what they had seen in Spain), but a permanent embassy under Sir Charles Cornwallis remained behind, first in Valladolid and after 1606 in Madrid, when it again became the capital. Here was a focus for English activity in Spain, a center for the merchants' factors scattered around the country and for the travelers who went there. Englishmen could visit Spain in comparative safety, and many of them did so.

The embassy produced a number of the early students of Spanish. It was as a member of the embassy staff that James Mabbe, the best of the Renaissance translators from Spanish, learned the language. And it was as secretary of the embassy in the first decade of the cen-

76. Cf. D. W. Maurer, "The Spanish Intrigue Play on the Restoration Stage" (Ph. D. diss., Ohio State University, 1935), p. 15.

77. Stiefel, "Die Nachahmung spanisher Komödien."

78. Edmund Malone, *Historical Account of the . . . English Stage* (Basel, 1800), prints (p. 131 n.) a record of payment to a Spanish company of actors that performed in London in 1635: "£10. paid to John Navarro for himself and the rest of the company of Spanish players, for a play presented before his Majestie, Dec. 23. 1635." Hugo Albert Rennert, *The Spanish Stage,* identifies the actor as "Juan Navarro Oliver, who, with his wife, Jerónima de Olmedo, had belonged to the company of Cristóbal de Avendaño in 1632," p. 139 n.

79. *English Travelers Abroad, 1604–1667* (London, 1952), pp. 325–90.

80. Hotson, *Shakespeare's Wooden O,* pp. 72 ff.

tury that Francis Cottington, who nearly fifty years later as Lord Cottington was an advisor of Charles II during his exile, acquired the interest in and knowledge of Spanish affairs that gave him an influential voice in Stuart politics. Other men who in time had Charles II's ear, including George Digby, second earl of Bristol, and Sir Richard Fanshawe, were connected with the embassy. Bristol was born in Madrid, the son of Sir John Digby, Cornwallis's successor as ambassador. Fanshawe, who after the Restoration was ambassador to Spain, was a member of the embassy staff in the 1630s.

Sir John Digby had the important and difficult task in 1623 of conducting the diplomatic negotiations connected with Prince Charles's courtship of the Infanta. This extravagant and romantic episode (known to students of the drama as the subject of Middleton's *A Game at Chess*) [81] took a number of cultivated Englishmen to Madrid, where some of them saw performances of Spanish plays. James Howell reported that "there are Comedians once a week come to the Palace, where, under a great Canopy, the Queen and the *Infanta* sit in the middle, our Prince and *Don Carlos* on the Queen's right hand, the King and the little Cardinal on the *Infanta's* left hand." [82] Among the two hundred Englishmen who accompanied Prince Charles in Madrid were Kenelm Digby,[83] nephew of Sir John, and Endymion Porter (the grandson of a Spanish lady), who had grown up in Spain.[84] The courtship of the Infanta came to nothing but frustration, and Prince Charles arrived home late in 1623 with anger rather than affection for the Spanish; English-Spanish diplomatic relations cooled. Yet prominent and influential Englishmen had acquired a knowledge of Spain and her literature in her golden age, when Lope was in full career and Calderón on the threshold of his. It is not implausible to think of this adventure as an important preliminary to the enlargement of English knowledge of Spanish literature.

The Spanish king was represented in England at this time by

81. For discussion of this highly allusive play and its historical background, see the edition prepared by R. C. Bald (London, 1929).

82. *Epistolæ Ho-elianæ: Familiar Letters,* ed. J. Jacobs (London, 1890–92), 1 : 169. Quoted from Shergold, *History of the Spanish Stage,* p. 266.

83. R. T. Petersson, *Sir Kenelm Digby; The Ornament of England, 1603–1665* (London, 1956), pp. 57–58.

84. Gervas Huxley, *Endymion Porter* (London, 1959), pp. 81–84.

Count Gondomar, ambassador from 1613,[85] who was a principal proponent of the Spanish match for Prince Charles. He was a powerful advocate for Spanish interests at James's Court, and to a small circle he brought knowledge and understanding of Spanish affairs and culture; [86] but to most Englishmen Gondomar was a symbol of Catholic duplicity and a threat to Protestantism. The frustration of his plans for an Anglo-Spanish alliance brought rejoicing. Throughout the first half of the century a fondness for Spain seems indeed to have been restricted to the courtiers. The House of Commons, representative of the nation at large, was consistently hostile.[87]

Soon after his accession in 1625 Charles chose a French wife, and with Henrietta Maria came the dynastic tie so important in mid-seventeenth-century history. Thereafter the usual ally of the Stuarts was France rather than Spain (though, as we shall see, the exigencies of Charles II's exile forced for a time a reversal of this pattern). England was intermittently at war with Spain during the reign of Charles I, the Interregnum, and the reign of Charles II. Yet the hostilities and the ever-changing pattern of alliances were compatible with a developing English interest in Spanish literature.

85. On Gondomar, see C. H. Carter, "Gondomar: Ambassador to James I," *Historical Journal* 7 (1964) : 189–208; and D. H. Willson, *King James VI and I* (London, 1956), pp. 362–65.

86. Cf. Randall, *The Golden Tapestry*, p. 16. Randall provides "A Sketch of Some Means of Learning Spanish," available to the English at this time (pp. 14–18).

87. Cf. C. V. Wedgwood, *The King's War* (London, 1959), p. 28: "in the summer of 1641, when so much urgent Parliamentary business was agitated at home, the Spaniards had landed in force on Providence Island in the Caribbean and utterly wiped out the English settlement there. John Pym was Secretary of the Providence Company; the principal shareholders were all leaders of the opposition to the King—the Earls of Warwick and Holland, Lord Saye, Lord Brooke and John Hampden. . . . The association between these men in politics and in commerce was not fortuitous: the same Protestant-Puritan sea-roving tradition that made them attack the King for oppressing the Puritans at home and favouring Spain abroad, had impelled them to this private venture against the Spaniard in the Caribbean."

II: THE ROYAL EXILE AND RESTORATION SPANISH STUDIES

CRITICS from Dryden to the present have recognized that Restoration drama is a courtier's drama, directed toward the taste and interests of the king and to some extent written by personal friends of the king in response to his suggestions. Charles II was a man of large intellectual capacity who was knowledgeable about and interested in drama; apart from Elizabeth I, he is the outstanding example among modern English sovereigns of a discriminating taste influencing the direction of dramatic history. Dryden's assertion, in *An Essay on the Dramatick Poetry of the Last Age,* that the alleged improvement in drama was attributable to him was oversimplification and overstatement; yet, given the assumptions of Restoration critical theory, it had some basis in fact. Dryden associates changes in drama with an improvement in conversation, and he calls attention to the king's travels during his exile as a determinant of his personal culture:

> Now, if they ask me, whence it is that our conversation is so much refined? I must freely, and without flattery, ascribe it to the court; and, in it, particularly to the King, whose example gives a law to it. His own misfortunes, and the nation's, afforded him an opportunity, which is rarely allowed to sovereign princes, I mean of travelling, and being conversant in the most polished courts of Europe; and, thereby of cultivating a spirit which was formed by nature to receive the impressions of a gallant and generous education. At his return, he found a nation lost as much in barbarism as in rebellion; and, as the excellency of his

> nature forgave the one, so the excellency of his manners reformed the other.[1]

The rhetoric of the royalist poet laureate includes a substantial residue of truth. Dryden's statement about the king's enforced exposure to foreign courts, and thus to foreign languages and literatures, is fact for which there is abundant documentation. And it counts for much in Restoration drama that he had acquired a knowledge of Spanish and an acquaintance with Spanish literature.

For Charles and many of his courtiers, the exile, however discouraging and even demoralizing, had some of the aspects of a grand tour. Several of the courtiers were poets or scholars—Thomas Hobbes (for a time the king's tutor), Thomas Killigrew, Sir William Davenant, the Marquis of Newcastle, among others—and they beguiled their tedium and frustration with travel, study, and writing. They were on the Continent during the minority of Louis XIV, a time of extraordinary achievement in French letters. The consequences for Restoration literature of their admiration for French dramatists and critics have long been emphasized, perhaps overemphasized. The courtiers remained Englishmen, and when they could go home again they looked to their native Renaissance literature as well as to what they had learned on the Continent; but they had become cosmopolitan in their knowledge and tastes as they had not been before. And an ingredient in their cosmopolitan culture was Spanish drama.

The most detailed assessment of Charles's intellectual attainments at the time of the Restoration comes from Samuel Tuke, known to us as the author of one of the early adaptations from Spanish drama, *The Adventures of Five Hours.* Tuke had been in exile with Charles and wrote from long acquaintance with him:

> He understand[s] *Spanish,* and *Italian;* speaks and writes *French* correctly; He is well vers'd in ancient and modern *History,* has read divers of the choicest peeces of the *Politicks,* hath studied some useful parts of the *Mathematicks,* as *Fortification,* and the knowledg of the *Globe;* but his chief delight is in *Navigation,* to which his *Genius* doth so incline him, that . . . I have heard

1. *Essays of John Dryden,* ed. W. P. Ker, 1 : 176.

> many expert Seamen . . . speak of it with delight and wonder; in *General,* here is a true friend to *Literature,* and to *Learned Men.*[2]

Tuke's emphasis would seem to be right: Charles knew languages, and he was interested in and generous to men of letters, but imaginative literature did not represent his deepest intellectual concerns, which were rather directed to speculative and applied science, including the science of navigation.[3] Bishop Burnet, writing much later, emphasized Charles's technical and scientific interests:

> He has knowledge in many things, chiefly in all naval affairs; even in the architecture of ships he judges as critically as any of the trade can do, and knows the smallest things belonging to it; he understands much natural philosophy and is a good chymist; he knows many mechanical things and the inferior parts of the mathematics, but not the demonstrative; he is very little conversant in books, and, young and old, he could never apply himself to literature.[4]

This would seem to be overstatement. Charles had studied languages systematically, and he often engaged in literary conversation. Clarendon, writing about his residence at Cologne in 1654, describes his daily routine:

> and he, being well refreshed with the divertisements he had enjoyed, betook himself with great cheerfulness to compose his mind to his fortune, and with a marvellous contentedness prescribed so many hours in the day to his retirement in his closet, which he employed in reading and studying both the Italian and French languages.[5]

Clarendon does not mention Spanish, but that Charles had some knowledge of it is corroborated, among many other ways, by the

2. Samuel Tuke, *A Character of Charles the Second* (London, 1660), p. 6.

3. On Charles II's literary accomplishments and influence, see Godfrey Davies, *Essays on the Later Stuarts* (San Marino, Calif., 1958), pp. 20–24; and James Sutherland, "The Impact of Charles II on Restoration Literature," in *Restoration and Eighteenth-Century Literature,* ed. Carroll Camden (Chicago, 1963), pp. 251–63.

4. Burnet, "The King's Character," in *A Supplement to Burnet's History of My Own Times* (from unpublished manuscripts), ed. H. C. Foxcroft (Oxford, 1902), p. 49.

5. Edward Hyde, Earl of Clarendon, *History of the Rebellion and Civil Wars in England,* ed. W. Dunn Macray (Oxford, 1888), 14 : 115.

fact that he used it to communicate with his Portuguese wife at the beginning of their marriage (see below, pp. 52–53).

A man of Charles's inquiring mind and enforced leisure could not have passed so many years in France and the Netherlands—in Holland in the earlier part of the exile and in Flanders (Belgium) in the later—without gaining some knowledge of Spanish drama. Though we know that he learned enough about it to recommend Spanish plays to two English dramatists, Sir Samuel Tuke and John Crowne, after the Restoration, we cannot say with precision, in the absence of references to plays he read or saw performed, how much he learned and through what channels. Yet a brief consideration of drama in mid-seventeenth-century France and the Netherlands will suggest that he had opportunity enough to gain a knowledge of the comedia in French and Dutch adaptations, if not in the original language as well.

The height of the Spanish vogue in French drama coincides with the years of the royal exile. The foremost historian of the French stage, H. C. Lancaster, points to occasional French borrowings from the comedia in the years before 1639, by Rotrou and Pierre Corneille (for *Le Cid*); but, he explains, these instances were few, nor were there many more instances in tragedy and tragicomedy in the years thereafter. The Spanish vogue, he writes,

> *was limited to comedy,* and began, not with Rotrou or with Corneille, but with d'Ouville. He had lived in Spain and knew the works, not only of the older dramatists, Lope and Tirso, but those of his contemporaries, Calderon and Montalván. His work as an *hispanisant* began about 1639, with his adaptation of Calderon in *l'Esprit folet.* Now he followed it up with four comedies, two from Calderon, one from Montalván, and one from Lope. He was supported by Corneille, who adapted Alarcón and Lope; by Brosse, who also imitated Calderon; and by Scarron, who turned to Tirso and introduced two more Spanish dramatists to the French public, Rojas and Solórzano. Half of the twenty comedies [1640–48] are adaptations of Spanish plays and we shall see that the fashion thus created continued in comedy during and after the Fronde.[6]

6. Henry Carrington Lancaster, *A History of French Dramatic Literature in the Seventeenth Century,* pt. 2 (Baltimore, 1932), 2 : 428.

Here is detailed and even statistical support for Dryden's reference in *Of Dramatick Poesie* to the recent French use of Spanish plays: "what was pleasant before," Neander says, "they have made regular." [7] It would seem to be more than coincidence that, as I shall explain later, the Restoration Englishmen writing adaptations of Spanish plays, like the Frenchmen before them, largely confined themselves to comedy. The fact that the Spanish vogue in France reached its height in the 1640s and 1650s meant that many Englishmen who were to be influential after the Restoration, and presumably the king himself, saw French adaptations of the comedia in Paris. Sir William Davenant, to cite a probable example, based his last play, *The Man's the Master* (1668), on Paul Scarron's *Jodelet ou le maître valet* (1645), which is in turn based on Rojas Zorrilla's *Donde hay agravios no hay celos.*

Charles spent the earlier years of his exile, both before and after the execution of his father, in Holland and in France, the latter country a natural refuge for him in view of his mother's nationality and residence there. The French royal house as well as the English had its troubles in those years of the Fronde, and Cardinal Mazarin, had he been so inclined, could have done little to aid Charles in regaining his kingdom. Neglect had changed to hostility toward him and friendship with his enemies by 1654, and in July of that year Charles thought it expedient to leave France and take up residence in Cologne. Negotiations between Mazarin and Cromwell came to a culmination in the Treaty of Westminster, signed in the autumn of 1655, a secret article of which provided that the French should expel Charles and his followers (with specified exceptions, including his mother) from their borders.[8] With prospects of French support and even hospitality cut off from him, Charles was forced to look elsewhere, and he found his most promising prospects with the Spanish, with whom the French had long been at war. Writing to Ormonde on March 19, 1656, as his negotiations for a treaty with King Philip approached a climax, he asked in his bantering way that he be sent a Spanish New Testament, because he expected to have "much need of that language." [9]

7. *Essays,* 1 : 69.
8. F. J. Routledge, *England and the Treaty of the Pyrenees* (Liverpool, 1953), p. 5.
9. *Calendar of the Clarendon State Papers Preserved in the Bodleian Library, 1655–1657,* ed. W. Dunn Macray (Oxford, 1876), 3 : 102.

Even before the Civil Wars, as already noted, the Stuart kings and their ministers had shown more liking for Spain than had Englishmen in general. "King James I and even more King Charles I," C. V. Wedgwood writes, "had pursued a pro-Spanish policy abroad, linked by King Charles with a pro-Catholic policy at home." [10] The Puritans, of course, had opposed the policy. Even on the eve of the first Civil War, Miss Wedgwood explains, Puritan trading ventures in the West Indies had led to armed conflict with Spain.[11] Cromwell's anti-Spanish policy of the 1650s had its origin in English resentment of Spain's exclusion of her trading ships from Spanish America: hostility to Spain was then and would long remain typical of London's business community, which supported Cromwell. Charles II's approach to Philip IV thus had political logic and historical precedent, however irrelevant it proved to be in accomplishing the Restoration.

In the wake of attacks by Cromwell's fleet on their West Indian possessions, the Spanish were receptive to overtures from Charles, who, his exile notwithstanding, could aid them against the English and French. He provided a point of focus for discontent in England; he could give malcontents within and without the British Isles a rationale and justification for making trouble. He had a considerable following among the exiled English, Scots, and Irish, and at his subsequent bidding some two thousand troops joined him. He commanded a certain amount of loyalty in the English fleet, and he held out the hope to the Spaniards that he could bring ships to them, as he could certainly lend a show of legitimacy to the activities of English privateers.[12] Reasons enough for Spain, facing the combined might of France and England, to enter into negotiations with him.

After preliminaries conducted from Cologne, Charles went to Brussels, capital of the Spanish Netherlands, and in March 1656 held conferences with the Spanish ministers Don Alonzo de Cárdenas and the Conde de Fuensaldaña, which resulted the following month in a secret treaty with Philip IV.[13] For his part, Charles, among other

10. C. V. Wedgwood, *Poetry and Politics under the Stuarts* (Cambridge, 1960), p. 154.

11. *The King's War, 1641–1647* (London, 1958), p. 28.

12. Eva Scott, *The Travels of the King: Charles II in Germany and Flanders, 1654–1660* (London, 1907), pp. 175–76.

13. Routledge, *Treaty of the Pyrenees*, pp. 6–7; Scott, *Travels of the King*, p. 195.

promises to be fulfilled when he should be restored, agreed that his loyal English, Scottish, and Irish troops should serve against France. In return Philip granted Charles and his followers permission to reside in the Netherlands; he promised financial support; and he promised, in the event that a port of debarkation could be secured in England, naval and military support for a royalist invasion. Charles was to spend the next four years mainly in the Spanish Netherlands, trying to induce the Spaniards to keep the promises made in this treaty. If all this did not contribute to his restoration, it did have the interesting consequence that he, his brothers, his courtiers, and some two thousand of his loyal officers and soldiers spent most of four years in a country in which Spanish was widely spoken.[14]

"In the sixteenth and seventeenth centuries," a Dutch scholar wrote in 1822, "the Spanish language was almost as common in our fatherland as French is today." [15] After the Peace of Münster in 1648, he adds, study of Spanish declined somewhat. Yet this would not necessarily have happened in the Southern Netherlands (modern Belgium), which unlike the independent Northern Provinces remained under Spanish domination. In any event, the court language of Brussels during the royal exile was Spanish.

Spanish rule in the Netherlands had already lasted a long time when Charles went there, and it had left its mark on letters: among other ways, in translations and imitations of the Spanish dramatists.[16] Vondel's biographer complained that his plays came in time to be less regarded than they deserved because other plays, primarily translations from the Spanish, came to be preferred to them.[17] Many of Lope's plays, in translation, were presented in the seventeenth century, understandably more than those of any other Spanish dramatist, but the plays of others including Calderón were presented too. His

14. Cf. C. H. Firth, "Royalist and Cromwellian Armies in Flanders, 1657–1662," *Transactions of the Royal Historical Society*, n.s. 17 (1903) : 67–119. See also P. H. Hardacre, "The Royalists in Exile During the Puritan Revolution, 1642–1660," *Huntington Library Quarterly* 16 (1953) : 353–70.

15. P. G. Witsen Geysbeek, *Biographisch Anthologisch en Critisch Woordenboek* (Amsterdam, 1822), 3 : 475 (my translation).

16. J. A. Van Praag, *Le Comedia espagnole aux Pays-Bas au XVII*e *et XVIII*e *siècle* (Amsterdam, 1922), passim.

17. Geeraerdt Brandt, *Het Leven van Joost van den Vondel*, ed. P. Leendertz, Jr. (The Hague, 1932), p. 54.

La vida es sueño, for example, appeared in both Brussels and Amsterdam in the middle of the seventeenth century as *Het Leven is Maer Droom.*[18]

Although in the absence of more precise records, we cannot speak confidently of Englishmen learning their Spanish drama—in either Dutch or Spanish—in the Netherlands, we may nevertheless assume that the prominence of that drama on the stages of Amsterdam and Brussels would not have escaped some of the many who were in the Netherlands during the exile. There is no reason to assume that Charles and his courtiers would have taken special interest in the Dutch translations and imitations of the comedia that appeared in large numbers both in print and on the stage; and yet they could scarcely have avoided hearing conversational allusions to Lope, Calderón, and other Spanish dramatists. Companies of Spanish players toured the Low Countries,[19] and it is not impossible that Charles saw them perform.

However futile his alliance with Philip IV may have been in producing political results, it had the interesting consequence for Charles of providing the occasion for a trip into Spain late in 1659. The episode, well documented in royalist correspondence, reveals Charles behaving in his characteristic manner, enjoying himself without inhibition, seeming to his older and more sober advisors Hyde and Ormonde unpredictable and even irresponsible, and yet finally conducting the important diplomatic conversations with tact and shrewd good sense.

The trip into Spain came when the Treaty of the Pyrenees ended the long war between France and Spain and opened the hope to Charles that those two countries might cooperate in accomplishing his restoration. Although the conference was held at Fuenterrabía, near San Sebastián and thus near the French border, Charles took a leisurely and circuitous route to it through much of northern Spain.[20] His ministers indeed complained that he conducted himself on the journey as though he were traveling more for pleasure than on important diplomatic business, and their fears were heightened

18. J. Te Winkel, "De Invloed der Spaansche Letterkunde op de Nederlandsche in Seventiende Eeuw," *Tijdschrift voor Nederlandsch Taal- en Letterkunde,* 1 (Leiden, 1881) : 59–114, 99–100.

19. Cf. Rennert, *The Spanish Stage in the Time of Lope de Vega,* p. 339.

20. Scott, *Travels of the King,* pp. 419–20.

by the fact that Charles had chosen as one of his companions the earl of Bristol, who was notoriously unstable.

Yet Charles's indirect route to the conference was partly a result of faulty intelligence. In consequence of a false report that the chief Spanish minister, Don Luis de Haro, had already left the conference to return to Madrid, Charles went first to Zaragoza, for reasons that are not altogether clear, perhaps planning to go on to Madrid, perhaps intending to intercept Don Luis de Haro on his homeward journey.[21] From Zaragoza the king wrote to Hyde in high spirits: "But I am very much deceived in the travelling in Spaine, for, by all reports, I did expect ill cheere and worse lying, and hitherto we have found both the beds and espetially the meate, very goode." [22] Only the dust troubled him, Charles wrote, no rain having fallen on that side of the Pyrenees for four months. He passed through Pamplona, and late in October 1659 finally reached Fuenterrabía, where he was received with appropriate dignity by Don Luis de Haro. "The King entered on Tuesday night, and stays in Don Luis's own quarter[s]," Sir Henry Bennet wrote to Hyde. "He is served by him as if he were the King of Spain." [23] In his subsequent diplomatic conversations with Don Luis, in which Bennet acted as interpreter, Charles acquitted himself well. "Now it is time I should tell you something of my master," wrote one of his attendants, O'Neil, to Hyde early in November; "Let me assure you that he hath behaved himself here as if he had been bred more years in Spaine than in France, and that the French that come to see him return very well satisfied with their receptions. We see what hee can do, when he is resolved." [24] But by this time Charles's endeavors were unnecessary: events in England were already in train to accomplish for him the restoration he had so long and vainly sought through diplomacy.

It would be difficult to overestimate the importance of the exile in determining the Spanish vogue in Restoration drama, a vogue that was a royalist phenomenon, a dramatic expression of tastes the Cava-

21. Cf. *A Collection of Original Letters . . . Found among the Duke of Ormonde's Papers,* ed. Thomas Carte (London, 1739), 2 : 251 (Letter of Hyde, November 1, 1659, to Ormonde).

22. Clarendon MSS, quoted in Scott, *Travels of the King,* p. 421.

23. *Calendar of the Clarendon State Papers, 1657–1660,* ed. F. J. Routledge (Oxford, 1932), 4 : 418.

24. Clarendon MSS, quoted in Scott, *Travels of the King,* p. 423.

liers acquired or had reinforced in their wanderings in Spain, the Low Countries, and France. Charles was surrounded by men who knew Spanish or had spent extended periods in Spain: his brother James, who served several years in the Spanish army and could speak the language; Sir Edward Hyde (Clarendon), who spent most of 1649 and all of 1650 in Madrid seeking Spanish support for the king, and who read Spanish literature in the original language; Lord Cottington, Hyde's associate in his Spanish embassy, an old man during the exile who had spent much of his youth in Spain before the Civil Wars and who, after he and Hyde were dismissed by Philip IV in January 1651, received permission from the Spanish king to remain in Valladolid; Sir Henry Bennet (Arlington), who was Charles's resident in Spain from 1657 until the Restoration and who learned the language and acquired an admiration for the formality of Spanish manners; George Digby, earl of Bristol, who as already noted had been born in Madrid during his father's embassy there; Sir Richard Fanshawe, famous for his translation of Camões's *Os Lusiadas* during the Interregnum, who after the Restoration was Charles's ambassador to Portugal and later to Spain.

The alliance with Philip IV brought the duke of York into a prolonged association with the Spanish. Before the Treaty of Westminster, he had served in the French army. Deprived of his command by the turn of events, he accepted a commission from the Spanish king, serving with distinction from 1657 until the Restoration as the field commander of Charles's loyal troops in Flanders, in the army led by Don Juan of Austria and the Marquis of Caracena. The duke's memoirs provide both a narrative of military action and a critical assessment of Spanish customs, especially as they inhibited rapid decision on the battlefield. Repeatedly he expresses irritation with Spanish formality, preserved even in the face of the enemy. "Don Juan observed on Campaign," he notes in his account of the events of 1657, "the same forms of gravity and reserve as if he had been in Brussels. He was everywhere equally difficult of access."[25] On one occasion, an opportunity for a surprise attack on an enemy convoy was lost because the two Spanish leaders could not be disturbed during their siestas.[26]

25. *The Memoirs of James II: His Campaigns as Duke of York, 1652–1660,* trans. and ed. A. Lytton Sells (Bloomington, Ind., 1962), pp. 234–35.
26. Ibid., pp. 231–32.

The memoirs reveal the duke in frequent association with the Spanish leaders, and they further imply that he could converse with them in Spanish. In discussing the relationships between the two generals, for example, he quotes and explains the force of a phrase (*No será de servicio del Rey*), by means of which the marquis of Caracena could veto a decision made by his superior, Don Juan.[27] For the duke, the climax of his Spanish service came in June 1658, when at the battle of the Dunes near Dunkirk he conducted himself courageously, gaining reputation for personal valor even in an engagement that ended in defeat.[28] A dozen years later when Dryden, in the dedicatory epistle to *The Conquest of Granada,* eulogistically reviewed the duke's military career, he cited the battle of the Dunes. "Where you charged in person," Dryden wrote, "you were a conqueror." And there seems to have been some factual basis for Dryden's hyperbole.[29] At any rate, the Spanish found him a useful ally, and after the war was over Philip IV made him a flattering offer "of commanding in Spain against Portugal, and also to be their High Admiral with the Title of Principe de la Mare," an offer which, his brother having acquiesced, he would have accepted had the Restoration not intervened.[30]

The duke of York knew the Spanish in war; Sir Edward Hyde knew them in diplomacy. He and Lord Cottington went to Madrid in 1649, and thus before the Treaty of Westminster, to seek Spanish support for Charles II not long after the execution of his father. The mission proved to be futile, and Hyde's account of it is a record of frustration. Yet it is also a record of a man of scholarly instincts observing customs, ceremonials, and entertainments, learning the language, and collecting books. His detailed and appreciative account, in *The History of the Rebellion,* of popular entertainments in Madrid—mock tournaments called "masquerades" staged by squadrons of horsemen, and bullfights, so popular that official discouragement could not stop them [31]—suggests a relish for exotic Spanish customs.

27. Ibid., p. 256.

28. His memoirs provide a detailed account of the engagement: ibid., pp. 255–75.

29. An anonymous "character" of the duke published just after the Restoration provides a circumstantial narrative of his conduct in the battle: *A Short View of the Life and Actions of the Most Illustrious James Duke of York* (London, 1660), pp. 21–22. The duke was accompanied in this engagement by his younger brother, the duke of Gloucester.

30. *Memoirs of James II,* trans. and ed. Sells, p. 291.

31. Clarendon, *History of the Rebellion,* 12 : 89, 90.

Hyde's careful relation of the sequence of events in a bullfight, conducted on horseback unless the horse was killed, can be read as a gloss on the account of a bullfight in the opening scene of *The Conquest of Granada,* in which the differences from modern custom would otherwise cause ambiguity.

In his autobiography Hyde, writing in the third person, alluded to his study of Spanish: "The Chancellor betook himself to the learning their language, by reading their Books; of which He made a good Collection." [32] As we shall see, he again alluded to his Spanish studies and book collecting while in Madrid in a letter he later wrote to Sir Richard Fanshawe (see below, p. 49). A record of his library survives in the form of a sale catalog, though because of its late date, 1756, it cannot be used with the confidence that all the books had been in his possession: [33] a few could not have been, for they were published after his death. Still, the nucleus of the library presumably represents his holdings, and some at least of the many Spanish books were probably acquired during the embassy in Madrid.

As we would expect of the great historian of the English Civil Wars, Spanish works of history are prominent in the catalog: among others, Mariana's *Historia general de España,* in an edition published in Madrid in 1649. There are works of imaginative literature as well: "Comedias de Fr. Zorrilla," "Comedias de Agust. Moreto y Cabana," "Poesias de Quevedo," "Araucana de Don Alonso de Erzilla y Zuniga," and "Novelas Exemplares de Miguel de Servantes," to name only a few. The sale catalog is the record of a scholar's library, including dictionaries and works of reference on many subjects, and yet it suggests the strength of the Hispanic interests of this very busy man, most important of the counselors of the young King Charles II.

Hyde's fellow ambassador in Madrid, Lord Cottington, was not a scholar, as Hyde himself explains in *The History of the Rebellion,* but he had spent much of his life in Spain and consequently knew

32. *The Life of Edward Earl of Clarendon . . . Containing, An Account of His Life from His Birth to the Restoration in 1660 . . . .* "Printed from his original Manuscripts, given to the University of Oxford by the Heirs of the late Earl of Clarendon" (Dublin, 1759), 1 : 234.

33. *Bibliotheca Clarendoniana: A Catalogue of the Valuable and Curious Library of . . . Edward Earl of Clarendon . . . . Containing a Great Number of Rare and Choice Books in the Latin, English, French, Italian and Spanish Languages* (London, 1756).

Spanish very well indeed. "It is true he was illiterate as to the grammar of any language," Hyde wrote, "or the principles of any science; but by his perfectly understanding the Spanish, (which he spake as a Spaniard,) French, and Italian languages, and having read very much in all, he could not be said [to be] ignorant in any part of learning, divinity only excepted." [34] Some thirty years older than his fellow ambassador, Cottington had first gone to Spain early in the reign of James I as a member of the embassy led by Sir Charles Cornwallis, and, in Hyde's words, "he remained there for the space of eleven or twelve years in the condition of secretary or agent, without ever returning into England in all that time." [35] His subsequent rise in England to several of the principal offices of state and to a peerage was owing in part to his usefulness as an expert on Spanish affairs. He was consulted in advance about Prince Charles's trip to Spain in 1623 and, his opposition to the undertaking notwithstanding, he was sent along with the prince. He was in Spain as ambassador in 1629. Having served in the first Civil War, he lived abroad following the defeat of 1646; and in 1648, at the request of the queen, he joined the Prince of Wales, who, as king, sent him with Hyde to Madrid the following year.

Cottington's devotion to Spain, like that of many others in the seventeenth century, was a corollary of his religion. Twice in the earlier years of his life, fearing death occasioned by grave illnesses, he had declared himself a Catholic only to recant when he recovered his health. He clearly wished to be a Catholic but found the religion an impediment in his political career. Old and tired when the Spanish king dismissed him and Hyde, he sought and received permission to remain in Spain, though not in Madrid. Hyde provides an illuminating glimpse of the two ambassadors not long before the end of their embassy: "when they both visited the *Presidente de la hazienda,* who carried them into his library, whilst the other [Hyde] was casting his eyes upon some books, (it being the best private library in Madrid,) the lord Cottington told the President that he was himself a Catholic but that his companion was an obstinate heretic." [36] Reconciliation with the church proved to be difficult for Cottington

34. *History of the Rebellion,* 13 : 30.
35. Ibid.
36. Ibid., p. 27.

because of his earlier apostasy, but it was accomplished in time through the mediation of a papal nuncio, and he went to Valladolid, to the same house in which he had lived many years earlier when that city was the capital, and there passed the remaining year of his life.[37]

Catholicism, too, seems to have been a factor in the liking for Spain of Sir Henry Bennet, though with him proof of a conversion is lacking.[38] In Flanders a trusted servant and friend of Charles II (and as the king's correspondence reveals, a cribbage partner), he was sent in 1658 as agent to Madrid, where he learned the language rapidly enough to serve the following year as Charles's interpreter in the diplomatic conversations at Fuenterrabía. He was reported to have been seen in a Catholic church with Charles, and Restoration gossip had it that it was fear of the consequences of having been seen there which made him slow to return to England after the Restoration.[39] In any event, his residence in Spain was formative in his career and even, it would seem, in his personal demeanor. He acquired a knowledge of foreign affairs and diplomacy which assisted his rapid rise in Restoration politics to a secretaryship of state and a peerage, and an admiration for Spanish manners and habits of dress that made him vulnerable to ridicule in Restoration society. *The Memoirs of the Life of Count de Grammont* includes a withering description of him:

> His first *Negotiations* were during the *Pyrenean* Treaty, where, tho' he had no Success, as to his Master's Interests, he did not altogether lose his Time; for he had perfectly learn'd and retain'd in his Behaviour the *serious Air* and *Gravity* of the *Spaniards,* and imitated pretty well their *slowness* in Business. He had a *Scar* cross the Nose, which was cover'd by a long *Patch,* or rather a little Plaister. . . . this remarkable *Patch* so fitted his *mysterious Looks,* that it seem'd to add to his *Gravity* and *Sufficienty.*[40]

37. Ibid., p. 29.

38. The *Dictionary of National Biography* (hereafter cited as *DNB*), s.v. Henry Bennet, Earl of Arlington.

39. Violet Barbour, *Henry Bennet, Earl of Arlington, Secretary of State to Charles II* (Washington, D. C., 1914), p. 43 n.

40. *Memoirs of the Life of Count de Grammont,* trans. Abel Boyer (London, 1714), pp. 139–40.

All this makes him sound like an equivalent in high life of the affected Hispanophiles of Restoration comedy, characters such as Wycherley's Mr. James Formal, alias Don Diego, of *The Gentleman Dancing-Master.*

Among those in exile with Charles who knew Spanish were two men of letters, the earl of Bristol, the king's companion on his trip to Spain and after the Restoration the author of three adaptations of plays by Calderón, and Sir Richard Fanshawe, the translator of Camões. Their careers will repay attention in our effort to understand the English interest in Spanish literature.

The impression of Bristol that emerges from Clarendon's *History* is unflattering in the extreme.[41] Clarendon had strong personal reasons for disliking Bristol, but he seems nevertheless to have conveyed a just impression of this erratic if brilliant man. Bristol was self-confident to the point of egotism; he was unpredictable and even irresponsible in behavior; and yet he was eloquent, witty, and gay, an agreeable companion—at least for a time. He had an extraordinary capacity for winning the friendship of persons in high places. Before the treaty of 1655 between France and England, he enjoyed the patronage of Cardinal Mazarin. After the change in national alliances, he joined Charles; and soon, as Clarendon explains, he charmed the Spanish leader in Flanders, Don Juan of Austria:

> He was present when don Juan eat, and when he used to discourse of all things at large, and most willingly of scholastical points, if his confessor or other learned person was present. The earl always interposed in those discourses, with an admirable acuteness, which, besides his exactness in the Spanish language, made his parts wondered at by every body.[42]

And he charmed Charles himself, who apparently took him along to Spain in 1659 as much for his social qualities as for his knowledge of Spanish. Charles's tardiness in reaching the conference was attributed to Bristol's influence. "The Marquis of Caracena speaks sharply," Secretary Nicholas wrote to Lord Ormonde about Charles's delay, "and, being told that the Earl of Bristol was with him in his

41. Cf. *History of the Rebellion,* 4 : 127–28.
42. Ibid., 15 : 79.

dilatory proceedings on his journey, he shrugged his shoulders."[43] At the conference Bristol won the favor of the chief Spanish minister, Don Luis de Haro, who on the termination of the meeting took him back to Madrid and secured him employment in the service of the king of Spain. Bristol remained in Madrid until after the Restoration.[44]

A man as knowledgeable and as talkative as Bristol, with access to the highest circles of society, would have provided in the early years of the Restoration an important source of information about Spanish drama. He was a major figure in introducing the comedia into England. He may have assisted Sir Samuel Tuke in writing *The Adventures of Five Hours;*[45] he wrote *Elvira; Or, The Worst Not Always True,* an adaptation of Calderón's *No siempre lo peor es cierto,* and two other adaptations of Calderón's plays that have not survived (though according to John Downes they were performed): *'Tis Better than It Was,* presumably from *Mejor está que estaba,* and *Worse and Worse,* presumably from *Peor está que estaba.*[46]

The sale catalog of his library provides a glimpse of a collection of Spanish books in Restoration England. The catalog cannot be used with complete confidence that all the books had belonged to Bristol since, as the bookseller explains in his preface, it also lists the books of another person: "This Catalogue consists principally of the Library of the Right Honourable *George* late Earl of *Bristol,* a great part of which were the Curiosities collected by the learned Sr. *Kenelme Digby.* Together with the Library of another Learned person."[47] We could wish that the bookseller had been more specific about which books had belonged to the other "learned person." Yet in view of Bristol's known interests, it seems safe to assume that most of the Spanish books were his. At any rate, in the Spanish section of the catalog the following volumes of plays are listed:

43. Flanders Papers, Oct. 29–Nov. 8, 1659, quoted in Scott, *Travels of the King,* p. 422.

44. H. M. Digby, *Sir Kenelm Digby and George Digby, Earl of Bristol* (London, 1912), p. 263.

45. Cf. Samuel Pepys, *Diary,* July 20, 1664; John Downes, *Roscius Anglicanus* (London, 1708), p. 22.

46. *Roscius Anglicanus,* p. 26. Pepys saw *Worse and Worse* on July 29, 1664.

47. *Bibliotheca Digbeiana, sive Catalogus Librorum In variis Linguis Editorum, Quos post Kenelmum Digbeium eruditiss. Virum possedit Illustrissimus Georgius Comes Bristol: nuper defunctus* (London, 1680). Cf. Alfred W. Pollard, "English Book-Sales, 1676–1680," *Bibliographica,* 1 (1895), 373–84.

Comedias Varias, escritas por Varios Autores, 13 vol. Madrid, 1652
Comedias Famosas de Don Francisco de Roxas, 2 vol. Madrid, 1640
Las Comedias del Dotor Juan Perez de Montalvan, 2 vol. Valencia 1652
Las Comedias Famosas de Don Pedro Calderon, 3 vol. Madrid
Las Comedias de D. Augustin Moreto y Cabana. Madrid 1654
Las Comedias de Don Juan de Matos Fragoso. Madrid 1658
Autos Sacramentales, y Varias Poesias, por Varios Autores. ib. 1655
Comedias Varias, por Varios Autores, 2 vol. (some MSS.)
Comedias Humanas, y Divinas, y Rimas Morales, por Diego Muxet. 1624.[48]

The three volumes of Calderón's plays are significant, and so are the thirteen volumes of "Comedias Varias," which may well have included some of Lope's and Tirso's works. This must have been a handsome collection of plays, since in the auction it brought the high price of forty-six shillings. The fact that so many of the volumes were published in the 1650s would suggest that Bristol acquired them when he was in Madrid in 1659 and 1660. At the least, this sale catalog reveals that editions of the comedia were available in Restoration England (and other catalogs, now in the British Museum, provide ample corroborating evidence).[49]

Judging from his library, his adaptations from Calderón, and his qualities of mind and personality, we may assume that Bristol, who had resided in Madrid for long periods of time, was a propagandist for and a popularizer of the comedia at Charles's court. If he lacked the ability to write good plays himself, he still would have aroused the interest of more able men in Spanish drama.

The Cavalier poet, translator, and diplomatist Sir Richard Fanshawe, despite his greater prominence in literary history than Bristol's, does not have the same kind of direct relationship to Restoration drama because he was primarily a translator of nondramatic poetry. Yet he translated one Spanish play (which did not reach the Restoration stage, though it was read by Hyde, among others), and he brought a knowledge of Spanish literature to the circle around the king that would have had an impact on the drama. Abundant infor-

48. *Bibliotheca Digbeiana,* p. 67.
49. On the nature of the catalogs, see Pollard, "English Book-Sales."

mation about him survives, not only because of his political prominence but also because his wife wrote her memoirs; and in the records of his career we may observe the devotion to the literature of Spain—and in his case of Portugal as well—that led to the Spanish plays of the Restoration.

In his youth, following study at Cambridge and in the Inner Temple, he went to France in 1632 and after some months on to Spain, where except for occasional visits to England he remained until 1638, spending the last three years there in the service of the English ambassador, Lord Aston. His wife's account of this period abroad, so decisive for his later career, merits attention, though with the caution that she is not accurate as to duration of time:

> After a year's stay in Paris he travelled to Madrid in Spain, there to learn that language. At the same time for that purpose went the late Earl of Carnarvon and my Lord of Bedford, and Lord John Berkeley, and several other gentlemen. Afterwards having spent seven years abroad, he returned to London, and gave so good an account of his travels, that he was, about the year 163[5], made Secretary of the Embassy, when my Lord Aston went Ambassador. . . . Upon the return of the Ambassador, your father [i.e., Fanshawe] was left resident until Sir Arthur Hopton went Ambassador, and then he came home, about the year 1637 or 1638.[50]

He spent only about two years in Spain—not six as his wife here implies—before his three years in diplomatic service, but the total of five years was enough to give him a knowledge of the language and the country sufficient for him to be regarded as an expert on Spain for the rest of his life.

Lady Fanshawe's passing reference to other Englishmen—noblemen and gentlemen—who went to Madrid in the 1630s to learn the language reminds us that there was an intensification of English literary interest in Spain in the final decade before the Civil Wars. The young men to whom Lady Fanshawe alludes were in Spain at the end of Lope's career and at the high tide of Calderón's, a glorious time in the history of drama, and it may be assumed that some of

50. *Memoirs of Ann Lady Fanshawe*, ed. H. C. Fanshawe (London, 1907), pp. 28–29 (hereafter cited as Lady Fanshawe, *Memoirs*).

them took back to England reports of what they had seen on the Spanish stage.

The foreign travel Fanshawe voluntarily undertook in the 1630s was followed in the 1640s by travel forced upon him by war. His wife's memoirs record in moving detail the adventures and privations of the years after their marriage in 1644, years that included service in the train of the Prince of Wales and that for Fanshawe reached an unhappy climax at the side of Charles II (as the prince had then become) at the Battle of Worcester. Following the defeat, Fanshawe was captured by the parliamentary forces. After some two months in prison at Whitehall, he obtained a release on bail through his wife's intercession with Cromwell, and during the years of the Protectorate he lived quietly in England. These years of enforced leisure led him back to his studies. In March 1653 he took up residence on the estate of his friend the earl of Strafford (son of the executed minister) at Tankersley in Yorkshire, and there he devoted himself assiduously to translation. In somewhat over a year he translated the Portuguese national epic, Camões's *Os Lusiadas;* a Spanish play, Antonio Hurtado de Mendoza's *Querer por solo querer;* and a Spanish dramatic entertainment by the same author, *Fiestas de Aranjuez.* The first of these was by far the most considerable task.

Fanshawe's translation of Camões is deservedly famous for its reflection of the verve of the original. A man of action who had traveled and known adventure, Fanshawe surely found much to his liking in this Portuguese poem, the supreme Renaissance epic of exploration and discovery. Portuguese was then little studied in England. "I Can *not* tell how your Lordship may take it," he wrote in his dedicatory epistle to Lord Strafford, "that in so *uncourted* a *language,* as that of PORTUGALL, should be found extant a *Poet* to rival your beloved TASSO." High but just praise. So far as we know, he had not studied Portuguese before undertaking this task,[51] but with a thorough knowledge of Spanish he would not have had difficulty in reading the poem, and in any event he seems to have had available the elaborate edition prepared by Manuel de Faria y Sousa (Madrid, 1639), which included after each stanza a prose translation

51. Sir Richard Fanshawe, trans., *The Lusiads,* ed. Geoffrey Bullough (Carbondale, Ill., 1964), p. 33.

into Spanish.[52] He succeeds perhaps better than any subsequent English translator of this epic in reproducing its narrative pace.

The translation from Camões was published in 1655; those from Antonio Hurtado de Mendoza not until 1671, some five years after Fanshawe's death. But that they were earlier circulated in manuscript is implied by a letter written to him in 1659 by Sir Edward Hyde. The letter will repay quotation for what it reveals about Fanshawe and even more for its indication that Hyde (who as the earl of Clarendon was soon to preside over the Restoration settlement) read Spanish literature in the original language. Hyde wrote from Brussels on July 16–26, 1659:

> I thank you for your poetry, which I see you refresh yourself [with] in both languages. I do very much long to see your *Querer por solo querer,* both in the translation and the original, I have heard it much commended, but could not procure it whilst I was in Spain. If you will needs exercise yourself in translations, which methinks you should not choose to do, when you can so well digest your own thoughts upon many subjects, I wish you would collect a parcel of Spanish letters, which though you will not find together in any one volume, at least that I have seen, you may out of several authors bring together such a collection of letters, both serious and light, which will appear better in English than any volume of letters that I ever saw in any language.[53]

This is a pleasing glimpse of the literary side of the exile less than a year before the Restoration, when Hyde himself could write a letter —in his own hand—about poetry and make an informed suggestion for a new book.

Fanshawe's choice of a Spanish play to translate or, to use his own more accurate word, *paraphrase,* reinforces our conception of him as essentially nondramatic in his literary interests and aptitudes, for it is not in the strict sense a comedia but an elaborate court entertainment: Antonio Hurtado de Mendoza's *Querer por solo querer,* first presented in 1622 as a birthday celebration before the young

52. Ibid., p. 21.

53. Historical Manuscripts Commission, *Report on the Manuscripts of J. M. Heathcote, Esq., of Conington Castle* (1899), p. 11.

King Philip IV by amateurs, the *meninas* (high-born ladies-in-waiting) of the queen, at the royal palace of Aranjuez.[54] This very long Spanish play, about the rescue of a bewitched maiden in an enchanted castle, seems a curious choice for Fanshawe to have made as the subject of an extended work. Perhaps he had had some connection with the author (a nobleman who held high office at the Spanish court) when he was in Spain in the 1630s; perhaps he had heard about the splendid performance at the royal palace; perhaps, as a translator of Góngora, he was attracted by the Gongorism of Hurtado de Mendoza's style. In any event, his translation can be read only by an act of the will, and the original has itself fallen into oblivion.

The Restoration meant to Fanshawe a return to the world of affairs and an end to his translations. Charles II remembered his old friend with gratitude. Lady Fanshawe wrote that the king had earlier promised her husband an appointment as secretary of state, and her memoirs betray a sense of resentment that the position was not forthcoming. But other marks of the royal favor did come to Fanshawe, including a mission to Portugal in 1661 to take Charles's portrait to his contracted bride; and, in May 1662, an assignment to meet her when she arrived in England. Fanshawe's special qualifications for these honors, we may assume, were his prestige as translator of *Os Lusiadas* and his ability to speak Spanish, which would have been intelligible to the Portuguese.

Then came two final diplomatic missions, as ambassador to Portugal (September 1662 until August 1663) and, after a short interval in England, to Spain in February 1664 until his sudden death in Madrid in June 1666. In his wife's memoirs we hear much about the court ceremonial of their reception in Portugal and Spain; she relished the pomp enjoyed by an English ambassador's wife, and she described it in detail. Of special relevance here, her account of their stately progress from Cadiz to Madrid in the spring of 1664 includes allusion to attendance at several plays. Referring to their residence at Seville, she writes: "During our stay in this palace we were every day entertained with variety of recreations—as, shows upon the river, stage plays, singing, dancing, men playing at legerdemain;" and

54. N. D. Shergold, *A History of the Spanish Stage from Mediaeval Times until the End of the Seventeenth Century* (Oxford, 1967), pp. 270–74.

referring to Cordoba: "At night we had a play acted;" and to Toledo: "We were there entertained during our stay with comedies and music and *juego do toros.*"[55] Obviously the ambassadorial party, which included, in addition to Sir Richard and Lady Fanshawe, a number of English gentlemen, had frequent opportunity to see the comedia. And it is possible that among the English gentlemen was William Wycherley, whose first two plays, *Love in a Wood* (1671) and *The Gentleman Dancing-Master* (1672), include borrowings from Calderón.[56]

Fanshawe's translation of Camões and his missions to Portugal provide a reminder that Spanish and Portuguese are mutually intelligible languages—different languages, to be sure, with different patterns of pronunciation and systems of inflection, but yet having supplies of words which for the most part resemble their counterparts closely enough to be recognizable in print and, less easily, in conversation. The connection between the two languages was described in 1662, the year of Charles's marriage to Catharine of Braganza, by James Howell, who hoped to assist those who knew Spanish to learn something about Portuguese.[57] "As *Scotland* is to *England,*" Howell wrote, and we must remember that he was using the linguistic terminology of the seventeenth century, "so *Portugall* may be sayed to be in relation to *Spain,* in point of Speech; The *Scott* speaks somewhat broader, and more gaping; so doth the *Portugues* compared to the *Castilian,* and shorter farr."[58] And he includes in his book, which is an English grammar dedicated to the new English Queen, who was trying to learn her husband's language, "A Short

55. Lady Fanshawe, *Memoirs,* pp. 139, 141, 143.

56. Lady Fanshawe refers to one of the gentlemen attendants on Sir Richard as a "Mr. Wycherly" (*Memoirs,* p. 146). A closer identification of this man would seem to be impossible, though the fact that the dramatist later borrowed from Calderón's plays suggests Lady Fanshawe is referring to him. Cf. Willard Connely, *Brawny Wycherley* (London, 1930), pp. 45–48. James Urvin Rundle, "Wycherley and Calderón: A Source for *Love in a Wood,*" *PMLA* 64 (1949) : 701–07.

57. Howell had petitioned to be made tutor to the queen, *Calendar of State Papers, Domestic, 1661–62,* p. 37: "July 11, 1661. 52. James Howell to the Lord Chancellor. Requests his influence with the King to obtain him the place of Tutor in Foreign Languages to the Infanta who is coming to be Queen. Knows the Spanish tongue with the Portuguese dialect, also Italian and French, and has published a great dictionary with grammars to all three languages, dedicated to the King. Has a compendious, choice method of instruction."

58. James Howell, *New English Grammar* (London, 1662), p. 83.

Dictionary or, Catalog of such Portuges Words that have no Affinity with the Spanish."[59] Howell recognized clearly enough that the royal marriage would bring both the peninsular languages into increased prominence in England. Their political hostility notwithstanding, Portugal and Spain were linguistically allied, and it counts for much in the Spanish studies of Restoration Englishmen that their queen and a number of her attendants spoke Portuguese.

Like any other royal marriage in the seventeenth century, Charles's marriage was intended to serve, and in this case did serve, a political purpose. Negotiations for it were under way even before the Restoration, General Monck taking an important part in them; but the marriage was not contracted before other possibilities had been canvassed.[60] Netherland, French, and Spanish candidates were suggested. The Queen Mother understandably urged a French choice. The earl of Bristol, among others, urged a Spanish; and, hostile to Charles's proposed marriage to Catharine, he brought reports alleging her sterility as well as her personal unattractiveness. That Charles ultimately chose the Portuguese bride turned on, among other considerations, the advice he received from Clarendon, the encouragement of the French king (who, despite his recent marriage to the daughter of Philip IV, wanted English support of the Portuguese against the Spaniards), and the immensity of the dowry offered. The dowry indeed included Bombay, Tangier,[61] and two million cruzados (about £330,000) in money, sugar, and Brazilian wood; it was to have the long-range consequence of opening up India to English commercial exploitation.[62] With all this, Charles had little reason to complain that his Portuguese bride was not beautiful and had received such a limited education she could not even speak French, much less English.

She arrived off the coast of Portsmouth, in a squadron commanded

59. Ibid., pp. 85 ff.

60. David Ogg, *England in the Reign of Charles II* (Oxford, 1963), 1 : 185.

61. The acquisition of Tangier would in time bring some Englishmen to an acquaintance with Spanish drama: see Paul Kaufman, "Spanish Players at Tangier: A New Chapter in Stage History," *Comparative Literature* 12 (1960) : 125–32; and Shergold, *History of the Spanish Stage*, p. 543 n.

62. Ogg, *Reign of Charles II*, 1 : 187. For an extended study of the consequences for England of Queen Catharine's dowry, see Gertrude Z. Thomas, *Richer than Spices* (New York, 1965).

by the earl of Sandwich, in May 1662, and the duke of York sailed out to greet her—and to talk to her in Spanish.[63] Charles himself talked to her in Spanish when he met her in Portsmouth, where they were married before a small group of courtiers, including Sir Richard Fanshawe and his wife, who describes the occasion in her memoirs. Later that month the king and queen proceeded in easy stages to Hampton Court, where they spent much of the summer. "Here the Queen receiv'd the Addresses of all the Nobility," wrote an early eighteenth-century historian, "and Submissions of the several Deputies for the Cities of *England;* more particularly from the Lord-Mayor and Aldermen of *London,* who, by Sir *William Wylde* their Recorder, pronounc'd a *Spanish* Oration, and presented her with a rich Purse of Gold."[64] We may guess that persons who could speak Spanish, or some approximation to it, were much in demand that summer, and that such skill in the language as Charles himself had was frequently put to the test.

The inadequacy of her English notwithstanding, the queen saw a number of plays at court[65] and, after she had been in England a few years, in the public theaters as well. Several of the plays she saw had Spanish or Portuguese subjects: presumably they would have been recommended to her. Thus she saw at court in December 1662 a play called *The Valiant Cid,* an adaptation of Corneille's play, which in turn derives from Guillén de Castro's *Las mocedades del Cid.* In January 1668 she saw, in the King's Company's Bridges Street Theatre, Dryden's *The Indian Emperour,* his dramatization of Cortes's conquest of Mexico; and in June of the same year, in the same theater, his *An Evening's Love; Or, The Mock Astrologer,* a play that, whatever the complicated facts of its immediate sources, derives from Calderón's *El astrólogo fingido.* In November of that year Catharine saw the King's Company perform an adaptation of

63. A detailed account of the marriage and its preliminaries was written by a Portuguese historian: D. António Caetano de Sousa, *História genealógica da casa real portuguesa,* a multivolume work of which the first volume appeared in 1735. The work has recently been edited by M. Lopes de Almeida e César Pegado (Coimbra, 1946); the account of the marriage (in vol. 7 of the new edition) includes specific reference to both the duke of York's and Charles II's conversing with Catharine in Spanish.

64. Laurence Echard, *The History of England* (London, 1718), 3 : 84.

65. Caetano de Sousa, *História genealógica,* 7 : 171, refers to performances of plays at Hampton Court in the summer of 1662.

Fletcher's *The Island Princess; Or, The Generous Portuguese,* a title with an application that could scarcely be missed.[66] All this is not to imply that there was a sustained effort to produce plays for the delectation of Charles's Portuguese wife; rather, that courtiers and managers of theaters would have been sensitively aware that certain plays might hold special interest for her.[67]

Because she was attended by Portuguese ladies and by Portuguese chaplains, her language was frequently heard at court. She remained a Catholic, and the Portuguese clergymen around her were granted immunity from the legal sanctions against Catholic worship; they preached sermons at court in Portuguese. On this subject, as on so much else about Restoration England, Samuel Pepys provides information. As will be noted below, he knew Spanish well enough to be a devoted collector of Spanish books; and from his diary, March 17, 1667, we learn that he knew it well enough for him partially to comprehend a Portuguese sermon:

> I to walk in the Parke, where to the Queene's Chapel, and there heard a fryer preach with his cord about his middle, in Portuguese, something I could understand, showing that God did respect the meek and humble, as well as the high and rich. He was full of action, but very decent and good, I thought, and his manner of delivery very good.

Pepys was an uncommon man, in his linguistic skills as in everything else; and yet he would not have been alone in taking an interest in the foreign language frequently heard at court, which was so closely allied to Spanish.

As we seek to determine how widely Spanish language and literature were known in the court of Charles and Catharine, we find a major source of information in the full documentation surrounding the career of Pepys. He was a man of genius with an inquiring mind and a capacity for intellectual enthusiasm, and he can be regarded

66. My references to performances are drawn from *The London Stage,* part 1: 1660–1700, ed. William Van Lennep (Carbondale, Ill., 1968).

67. There are no records of Spanish theatrical companies playing in England during Charles II's reign: see Sybil Rosenfeld, *Foreign Theatrical Companies in Great Britain in the 17th and 18th Centuries,* Society for Theatre Research, Pamphlet Series, no. 4 (London, 1955).

as typical only in the way that a man of great capacity can represent persons of lesser capacity. Yet he shared the tastes of his age. Like many others he learned to read Spanish, and he amassed a collection of Spanish books;[68] unlike others, he arranged for all his books, including the Spanish ones, to be preserved intact—and they have survived to the present, a record of his varied interests.

Where and how he learned Spanish is not known; he knew it when he began his diary in 1660. Grammars, dictionaries, and teachers were available in London, and presumably he made use of them. Early in his diary, on February 11, 1660, he wrote, referring to a guidebook: "This morning I lay long abed, and then to my office, where I read all morning my Spanish book of Rome"; and at nearly the end of the diary, on April 28, 1669, he mentions a gift he had received of Mariana's history of Spain, specifically remarking that it was in Spanish. He several times mentions visits to booksellers in quest of Spanish books, as on March 27, 1663: "Staying a little while in Paul's Churchyard, at the foreign booksellers, looking over some Spanish books and with much ado keeping myself from laying out money there." He seems indeed to have felt such affection for Spanish books that he had to discipline himself against spending too much on them, if we may judge from such an entry as this for Jaunary 13, 1664: "Through Bedlam, calling by the way at an old bookseller's, and there fell into looking over Spanish books and pitched upon some, till I thought of my oath when I was going to agree for them, and so with much ado got myself out of the shop glad at my heart and so away." Testimony to Pepys's strength of character—and also to the availability of Spanish books in London.

Pepys continued to buy Spanish books in the years after he terminated the diary, sometimes apparently employing friends who were traveling abroad as agents, and he seems to have bought books himself when he went to Spain in the winter of 1683–84.[69] He made this trip in line of duty, in the company of Lord Dartmouth, who was sent to bring home the British garrison from Tangier (which, it will be recalled, had been acquired as part of Queen Catharine's dowry), but he characteristically combined travel and sightseeing

68. See Sir Stephen Gaselee, *The Spanish Books in the Library of Samuel Pepys* (Oxford, 1921). My discussion of Pepys's interest in Spanish is largely based on Gaselee.

69. Edward M. Wilson, "Samuel Pepys's Spanish Chap-books," part 1, *Transactions of the Cambridge Bibliographical Society*, 2 (1955) : 127–54.

with his work for the navy. Stimulated by the adventure, he again kept a shorthand diary, the so-called "Second Diary," in which we can trace his movements as he journeyed from Tangier to Cadiz to Seville. This time he wrote as an important man of affairs, having lost the expansiveness of his youth, with the result that we learn much about the administration of the navy and little about his response to Spain. His visit to Seville was a disappointment, partly because it coincided with heavy rains and flooding.[70] Yet his instincts as a book collector survived the rain and his preoccupation with business; it was apparently while he was at Seville that he bought a large and valuable collection of chapbooks: seventy-five Spanish pamphlets published after the middle of the century, many containing work by important Spanish authors.[71]

His earlier diary would be sufficient, even if abundant corroborating evidence did not exist, to establish the availability of Spanish books in London bookstores. Many of them were printed in the Netherlands, just across the Channel. A comprehensive *Bibliographie des impressions espagnoles des Pays-Bas Meridionaux*[72] reveals with precision how many were printed in the region that is now Belgium. A bibliographical study of the production of Spanish books in the sixteenth century concludes that "the Netherlands were the chief source of supply of Spanish books for the English market at this time. This is only natural in view of the proximity of the two countries, the ease with which books could be transported by water from Antwerp to London, and the common cause which England and the Netherlands made against Spain late in the century."[73] At least the first two of these conditions held true of the seventeenth century, and library lists continue to show books printed there. With more frequent travel to Spain, however, there seems to have been an increase in the direct importation of books. Pepys's library includes more

70. *Letters and the Second Diary of Samuel Pepys*, ed. R. G. Howarth (London, 1932), pp. 166–67.

71. Wilson, "Samuel Pepys's Spanish Chap-books," p. 128. See also Wilson, "Some Poems from Samuel Pepys's Spanish Chapbooks," *Bulletin of Hispanic Studies* 32 (1955): 187–93.

72. Compiled by Jean Peeters-Fontainas (Nieuwkoop, 1965).

73. Henry Thomas, "The Output of Spanish Books in the Sixteenth Century," *The Library*, 4th ser., 1 (1920–21): 69–94. See also Thomas, *Short-title Catalogue of Books printed in Spain and of Spanish Books printed elsewhere in Europe before 1601 now in the British Museum* (London, 1921).

books printed in Spain than in the Netherlands, though his might not be a typical case because of his navy connections and his travels in Spain.

The catalog of Pepys's Spanish books, prepared in this century by Sir Stephen Gaselee, lists 185 separate works, of which twenty-six are dramas bound together in a single volume, including plays by Lope, Tirso, Calderón, Moreto, and Rojas Zorrilla. Most of the plays have religious subjects, which is surprising, since we do not think of Pepys as having been especially pious. Calderón, for example, is represented by *El ángel de la guarda, Las cadenas del Demonio, El esclavo de María, La gran comedia de la exaltación de la Cruz,* and *El mejor padre de pobres.* It is improbable that Pepys anticipated the twentieth-century esteem for the Spanish allegorical drama. More likely, he bought a collection of religious plays that had been formed by someone else.

Pepys's collection of Spanish books is unique in that it is preserved along with the rest of his library.[74] But the private libraries of many Restoration gentlemen contained Spanish books; and the large number of late-seventeenth- and eighteenth-century sale catalogs in the British Museum, most of them comprehensive listings of the books of persons recently deceased, enable us to determine with precision what those books were.[75] There has already been occasion to comment on the sale catalogs of the earl of Clarendon and of the earl of Bristol. Bristol's was, of course, a special case, because of his lifelong associations with Spain. Other catalogs are less remarkable, but they nevertheless repay study.

The catalogs provide a warning against an anachronistic projection of modern indifference to language study into the seventeenth century. In reading them one is impressed by the prominence in private libraries of books in foreign languages, modern languages as well as Latin and, though with less frequency, Greek. Customarily the catalogs are subdivided by language as well as by size of book; and nearly all the libraries for sale included a large component in one, and usually several, foreign languages. The catalogs provide a

74. On Pepys's library, see H. B. Wheatley, "Two English Bookmen: Samuel Pepys; Henry Fielding," *Bibliographica* 1 (1895) : 155–62.

75. *List of Catalogues of English Book Sales 1676–1900 Now in the British Museum* (B.M., BAR.T.19.b). See also Pollard, "English Book-Sales," pp. 373–84.

warning too, in the number and variety of books listed, against overconfidence in assuming that we can fully and surely trace the literary background of seventeenth-century drama. Englishmen obviously read many books of which the modern memory is dim.

It should be said at once that Spanish books are less prominent in these catalogs than books in the classical languages and in French, and perhaps less prominent than books in Italian. Yet the catalogs remove any doubt that Spanish books and books in English (some of them translations) on Spanish subjects were widely read in Restoration England. Works of Spanish history, especially the history of the Spanish and Portuguese conquests, are conspicuous: Acosta, Gómara, and above all Mariana, in both the original language and translation, make frequent appearances. Many of the libraries had belonged to clergymen, and they predictably include concentrations of books, in English and other languages including Spanish, on biblical and theological subjects. As P. E. Russell has pointed out, referring to works of Spanish theology in libraries of Oxford colleges, the religious differences between the two countries did not prevent Englishmen from reading the Spanish theologians.[76]

It will be useful to examine several of the catalogs. The duke of Lauderdale's library, sold May 14, 1690, included an extensive collection of Spanish books: among others, a volume of comedias by Lope and other dramatists, *Don Quijote* and the *Novelas ejemplares* of Cervantes, the works of Quevedo, Góngora, Bartolomé Leonardo de Argensola, Fernando de Herrera, as well as the edition by Manuel de Faria y Sousa, with Spanish translation, of the Portuguese *Lusiadas.* The library included Spanish historical works: Gómara's *Historia de la conquista de Méjico,* the Inca Garcilaso de la Vega's *Historia general del Perú,* Herrera's *Historia de las Indias Occidentales,* and Mariana's *Historia general de España.* Lauderdale's was a ducal library, of an amplitude beyond the reach of private gentlemen; and yet the catalogs of persons of lower rank show impressive Spanish holdings. For example, the library of the Reverend Timothy Puller of London, sold December 10, 1695, included "Comedias varias de Lope de Vega," four volumes; "Altras [sic] Comedias de Lope de

76. "It is . . . abundantly clear from printed sources and from the seventeenth-century catalogues of some Oxford libraries that the writings of pre-Reformation and contemporary Spanish theologians were readily accessible to those who cared to study them." P. E. Russell, "English Seventeenth-Century Interpretations of Spanish Literature," *Atlante* 1 (1953): 68.

Vega," two volumes; "Ocho Comedias nuevas compuestas por . . . Cervantes"; "Querer por Solo Querer Comedia"; as well as many other works by Spanish authors including Cervantes, Quevedo, Guevara, Garcilaso de la Vega, and Ercilla.

Nicholas Rowe's library, sold August 26, 1719, included, in Spanish, *Don Quijote* and Mariana's history and, in English, Quevedo's *Visions* and several volumes on Spanish history. William Congreve's library list (not a sale catalog in this instance) shows, in addition to a Spanish-English dictionary, two different editions of *Don Quijote* in the original language and an edition in French translation, as well as another translation from Cervantes's works in French and still another in Italian.[77] Congreve also had, translated into French or English, Quevedo's *Visions,* Mateo Alemán's *Guzman, Lazarillo de Tormes, The Lusiads* (in Fanshawe's translation), as well as a series of volumes on Spanish and Portuguese history. This library list would seem to be typical of those of many Restoration men of letters; Congreve presumably had some knowledge of the language and more than a casual interest in Spanish civilization, but he was not, judging from his books, an accomplished student of the language and the literature.

There was no lack of aids in England for learning Spanish, of books—dictionaries, grammars, and manuals—or of teachers. Dale Randall has described the means of study available to an earlier generation of Englishmen, and much of what he says is relevant to the Restoration. "One may readily count more than twenty texts," he writes, "which could have been useful to translators writing between 1535 and 1662. . . . And, of course, if one adds to these the books which made it possible to learn or polish one's Spanish through the convenient intermediaries of French or Latin, the number of titles is greatly multiplied." [78] The Restoration and early eighteenth-century sale catalogs provide an indication of the grammars and dictionaries widely used in this later period.

The *Bibliotheca Digbeiana* (which, as noted, lists books owned in

77. *The Library of William Congreve,* ed. John C. Hodges (New York, 1955).

78. Randall, *The Golden Tapestry,* p. 19. See also Robert Spaulding, *How Spanish Grew* (Berkeley and Los Angeles, 1943), pp. 178–81. Amado Alonso, *De la pronunciación medieval a la moderna en español* (Madrid, 1955), pp. 231–70, provides a detailed account of the manuals published in the sixteenth and seventeenth centuries to aid Englishmen in learning Spanish. For an older but still useful treatment of the same subject, see Leo Wiener, "Spanish Studies in England in the Sixteenth and Seventeenth Centuries," *Modern Quarterly of Language and Literature* 2 (1899): 3–10.

turn by Sir Kenelm Digby and the earl of Bristol, as well as by another and unidentified person) includes a series of books useful in the study of Spanish, among others John Minsheu's dictionary of Spanish and English (1623) and James Howell's dictionary of English, French, Italian, and Spanish (1660). Pepys had Minsheu's dictionary: "A dictionary in Spanish and English: first published into the English tongue by Ric. Percivale Gent. Now enlarged . . . by John Minsheu, Professor of Languages in London" (1623),[79] a work described by a modern authority as "probablemente el más famoso de los libros sobre la lengua española, escritos en inglés." [80] Nicholas Rowe had "Minsheu's Dictionary of 9 Languages" (1626), "Stevens's Spanish Dictionary" (1706), and "Anton's Spanish Grammar" (1711). This would seem to lend bibliographical support to an anecdote, widely circulated in the eighteenth century, that Robert Harley (Oxford) suggested to Rowe that he learn Spanish. Rowe did so, the story goes, expecting a diplomatic assignment, only to be told when he reported his accomplishment to Harley that he could now read *Don Quijote* in the original language.[81]

That Rowe's interest in Spanish (if not the motive that prompted it) was not unusual in early eighteenth-century England is implied by a notice in *The Daily Courant,* February 25, 1716:

> On the First of March next, being Thursday, the Publick Prayers will be Read, and a Sermon preached in the Spanish or Castillian Tongue, at the Parish Church of St. Peter le Poor, Broad-street, near the Royal-Exchange, beginning exactly at 11 a Clock in the Forenoon, and will (God willing) be continued weekly every Thursday at the same Place and Hour. It is humbly hoped, and earnestly desired, that all Gentlemen and others, who love and use the Spanish Tongue, will personally assist and encourage so pious an Undertaking. The Person who is to officiate is the Reverand Mr. Felix Antony de Alvarado, by Birth a

79. Gaselee, *Library of Samuel Pepys,* p. 35.

80. Cyril A. Jones, "El estudio del Español en Inglaterra," *La Torre: Revista general de la Universidad de Puerto Rico* 2 (1954): 168.

81. According to his contemporary biographer, Dr. James Welwood, Rowe "was Master of most Parts of Polite Learning, especially the Classical Authors both *Greek* and *Latin,* understood the *French, Italian* and *Spanish* Languages, and spoke the first fluently, and the other two tollerably well. . . ." Welwood, preface to Rowe's translation of Lucan's *Pharsalia* (London, 1718), p. xxiv.

> Spaniard, a Native of the City of Seville, some Years since Naturalized in this Kingdom, converted to the Protestant Religion, and now a Minister of the Church of England as by Law established.[82]

If Spanish was never considered part of the necessary equipment of an educated gentleman, many Englishmen nevertheless learned it, or at least learned to read it. Milton, according to Samuel Johnson, "read all the languages which are considered either as learned or polite: Hebrew, with its two dialects, Greek, Latin, Italian, French, and Spanish." [83] Men as varied in position and temperament as Archbishop Sancroft and Daniel Defoe knew some Spanish. Sancroft resided in Amsterdam from November 1657 until the summer of 1659, and he traveled in Belgium and France before he returned to England several months after the Restoration. Presumably he learned Spanish while on the Continent; in any event, his library included Spanish books.[84] Defoe's knowledge of the language was not extensive, though he read works of the Spanish geographers.[85] Sir William Temple knew Spanish and in his essays made informed references to the language and literature. "The three modern Tongues most esteemed are *Italian, Spanish,* and *French,*" he wrote in *On Ancient and Modern Learning,*[86] and his opinion on this subject was not controversial. His sister made translations from Spanish poetry, which the young Jonathan Swift was employed in copying out.[87]

Gerard Langbaine, in the first major bibliographical work devoted to English drama, *An Account of the English Dramatick Poets* (1691), not only implied that he himself could read Spanish but also that the audience to whom he directed his book could do so. Dryden,

82. A similar notice appeared in *The Daily Courant,* April 14, 1716. This time it is stated that Mr. Alvarado "teaches the Spanish, Latin, Italian, and French Tongues, at Home: And waits upon any Gentleman at his House."

83. "Milton," *Lives of the Poets,* ed. Hill, 1 : 154.

84. George D'Oyly, *The Life of William Sancroft, Archbishop of Canterbury* (London, 1821), 1 : 93–107. Edward M. Wilson, "Spanish and English Religious Poetry," *Journal of Ecclesiastical History* 9 (1958) : 47.

85. A. E. Levett, "Daniel Defoe," in F. J. C. Hearnshaw, ed., *Social and Political Ideas of Some English Thinkers of the Augustan Age* (London, 1928), p. 186; James Sutherland, *Defoe* (London, 1937), p. 22.

86. Irwin Ehrenpreis, *The Personality of Jonathan Swift* (London, 1958), p. 94. *Critical Essays of the Seventeenth Century,* ed. J. E. Spingarn (Oxford, 1908–09), 3 : 63.

87. Carl Van Doren, *Swift* (New York, 1930), pp. 22–23.

he writes, "has plunder'd the chief *Italian, Spanish,* and *French* Wits for Forage, notwithstanding his pretended contempt of them." [88] And again, referring to Sydserf's *Tarugo's Wiles,* he writes that the main intrigue of the play is "founded (as I suppose) on the *Spanish* Play *No puedeser,* or *It cannot be;* but not having the Original, I cannot be positive." After calling attention to the resemblance of Crowne's later *Sir Courtly Nice* to *Tarugo's Wiles,* he suspends judgment on the relationships between the Spanish and the two English plays: "I leave it to the Decision of Mr. *Crown,* or any other who have seen the *Spanish* Play." [89] The number of those who knew the language included the poet and translator Philip Ayres, who at least once experimented in writing Spanish verse, and the English ambassador to Spain from 1671 until 1678, Sir William Godolphin, who when he was recalled in the turmoil of the Popish Plot chose to remain in Spain, an avowed Catholic.[90] More names could be cited, but these will suffice to suggest the prominence of Spanish studies in Restoration England: knowledge of the language was a common if not a usual accomplishment of gentlemen with literary interests.

Before the theaters were closed in 1642, English dramatists made curiously little use of the comedias as sources or formal models for their own plays. Shirley turned to them and probably, on a few isolated occasions, Fletcher and several other dramatists did so too. Yet in view of the wealth of Spanish Renaissance drama, and the wide-ranging English search for promising materials to be dramatized, the number of established instances of borrowing from the comedia (as differentiated from Spanish prose narrative) is small. After the Restoration the number is larger. Spanish drama became fashionable in part as a delayed consequence of the royal exile, the last four years of which were passed in alliance with the king of Spain and in a country in which Spanish was the language of the court. No doubt also the mere passage of time intensified English

88. P. 149.

89. Pp. 434–35.

90. George Saintsbury, "Philip Ayres," in *The Bibliographer,* 2 (1903): 215–24. *DNB,* s.v. Sir William Godolphin. An important collection of Godolphin's letters is printed in *Hispania Illustrata: Or, The Maxims of the Spanish Court, And most Memorable Affairs, From the Year 1667, to the Year 1678* (London, 1703).

awareness of the comedia. The interval between 1642 and 1660 was long enough for knowledge of Spanish drama to be diffused throughout western Europe—Germany, France, the Netherlands, as well as England. By the time of the Restoration, Englishmen were becoming aware that Spain had experienced a literary golden age comparable in achievement to England's own.

III: THE RETURN OF THE CAVALIERS AND THE ESTABLISHMENT OF THE "SPANISH PLOT"

THE appearance in 1668 of Etherege's *She Would If She Could* and John Dryden's *Of Dramatick Poesie*—the one a foreshadowing of the comedy of manners to come, the other a critical assessment of what had already been since 1660—make that year a convenient dividing point between the first, experimental phase of Restoration drama and the second phase, which was soon to reach maturity in the plays of Etherege, Wycherley, and Dryden. The first eight years of the Restoration are formative in the drama: theater managers, lacking a repertory of plays less than twenty years old, were searching for talent, and playwrights were searching for dramatic forms with which to make their reputations.

Conditioned by the analogy of organic evolution (which has at least limited usefulness in literary history so long as it does not confound evaluations of individual works), we look to the plays of 1660 to 1668 for insight into the ancestry of Restoration drama. If the heroic play, including its derivatives in blank verse, and the comedy of manners emerged as what seem in retrospect the most distinctive of Restoration dramatic forms, their preeminence was not established at once nor did it exclude other forms of drama, including adaptations from and imitations of the comedia. The oversimplifications of modern scholarship have taken their toll of late seventeenth-century plays—the more destructively since the dramatic texts, except for a handful of anthology pieces, have been difficult to find except in large libraries. Among the results has been an obscuring of the Hispanic strain in the drama. I have already considered Dryden's comments on the comedia in *Of Dramatick Poesie,* and I have referred to his plays of that year and earlier which have Spanish themes and characters and have, or may have, Spanish sources: *The Rival Ladies, The Indian Emperour,* and *An Evening's Love.* As will become apparent, a number of his fellow dramatists were writing plays in the Spanish manner.

The reasons for the exploitation of Spanish drama on the Restoration stage are complex. But exploited it was, soon after 1660. In fact, we have it on the authority of the editors of *The London Stage* that the first new subgenre to appear was the "Spanish romance":

> From the increased record of performances that we have compiled, the Calendar shows that it was neither the comedy of manners nor even the rimed heroic drama that emerged first; it was, instead, a type of comedy which may be called the Spanish romance. This kind of play, based upon a Spanish source, placed its emphasis upon a rigid code of conduct, had a plot filled with intrigue, and emphasized one or more high-spirited women in the *dramatis personae.* In this category falls Sir Samuel Tuke's *The Adventures of Five Hours* [January 1663], then attributed to Calderón, which became the first highly successful drama of the Restoration. . . . Other plays in the same category that soon followed were Lord Digby's *Elvira* (November 1664), Thomas Porter's *The Carnival* (ca. 1664), John Dryden's *The Rival Ladies* (June 1664), and, later, St Serfe's *Tarugo's Wiles* (5 October 1667) and Dryden's *An Evening's Love* (12 June 1668).[1]

Here is an outline history of the first phase of the "Spanish plots."

Theatrical production having been interrupted for nearly a generation when the theaters reopened in 1660, managers at first were forced to present plays written before 1642. Dramatists promptly went to work and soon were writing new plays in quantity, but several years elapsed before a new repertory could be created, and in the interval old plays had to serve. Among the revivals were Renaissance plays taken from Spanish sources. As early as November

1. *The London Stage,* pt. 1, pp. cxxii–cxxiii. For a critique of the conception of "Spanish romance" presented in *The London Stage,* see Dryden, *Works,* 10 : 443 n.–44 n.

1660, Shirley's *The Opportunity,* based on Tirso's *El castigo del penséque,* was acted by the King's Company at the Vere Street Theatre; and in November 1662 Shirley's *The Young Admiral,* based on Lope's *Don Lope de Cardona,* was acted by the same company at court.[2] It counts for something in the rapid establishment of the Spanish plots that the single group of old plays most frequently performed were those attributed to Beaumont and Fletcher. Sixteen of them were performed in the season 1660–61, fifteen the next season, and some forty in all before the end of the century.[3] As Dryden noted in a passage already cited, Beaumont and Fletcher (it would be more accurate to say Fletcher) went often to Spanish prose fiction for their plots. Many of their plays are dramatic romances, even many that do not have Spanish sources, and they have a strong narrative line in the manner of the comedia. An audience accustomed to the romances of Beaumont and Fletcher would have been receptive to adaptations from Spanish drama.

Yet the impulse primarily responsible for the establishment of the Spanish plots on the Restoration stage was provided, not by the older English drama, but by the comedia. Except for Dryden's *The Rival Ladies* and the doubtful case of Thomas Porter's *The Carnival* (which looks as though it is an adaptation of a Spanish play, though no specific source is known), the important and distinctive plays of the subgenre produced in the years just after the Restoration can be traced to the comedia. They are adaptations of Spanish plays, so close to the originals in several instances—Tuke's *The Adventures of Five Hours,* for example, and Lord Bristol's *Elvira*—as to be little more than free translations.

In two instances, Davenant's *The Man's the Master* and Dryden's *An Evening's Love,* French plays intervene between the Spanish and the English, and there is some deflection of tone from the comedia, but even so, much of the original remains. Davenant and Dryden would seem to be alone in the group of those writing adaptations in the first few years who used French intermediaries, just as they were

2. Records of performances are taken from *The London Stage,* pt. 1.

3. Louis B. Wright plausibly associates the popularity of the Beaumont and Fletcher plays on the Restoration stage with the frequency with which they were read in mid-century while the theaters were closed: "The Reading of Plays during the Puritan Revolution," *Huntington Library Bulletin* 6 (Nov. 1934): 73–94. *The London Stage,* pt. 1, p. cxxviii.

alone in having written many plays. Most of the early Spanish plots were the work of gentlemen, Cavaliers in their backgrounds, who were essentially amateurs. Through family connections or the experiences of exile they had gained a knowledge of the comedia, which they could turn to advantage in the experimental years of the Restoration stage.

The close link with the comedia accounts for the consistency with which these early Spanish plots exhibit a set of distinctive formal conventions—conventions that made them recognizable to contemporary audiences and that make them a coherent and intelligible strand in the development of Restoration drama. After the early years of the Restoration, the conventions were not often observed comprehensively, though dramatists long continued to employ variations on them in plays that, in sources, settings, plots, and themes, bear relationships to the comedia. The inventive variations on the Spanish plot by Dryden, and slightly later by Wycherley and Aphra Behn, resulted in better plays than the early and faithful adaptations from the comedia. Still, the variations gain in interest from the fact that they depart from a pattern of Spanish intrigue drama established by Tuke, Bristol, and their fellow Cavaliers. Their inexpertness notwithstanding, the Cavaliers deserve such credit as attaches to the establishment of the Restoration Spanish plot.

The easiest of the distinctive conventions to isolate and describe, and probably those with the most important corollaries of theme and tone, are the obvious ones of Spanish setting and characters.[4] The term "Spanish plot," insofar as it is useful in describing late seventeenth-century plays, applies only to comedies portraying Spaniards (or Portuguese; for much of the century the two countries were united politically) in their native country or in the parts of Italy controlled by Spain. When major borrowings from the comedia appear in plays with English characters and settings—for example, in Wycherley's *Love in a Wood* and *The Gentleman Dancing-Master*

4. David W. Maurer, "The Spanish Intrigue Play on the Restoration Stage" (Ph.D. diss., Ohio State University, 1935), includes an excellent account of the nature of the "Spanish plot," to which I am indebted. The dissertation was published in part in *Ohio State University Abstracts of Doctors' Dissertations,* no. 18, pp. 275–82. On this subject, I am also indebted to Allison Gaw, "Sir Samuel Tuke's *Adventures of Five Hours* in Relation to the 'Spanish Plot' and to John Dryden," in *Studies in English Drama* (University of Pennsylvania, 1917).

and Crowne's *Sir Courtly Nice*—the change in nationality alters the values by which the plays are ordered. Spanish setting and characters are functional in Restoration plays in a way that those of other nationalities, with the dubious exception of Italian, are not.

Curiously little, by comparison, is made of French settings and characters, and this notwithstanding the frequency with which Englishmen borrowed from Molière and his contemporaries; frenchified Englishmen are a common enough subject of ridicule, and Frenchmen in England sometimes appear, but comedies in which some special point is made of a French setting are rare. Italian locales and characters are more frequent; they occur, in fact, with approximately the same frequency as the Spanish, and often, like the Spanish, they seem to determine action, theme, and tone. But whereas the English dramatists thought of the Italians as subtle, treacherous, and volatile, they envisaged the Spaniards as grave and dignified though suspicious, and from the differences in conception of national character arose differences in plays.

Plays with Italian and Spanish characters and settings are often alike in having a strong plot-line of love intrigue; they differ in the retention in the Spanish plots of character types and codes of conduct, above all the code of honor, peculiar to the comedia. The distinction will perhaps be more convincing if, before turning to the early adaptations of Spanish drama, we consider briefly a play contemporary with them that has Italian characters and a setting in Verona: Richard Rhodes's *Flora's Vagaries,* produced by the King's Company during the winter of 1662–63. A lively comedy of intrigue having a plot as full of "turns" as the adaptations of the comedia about which Dryden complained, it bears more than a superficial resemblance to the Spanish plots. Flora, a gay and irrepressible young woman, and Otrante, her more serious cousin, have been immured by the father of Otrante, Grimani, a type of the suspicious old man of seventeenth-century comedy. A young villain, Francisco, looking to Otrante's wealth as well as her beauty, gains entrance to her garden, having treacherously enlisted the aid of an honorable young man, Ludovico, by a false claim that he was acting with her consent. Francisco kidnaps her, though Ludovico, soon disabused, rescues her. Ludovico's courtship of Otrante follows, paralleled by that of his friend Alberto, of Flora: the former the sober and more reluctant pair of lovers, the latter the more uninhibited and open.

Now in all this there would seem to be little that is different, in episodic detail, from the plays based on the comedia. Yet a stern conception of personal and family honor is absent. Grimani, far from being a dignified father and uncle, preoccupied with the point of honor, emerges as a ludicrous figure of fun, whose provenance would seem to be the *commedia dell'arte*. "*Enter* Flora *running*," goes a stage direction in act 3, "Grimani *following her with a stick*." And from his servant we learn something of his past: "he was first a Merchant, there he broke compounded for his debts, and with forty Crowns set up for a pawn Broker, thriv'd upon that and grew into an Usurer, from thence into a Senator." His lack of dignity and inability to command respect frees his lively niece for the uninhibited exercise of her wit. The complex turns of the love intrigue notwithstanding, the texture of the play finally has more in common with the relaxed love banter of Dryden's *Secret Love* than with the adventures, motivated by sensitive personal honor, of the Spanish plots.

Except in the work of Dryden and perhaps later of Aphra Behn, the English plays with Spanish locale and characters include few memorable trials of wit in verbal exchanges. The multiplicity of episode and the elaboration of suspense rarely permitted leisurely conversation unnecessary to the advancement of dramatic action. The witty irreverence of the Restoration gay couple, if compatible with an Italianate comedy of intrigue such as *Flora's Vagaries,* would produce tension in the more solemn Spanish plots, preoccupied as they are with the point of honor. The close adaptations of the comedia in the first years of the Restoration largely avoid conversational banter among gentlefolk, relegating it to the *graciosos* of inferior rank. Perhaps only in Dryden's *The Rival Ladies* and *An Evening's Love,* the most attractive of the Spanish plots of the first decade but ones in which any borrowings from the comedia are at a remove, is there approximation to the conversational texture of the later comedy of manners.

The Spanish conception of honor used as a complicating force permits us to make useful discriminations between the Spanish plots, as contemporaries called them, and other Restoration intrigue plays, whether Italian or English in setting. In the Spanish plays sensitivity to punctilios among the gentlemen and fear among the ladies lest they reveal information which could occasion duels provide, in combination, a motive for the otherwise inexplicable silences of female characters that are so prominent as complications in the plays. The concept of honor leads to hostility between the generations and rivalry between young men. The frequency of duels derives from the code of honor, from the readiness of brothers and fathers to resort to the sword to protect the chastity and good name of sisters and daughters. In some of the later Spanish plots, to be sure, there is an intermittent relaxation of the stern code controlling the comedia—an intermittent intrusion of the relaxed attitudes toward sexual relations customary in the comedy of manners. Some of the English plays also depart from the Spanish by not altogether neglecting the role of the mother. The virtual absence of this character in the Spanish cape and sword plays [5] is presumably a corollary of the preoccupation with family honor, of which brothers and fathers are the usual custodians. Mothers are, on the other hand, prominent in the English comedy of manners (in Etherege's *The Man of Mode,* for example), and they occasionally appear in later English cape and sword plays such as Aphra Behn's *The Dutch Lover* and Durfey's *The Banditti.* Yet in the Spanish plots, as in the comedia, the customary antagonists of the young gallants are brothers and fathers.

It could be argued that, as wealth is the dominant consideration of prudent relatives in the English comedy of manners, and thus is the most frequent obstacle to the matrimonial schemes of the young, so concern to protect the family honor is uppermost in the Spanish plots. The characters of most Restoration comedies, the young as well as the old, are curiously prudent about financial affairs. Money is sometimes a barrier in the comedia, for example, in Rojas Zorrilla's tragedy *La traición busca el castigo,* which was the ultimate source of Vanbrugh's comedy *The False Friend.* But prudent practicality in arranging marriage settlements is less conspicuous in the comedia than in the English comedy of manners, and it is less conspicuous in the Spanish plots as well. The financial concerns of Restoration England could scarcely be expected to intrude in these dramatic ro-

5. Cf. Rudolph Schevill, *The Dramatic Art of Lope de Vega* (Berkeley, 1918), pp. 17–19.

mances set in a chivalric country of long twilights and temperate nights.

In their English versions as in the Spanish originals the cape and sword plays are disproportionately nocturnal, the obscurity of night in a candlelit age providing at once an emblematic expression of the confusion that envelops the characters and a necessary condition for the mistaken identities on which plots turn. The long Spanish evening, the night, and often too the dawn are benign backgrounds for romantic young love in a country in which the day can be harsh. And the night provides a cover for swordplay—both a reason why duels are inadvertently joined and a means by which reluctant duelists may escape unharmed. These plays are after all comedies—or tragicomedies—and by literary convention not many people die, no matter what the danger to which they are exposed.

It is apparent from Dryden's writings, as well as from the comments of others, including Samuel Pepys, that the decisive play in establishing the vogue of the Spanish plots was Samuel Tuke's *The Adventures of Five Hours,* translated and adapted from a Spanish play at the suggestion of the king himself. Dryden referred to the play with humorous disdain in the prologue to *The Wild Gallant* (1663), which had suffered from the competition provided by Tuke's play. An "astrologer" speaking in the prologue concludes that it is Dryden's fate *"To be indanger'd by a* Spanish *Plot";* and so indeed in *The Wild Gallant* he was, for the play failed. Again, in *Of Dramatick Poesie,* he is critical of *The Adventures,* which seems to have represented for him, as for others of that decade, the type of the Spanish intrigue play. Referring to Jonson's limiting of imagined time in *The Silent Woman* to the time of performance, he adds in the querulous tone he adopts whenever he refers to Tuke's play: "A beauty perhaps not much observed; if it had, we should not have looked on the Spanish translation of *Five Hours* with so much wonder." [6] The remark suggests that the play had a critical as well as a popular success. Elsewhere in the essay he refers depreciatingly to Tuke's character Diego,[7] a version of the gracioso of the comedia; and it is noteworthy that Dryden in *The Rival Ladies,* though in

6. *Essays,* 1 : 83.
7. *Essays,* 1 : 69.

other respects he imitates the pattern of the Spanish intrigue play, does not include that famous character type. In the most important of the references to the comedia in *Of Dramatick Poesie,* Dryden presumably had *The Adventures* and Lord Bristol's adaptations in mind. I have quoted the passage before, but it bears repeating in this context; Lisideius speaks:

> But by pursuing close one argument, which is not cloyed with many turns, the French have gained more liberty for verse, in which they write; they have leisure to dwell on a subject which deserves it; and to represent the passions (which we have acknowledged to be the poet's work), without being hurried from one thing to another, as we are in the plays of Calderon, which we have seen lately upon our theatres, under the name of Spanish plots.[8]

Dryden's disdain for *The Adventures of Five Hours,* though consistent enough with the theory of drama expressed in *Of Dramatick Poesie,* was not characteristic of the general response to the play. Samuel Pepys's enthusiasm for it was much more typical. He saw its première on Jaunary 8, 1663:

> There being the famous new play acted the first time to-day, which is called "The Adventures of Five Hours," at the Duke's house, being, they say, made or translated by Colonel Tuke, I did long to see it; and so made my wife to get her ready, though we were forced to send for a smith, to break open her trunk . . . and though early, were forced to sit almost out of sight, at the end of one of the lower forms, so full was the house. And the play, in one word, is the best, for the variety and the most excellent continuance of the plot to the very end, that ever I saw, or think ever shall, and all possible, not only to be done in the time, but in most other respects very admittable, and without one word of ribaldry; and the house, by its frequent plaudits, did show their sufficient approbation.

Evelyn, who had earlier seen the play in rehearsal, was also present on January 8: "I went to see Sir S: Tuke (my kindsmans) Comedy acted at the Dukes Theater, which so universally tooke as it was acted

8. Ibid., p. 60.

for some weekes every day, & twas believed would be worth [to] the Comedians 4 or 500 pounds: Indeede the plot was incomparable but the language stiffe & formall"—more judicious criticism than that of Pepys, whose enthusiasm grew with the passage of time. On August 20, 1666, in an extravagance of praise that has damaged his reputation as a critic, Pepys wrote that he had been reading *Othello,* "which I ever heretofore esteemed a mighty good play, but having so lately read 'The Adventures of Five Houres,' it seems a mean thing."

Tuke's title, an adaptation of the Spanish with a reduction in the number of hours from six to five, provides a tactful reminder that the time scheme corresponds with that recommended by the critics. In those years the doctrines of neoclassicism were lively topics of conversation in court circles. The king himself in 1667 made an objection to *Secret Love* that involved a subtlety of neoclassical theory.[9] The publication in 1660 of Corneille's collected works—the plays he had by then written with commentaries on each of them and three critical discourses, one of them on the unities—had provided a stimulus to and a focus for critical speculation.[10] *The Adventures of Five Hours* gained in reputation from the fact that it was in the specialized sense "regular," as well as orderly in the contrivance of its plot.

Yet, in the English as in the Spanish play of which it is a faithful rendering, the limitation of time is achieved at the cost, paradoxically, of verisimilitude, a quality the unities of time and place were intended to enhance. Unlike French classical plays, in which the unities are a corollary of simplicity in narrative line, cape and sword plays such as Coello's and Tuke's have plots in which characters undergo repeated changes of expectation and fortune. In the French drama the unities could enforce close and extended analysis of states of mind; in *The Adventures of Five Hours* and its Spanish predecessor, complications and reversals come too fast for states of mind to receive much attention. Emphasis falls, not on credibility of character in relation to events, but rather on adroit manipulation of events. Pepys's choice of terms in praising *The Adventures of Five Hours* was discriminating; the play was "the best, for the variety

9. Dryden, *Works,* 9 : 117.
10. Cf. Pierre Legouis, "Corneille and Dryden as Dramatic Critics," in *Seventeenth Century Studies Presented to Sir Herbert Grierson* (Oxford, 1938), pp. 269–91.

and the most excellent continuance of the plot to the very end." That is to say, he admired the artistry revealed in the contrivance of the plot, a quality that we may also admire if we suspend our modern preoccupation with plausibility of characterization.

The turns and counterturns of the plot are too complex for it to be profitable to describe them here. But the psychic distance Tuke's characters must travel in five hours before they achieve matrimony may be suggested by an account of the plight of the two heroines at the opening of the play. Much of the essential action has taken place before the first act begins and must be presented retrospectively, in expository conversation. Later English dramatists sometimes "regularized" Spanish plots by the use of retrospective conversation; in this instance, Tuke had no need to modify his original. Early in the first act of the Spanish as well as the English play the two young women compete with one another in describing their predicaments. The beloved of the one is unknown to her except for his name, she having seen him only once on her travels when he saved her life; the beloved of the other has killed her brother's friend in self-defense, and to further compound her difficulties she has been betrothed by her brother against her will to an unknown man—in fact, though she does not know it, to the other young woman's beloved. With these events in the past, the play can move rapidly through misadventures and misunderstandings, complicated by the Spaniards' sensitivity about family honor and readiness to use the sword in defense of it, to a conventional pairing of couples. All this is indeed accomplished in five hours, only about twice as long as the elapsed time of representation; and it is accomplished with a neatness of complication and resolution of plot that compels admiration for craftsmanship—Coello's craftsmanship, however, rather than Tuke's.

Dryden's criticism of the hurried plot of *The Adventures of Five Hours* is more consonant with modern taste than Pepys's praise of the excellence of its design. *The Adventures* has the advantages and liabilities of cape and sword drama in superlative measure. It is a better play than modern students commonly assume, more artful in its intrigue and more entertaining. If conventional, the characters nevertheless possess sufficient individuality for us to be concerned about what happens to them; and they carry on their troubled courtships with an attractive zest and resourcefulness. We can imagine the half-humorous excitement caused by the appearance on the darkened stage of two pairs of armed men, brothers and lovers of the heroines, who become aware of one another, draw their swords and engage—and part without knowing their opponents' identity. Tuke's tone is right: not wholly comic or serious but both by turns, romantic but not absurdly so. He follows the Spanish in his use of the gracioso, who, Dryden's disparagement of him notwithstanding, serves the purpose, traditional to that character type in the comedia, of reducing the heroics of other characters to credibility. *The Adventures* is a good example of the cape and sword play, perhaps the truest and most successful naturalization of this Spanish form in English. And yet it does not commend itself to modern students of literature, largely for the reason that Dryden specified: the plot hurries from one thing to another so rapidly that there is little opportunity "to represent the passions."

The circumstances surrounding Tuke's writing of *The Adventures* provide a reminder of the importance of the king's exile in introducing the Spanish plays to England. Charles himself proposed to Tuke that he write an adaptation of *Los empeños de seis horas* (or did he merely praise the Spanish play in Tuke's presence?), presumably having learned about it on the Continent; and Tuke was able to act on the suggestion as he could not have done had he not known Spanish, presumably having learned it in the Spanish Netherlands while he was there in the final decade before the Restoration.[11] Tuke's is a courtier's play, royalist in frequent innuendo (including a respectful glance at the king's recent Portuguese marriage [act 1]). In the prologue recited when the play was performed at court, Tuke refers, in appropriate hyperbole, to the king's command, which came at a time when he was planning a retirement:

> He chanc'd to hear his Majesty once say
> He lik'd this Plot: he staid; and writ the Play.

In the preface to the third edition of the play, published in 1671, he adds more detail:

> certainly the *Plot* needs no *Apology;* it was taken out of *Dom Pedro Calderon,* a celebrated *Spanish* Author, the Nation of the World who are the happiest in the force and delicacy of their *Inventions,* and recommended to me by *His Sacred Majesty,* as

11. Cf. Gaw, "Tuke's *Adventures,*" p. 4.

an *Excellant Design;* whose Judgment is no more to be doubted, than his Commands are to be disobey'd.

Tuke's use of the phrase "excellent design" sounds as though Charles would have sided with Pepys rather than Dryden in evaluating the play.

Colonel Samuel Tuke—Sir Samuel as he became in 1664—had shared the king's exile. After distinguished service in Charles I's army, he spent the years of the Protectorate on the Continent, in France and in Flanders. Although references to him are frequent in the royalist state papers of the 1650s and reveal that he was well and favorably known to the king, the duke of York, and their mother,[12] the known records provide no information, apart from showing that he passed time in Flanders, about his study of Spanish. In any event, Tuke was not an accomplished man of letters. The dialogue of *The Adventures,* in the phrase of Tuke's perhaps overly severe kinsman John Evelyn, is "stiffe & formall"; the plot, on the other hand, again according to Evelyn, is "incomparable," and this Tuke took from his Spanish original. Though he could presumably read Spanish (perhaps with assistance from Lord Bristol), he seems not to have had a sustained interest in the language and literature.

In the preface to the third edition of his play, Tuke alluded to *Los empeños de seis horas* as the work of Calderón (a circumstance to be taken into account when interpreting Restoration criticism of the comedia). Calderón's name appeared in seventeenth-century editions of it; but he did not include it in his own list of his plays, and it is at the top of the list, compiled by his friend Vera Tassis, of plays falsely attributed to him.[13] Probably it was written by Antonio Coello, a dramatist and courtier of the reign of Philip IV: it is virtually identical to a play of different title published as his.[14]

12. For example, Queen Henrietta Maria wrote to her son the king on September 26, 1657, recommending the appointment of Tuke as one of the secretaries of the duke of York. She alluded to Tuke's loyal service to their family. The king in reply refused to make the appointment on grounds that Tuke lacked appropriate experience, assuring his mother that he would find some suitable employment for him: *Clarendon State Papers, 1655–1657,* ed. Macray, 3 : 365, 369–70.

13. Gaw, "Tuke's *Adventures,*" p. 23 n., provides a summary of the relevant bibliographical facts.

14. A. E. H. Swaen, ed., *The Adventures of Five Hours* (Amsterdam, 1927), p. xvi. This useful edition includes Tuke's texts of both 1663 and 1671, as well as the text of the Spanish play. See also the modern edition of *The Adventures of Five Hours* prepared by B. Van Thal, with an introduction by Montague Summers (London, 1927).

For the most part Tuke followed the Spanish play, even to the entrances and exits of characters.[15] Some of the changes he made were forced upon him by differences between English and Spanish dramatic conventions. He organized his play in five acts rather than the three customary in the comedia; and he broke up the long expository speeches of the original with questions and comments from the interlocutors. He introduced a love affair between servants, though he gave it little emphasis. He added an opening scene and expanded the closing scene, in both instances clarifying details of plot. He introduced a brief scene at the beginning of the fifth act, presumably to exploit a stage trick in which a virgin lights a candle with her breath.

Though he follows the narrative line of the comedia, he treats the language freely.[16] The rapidly moving short lines of the Spanish give way in the English to pentameters that are sometimes formal to the point of awkwardness. The movement of the dialogue is much slower than in the Spanish, Tuke often transforming matter-of-fact statement into sententious maxim. Even when he does not proceed to a generalization suggested by events of the play, he develops metaphorical allusion more fully and more explicitly than the Spanish dramatist does. The greater explicitness and elaboration of dramatic language look as though they are the result of too much straining for clarity and intensity.

When he revised his play for the third edition, Tuke unfortunately emphasized just these qualities. The later version is more consciously literary, less frequently colloquial (though it is also freer of such infelicities as inversions). The occasional solemnity has been intensified.

> Man's Joys do ne'r to their Perfection rise,
> Till when by Crosses heightned, they surprize.

says Antonio in the final scene of the first edition; and the next character changes the subject back to the business at hand. In the third edition Antonio's speech is more pompous, and it is reinforced by a remark of the next speaker:

> ANTONIO: *Ah! how the memory of our Crosses past,*
> *Heightens our joys when we succeed at last.*

15. Gaw, "Tuke's *Adventures*," pp. 25–26.
16. Ibid., pp. 41–42.

OCTAVIO: *Our pleasures in this world are alwayes mix'd,*
'Tis in the next where all our joys are fix'd.

Pious thoughts indeed for a gay comedy.

The changes apparently result from Tuke's desire to improve his perhaps unexpectedly famous play by taking into account both stylistic criticism of it and also developments in drama, such as the appearance of the heroic play with its supporting body of theory. It has been well argued that Tuke, in making the revisions, may have been influenced by Dryden's criticism, some of which was directed at *The Adventures,* and by the example of his heroic plays.[17] "As for those who have been so angry with this *Innocent Piece,* not guilty of so much as that Current Wit, *Obscenity* and *Profaneness*", Tuke wrote in his preface, in what would seem to be a bad-tempered allusion to Dryden's comedies as well as to his critical essays, "*These are to let them know,* that though the Author Converses but with few, he Writes to all, and aiming as well at the *Delight* as *Profit* of his *Readers.*" Tuke's sense of self-righteousness damages his syntax, though he could justifiably claim that his play was free of the sexual innuendo so prominent in Dryden's comedies. Whatever his motives in revising the play so comprehensively, he scarcely improved it. With his little knowledge of the theater, he heightened bad qualities even while alleviating minor faults.

Tuke may have had assistance from Lord Bristol in writing *The Adventures.* At least two contemporaries refer to Bristol as author or part author of the play. When Pepys, on July 20, 1664, saw Bristol's *Worse and Worse,* he wrote: "just the same manner of play, and writ, I believe, by the same man as 'The Adventures of Five Hours'; very pleasant it was." In this case Pepys perhaps attributed Bristol's play to Tuke rather than the other way around. But Lady Anglesey wrote to her husband on January 10, 1663, referring to *The Adventures:* "Lord Bristol has made a play which is much commended," while John Downes described it as "Wrote by the Earl of *Bristol,* and Sir *Samuel Tuke.*" [18] Although Downes did not write until over forty years later, he had been employed by Davenant's

17. Ibid., pp. 46–58.
18. Quoted from *The London Stage,* pt. 1, p. 61; Downes, *Roscius Anglicanus* (London, 1708), p. 22.

company at the time they first performed the play, and, judging from the completeness with which he lists roles played by individual actors, in *The Adventures* as in other plays, he had access to theatrical records which have since disappeared. Gerard Langbaine both in 1688 and 1691 attributed it to Tuke alone.[19] William Oldys, in his eighteenth-century marginalia to Langbaine's *An Account of the English Dramatick Poets,* added that the "E of Bristol is said to have joynd in it," [20] a remark probably derived from Downes: Oldys follows Downes in saying that the play "was richly dressd [and] took 13 nights successively." Yet even if Bristol had any part in the play, it was claimed by Tuke and was generally recognized as his literary property: he signed the dedicatory epistle of the first edition, he was the recipient of prefatory poems of congratulation printed in the second, and he put his name on the title page of the third. We may guess that Bristol might have helped him with the Spanish, which Bristol certainly knew and Tuke, apart from the play, left no evidence of having known; but we may merely guess.

That Lord Bristol should be credited with the authorship or part authorship of *The Adventures* is understandable in view of his known literary interests and his connection in the public mind with all things Spanish. I have already referred to his advocacy of a Spanish marriage for the king and his opposition to the marriage to Catharine of Braganza (see above, p. 52). He was deeply involved in the intrigues of the Restoration court, so much so that he could have given only limited attention to literary projects. Prevented from holding office by his Catholicism, and no doubt also by the unreliability of his judgment and the instability of his temperament, he resentfully turned against Clarendon. And for his pains he has had the ill fortune to be remembered by later generations through an acid characterization in *The History of the Rebellion.*

Bristol's three plays were all adaptations from Calderón: *Elvira; Or, The Worst Not Always True* (acted in 1664, published in 1667) [21] from *No siempre lo peor es cierto; 'Tis Better than It Was,*

19. *A New Catalogue of English Plays* (London, 1688), p. 25; *An Account of the English Dramatick Poets* (Oxford, 1691), p. 505.

20. Copy now in the British Museum (B.M., C.28.g.1).

21. The title page notes merely that the play was "Written by a Person of Quality." It was credited to Bristol by Anthony Wood, *Athenae Oxonienses* (London, 1691–92) 2, 430.

presumably from *Mejor está que estaba;* and *Worse and Worse,* presumably from *Peor está que estaba.* If the latter two adaptations were printed, as seems doubtful, they have not survived. We have John Downes's word for it that they were presented by the Duke's Company between 1662 and 1665, as well as a corroborating statement concerning *Worse and Worse* by Pepys, who saw it performed on July 20, 1664, and a record of its performance at court on November 26, 1666.[22] It has been suggested that *Elvira* may be one of the two lost plays renamed; [23] but since all three of Bristol's titles correspond closely to titles of Calderón's, I see no reason to doubt that the three adaptations were written. Judging from the carelessness with which *Elvira* was printed, Bristol took no interest in its publication; probably he did not bother to have the other two plays published at all. Our knowledge about them is limited to what can be inferred from Pepys's brief but informative comment, and from the two plays of Calderón with corresponding titles.

Like *The Adventures of Five Hours, Elvira* is more accurately considered a free translation than an original play. Bristol retains Calderón's characters, though he changes some names; and he follows with a minimum of difference the plot of the Spanish. It is in the texture of his verse—very loose blank verse—that his play is, predictably, most strikingly inferior to Calderón's.

The stylistic deficiencies notwithstanding, *Elvira* is readable, more so than many seventeenth-century plays written with greater skill, and Pepys reported that *Worse and Worse* (probably much like it) was entertaining on the stage. A special merit of the Spanish plots was their capacity to withstand translation, their durability even in such hurried hands as Bristol's. Not dependent on the analysis of motive, and thus not on the interaction of individualized characters either, the plays can command attention even in mediocre translated verse. In *Elvira* as in *No siempre lo peor es cierto* the intrigue is set in motion by a lady's withholding information lest she precipitate a duel. A gallant, secretly visiting his betrothed in her own apartment, discovers and severely wounds an unknown man. Despite his suspicion of his fiancée, he escorts her to another city and finds her refuge

22. *Roscius Anglicanus,* p. 26; *The London Stage,* pt. 1, p. 97.

23. Dorothea Townshend, *George Digby, Second Earl of Bristol* (London, 1924), p. 239. The suggestion had earlier been made in the *Dictionary of National Biography.*

as a gentlewoman attending the sister of his friend. The intruder proves to have been the erring suitor of the friend's sister, herself a spirited young woman who resolves the confusion by persuading her suitor to declare the other young woman's innocence.

This is the conventional matter of Spanish comedy of intrigue: ingenious young women scheming to put right difficulties arising from the impetuosity of young men who are oversensitive to affronts against honor. In Calderón's play conventionality of plot is no more damaging than it is in the best English comedies of manners. In Congreve, for example, plots as old as the Restoration are vehicles for language which, in its texture, determines characterization and theme. Calderón's verse is of course missing in *Elvira.* Yet Bristol saw and to some limited extent retained the pace of Calderón's play and its mood of Valencia with its orange trees blooming.

The changes he made again reflect differences between English and Spanish dramatic conventions. He divided his play into five acts rather than the three of the original, but this was merely an arbitrary and mechanical change, of little consequence. More important, he shortened Calderón's long speeches, sometimes breaking them up into dialogue, a change inevitable in a play to be performed on the English stage. This took its toll in *Elvira* as in other renderings of the comedia. In the Spanish the monologue provides concise exposition and also analysis of the emotional dimension of events; it provides compensation for the rapidity of plot movement by permitting reflective comment. In Calderón's play the wronged young woman, early in the first act, recalls to her doubting lover the tenderness of their courtship and the horror she felt at the sudden appearance of the intruder. The fact that Bristol must convey all this briefly and in conversational exchange inhibits his delineation of the young woman's plight.

Bristol's two lost adaptations, *'Tis Better than It Was* and *Worse and Worse* presumably resembled *Elvira:* at any rate, the plays of Calderón from which, to judge by their titles, they were adapted, resemble the original of *Elvira,* just as all three of them, cape and sword plays that they are, resemble the original of *The Adventures of Five Hours. Mejor está que estaba* and *Peor está que estaba* again portray young lovers temporarily frustrated by misunderstandings and by overscrupulous attention to honor and reputation; and both plays include a superabundance of what Dryden called "turns," changes in the direction in which events are moving. Dryden's criticism of the Spanish plots in *Of Dramatick Poesie* would apply to all three of the plays by Calderón, and probably he had one or more of Bristol's adaptations in mind, along with *The Adventures of Five Hours,* as he wrote. The dates of the composition of the essay on the one hand, and of the production of Bristol's plays on the other, coincide closely. Downes said that *'Tis Better than It Was* and *Worse and Worse* were performed between 1662 and 1665; *Elvira* was performed in November 1664 and printed in 1667.[24] Probably Dryden wrote a draft of the essay in 1665–66, and he revised and published it in 1668. The fact that Bristol had even less skill as a dramatic writer than Tuke may help to account for the severity of Dryden's remarks. Bristol's choice of cape and sword plays, to the exclusion of other forms of the comedia, would have reinforced the conception of Spanish drama, evident in *Of Dramatick Poesie* and elsewhere in Restoration criticism, as being severely limited in its resources.

Bristol's social prominence lent status to his plays that they did not deserve on their own merits. Although frustrated in his political ambitions, he had nevertheless shared the king's friendship in exile, he was an earl, and a Knight of the Garter. He was an English grandee who could command attention for anything he wrote, even something so slight as *Elvira* (accurately described by some seventeenth-century handwriting in a copy now in the British Museum as "Indifferent"). Along with Tuke he was a decisive figure in establishing the vogue of the Spanish plots, whatever the unknowable facts about his possible contribution to *The Adventures of Five Hours.* The type of play he chose for his adaptations and even the very plays themselves reappear as sources used by English dramatists in the later seventeenth and early eighteenth centuries.

Dr. F. T. Hogan has traced portions of Aphra Behn's *The Dutch Lover* (1673) to Calderón's *No siempre lo peor es cierto* and *Peor está que estaba,* and portions of her *The Rover,* part 1 (1677), to Calderón's *Mejor está que estaba.*[25] Dr. Hogan considers the borrowings to be *"direct"* from the Spanish; I think it more likely, since

24. *Roscius Anglicanus,* p. 26; *The London Stage,* pt. 1, p. 85.

25. Floriana T. Hogan, "Notes on Thirty-One English Plays and their Spanish Sources," *Restoration and Eighteenth-Century Theatre Research* 6 (1967): 57.

all three of the Spanish plays were adapted by Bristol, that Mrs. Behn used his English versions, perhaps remembering performances of them, perhaps having access to manuscript copies of the two plays which seem not to have been published. And as I shall explain later, I think that the translation from the Spanish recommended to Tom Durfey by the king, from which Durfey drew part of his *The Banditti* (1686), was Bristol's adaptation of *Peor está que estaba* (see below, pp. 150–52). Dr. Hogan has described Richard Savage's eighteenth-century adaptation from the comedia, *Love in a Veil* (1718), as an instance of direct borrowing from *Peor está que estaba.* Perhaps so; the English resembles the Spanish closely indeed.[26] But it would be an unusual coincidence if Savage's choice of this particular play as his source, from the vast number of comedias available, was uninfluenced by Bristol's adaptation of it. Could it be that Savage, an unscrupulous literary opportunist, merely published a manuscript of Bristol's adaptation, perhaps with some revision?[27] This is speculation, incapable of verification. But the recurrence as sources of English plays of precisely those comedias of which Bristol wrote adaptations is verifiable.

A better Spanish plot than *Elvira,* if a less influential one, is an obscure play, *The Carnival,* by an obscure young man, Thomas Porter, who was nevertheless a member of a distinguished family that had an even longer association with Spain than the Digbys. Thomas was the son of Endymion Porter, to whom reference has already been made as a member of the entourage attending Prince Charles in Madrid in 1623. Endymion Porter and Cottington had in fact traveled with the prince and the duke of Buckingham as they made their way to Spain, incognito and on horseback. The Porter family connection with Spain had begun in the preceding century,

26. Ibid., p. 57; Floriana T. Hogan, "Notes on Savage's *Love in a Veil* and Calderón's *Peor está que estaba,*" *Restoration and Eighteenth-Century Theatre Research* 8 (May 1969) : 23–29. See also Clarence Tracy, *The Artificial Bastard: A Biography of Richard Savage* (Cambridge, Mass., 1953), p. 40.

27. Tracy speculates that Savage may have worked from a translation of *Peor está que estaba* supplied him by a Mrs. Lucy Rodd Price, who had earlier translated Calderón's *La dama duende.* Tracy adds: "At any rate he could not have used the French translation produced in 1707 by LeSage, for the latter omits much of the dramatic material Savage used; and there was no other translation." We may amend this by saying that there had been a translation, Bristol's, though it has not survived into the twentieth century.

when about 1560 Giles Porter, Endymion's grandfather, had gone there, perhaps with an English embassy, and had married a Spanish aristocrat, Doña Juana de Figueroa y Mont Salve.[28] Their children were brought up in Spain, though Giles Porter returned to England with them in the 1580s and settled there. When in 1605 the earl of Nottingham led the large English mission to Valladolid for the ratification of the peace treaty, Giles Porter went along as interpreter, and he seems to have taken with him his grandson Endymion, then eighteen years old. Endymion remained in Spain for about seven years, serving for a time in the household of Count Olivares and no doubt enjoying social connections made possible by his grandmother's family.

In the history of the Porter family can be seen a continuing personal link with Spain, a renewal of ties over some four generations. As a biographer of Endymion Porter put it, "Whenever there was Spanish business to be done some of the Porter family generally had a hand in it." [29] The remark was suggested by Charles I's recommendation of Endymion's oldest son, George Porter, to Ormonde in 1641 as a leader of soldiers to be sent into service under the king of Spain. With such a family, it was natural enough for Thomas Porter, when soon after the Restoration he turned to writing plays, to look to Spain for dramatic materials.

His *The Carnival,* printed in 1664 and probably acted in that year,[30] is Spanish in locale and characters, and it resembles the comedia in tone and dramatic action; but it has no known source. I would assume that it is indeed based on a Spanish play, though one not as yet identified. The plot and the characters are in the familiar mold of the cape and sword play, even to the conventional motif of a young woman, disguised as a man, pursuing her errant lover. Several extended soliloquies look as though they are translations of Spanish monologues, as, for example, in act 2, when the central male character, Ferdinando, describes an emotional conflict arising from his obligation to one young woman and his love for another. Intermittently interrupting the serious action, again in the Spanish man-

28. Gervas Huxley, *Endymion Porter,* pp. 18 ff.

29. Dorothea Townshend, *Life and Letters of Mr. Endymion Porter* (London, 1897), p. 194.

30. *The London Stage,* pt. 1, p. 76.

ner, is the prattle of servants, one of whom, Sancho, approximates the gracioso.

Alfred Harbage has suggested that the play may have a common source with one by Davenant: "*The Carnival* . . . is filled with romantic intrigue certainly derived from some Spanish drama of cloak and sword, possibly the same that had suggested Davenant's *Spanish Lovers* of 1639." [31] Davenant had been a friend of Thomas Porter's father, and perhaps he gave assistance to the young man (though *The Carnival* was presented by Killigrew's company),[32] but the resemblances between the two plays seem to me to be insufficiently particularized to imply a common source. Yet Porter must have had a source. The excellence of *The Carnival,* which is much superior to Porter's other work, argues that it was not original and that Porter was able to draw on the skill of some other writer.

The plot of *The Carnival* is original enough, and in some details surprising enough, to repay summary. Don Ferdinando, in love with and betrothed to Donna Beatrice, is taken by her brother, Don Alvaredo, to meet his own beloved, Donna Elvira. Encouraged by Elvira, Ferdinando returns alone a little later to see her, and they converse and fall in love. But Ferdinando soon has qualms of conscience, and to escape from his dilemma, he leaves Seville to go to Salamanca. Beatrice learns of his abrupt departure and, like many another Spanish heroine, she disguises herself in man's clothes and sets out in pursuit. First Ferdinando and then Beatrice are captured by a band of thieves—amateur thieves, as it turns out, who soon release them unharmed. Complications arising from the adventure reunite not only Ferdinando and Beatrice but also the other couple, when Elvira, learning that Ferdinando has deserted her, turns to Alvaredo, her original suitor. Alvaredo, believing his honor to be injured by his sister's flight, promises to avenge himself on Ferdinando, whom he mistakenly holds responsible. Through the offices of Ferdinando's lively younger brother Felices (who has carried on a bantering courtship with Beatrice's younger sister Miranda), ex-

31. Harbage, *Cavalier Drama* (New York, 1936), p. 250.

32. Downes, *Roscius Anglicanus,* p. 8. Downes lists *The Carnival* among the "Old Plays" revived by the King's Company in the early years of the Restoration. Could Porter have merely revised a manuscript of an adaptation written before the Civil Wars? Yet Porter's name is on the title page, and he is credited with the play by Langbaine (*Account of the English Dramatick Poets,* p. 407).

planations are made, reconciliations accomplished, and marriages agreed to in a fifth act, which is enlivened by the carnival of the title.

Presumably, Porter's literary source, whatever that was, provided the unexpected complication, on which all else turns, of a young man betrothed to one young woman falling in love with another. This complication, calculated to emphasize the ambiguity of love, leads Ferdinando and Elvira to introspective musings that convey an impression of psychological authenticity, of freedom from conventions of love and courtship. The dramatic language, for which Porter was responsible, is competent enough to support the analysis of emotion. Porter's blank verse is curious; it is unobtrusive and usually, though not invariably, graceful but very irregular. Like Cavalier dramatists before him, he extends the process of relaxation in the formal patterns of verse observable in Caroline drama.[33] Yet some of the metrical irregularities could result from an attempt to imitate the polymetric structure of the comedia.

The obscurity into which *The Carnival* and its author have long since fallen notwithstanding, the play, to judge from the comments of Gerard Langbaine in 1691, had some contemporary popularity and reputation. Langbaine provides the only known seventeenth-century criticism of Thomas Porter:

> An Author that has writ in our Times two Plays, which are receiv'd with Candor, by all Judges of Wit; *viz.*
>
> *Carnival,* a Comedy acted at the Theatre-Royal, by his Majesties Servants; printed 4⁰. *Lond.* 1664.
>
> *Villain,* a Tragedy, which I have seen acted at the Duke's Theatre with great applause: the part of *Malignii* being incomparably play'd by Mr. *Sandford.*
>
> What this Author may have writ besides, I know not; and am sorry I can give no better Account of One, whose Writings I love and admire.[34]

We may give a tentative answer to Langbaine's final query by saying that Porter is now credited, though on the uncertain evidence of the

33. Cf. Harbage, *Cavalier Drama,* pp. 38–39.
34. *An Account of the English Dramatick Poets,* p. 407.

initials "T.P." on the title page,[35] with *The French Conjurer,* a comedy performed about 1677, and also with an earlier unacted tragicomedy, *A Witty Combat,* printed in 1663. Of all the plays, *The Carnival* alone would seem to have a relationship to the comedia, a circumstance that may, as I have suggested, account for its superiority to the others. Whatever its source, it provided, only four years after the Restoration (at about the time of Dryden's *The Rival Ladies,* in which the motif of a young woman disguised as a man and captured by bandits reappears), an example of a Spanish plot in which the rapid "turns" of action did not prevent the sensitive depiction of passion and emotional conflict. No more than other English dramatists of the decade did Porter succeed in naturalizing the gracioso; the comic scenes interrupt, they do not comment on or interpret the serious plot, a circumstance perhaps relevant to the disdain for the gracioso expressed in *Of Dramatick Poesie.* In its weakness as in its strength, the play would have contributed to the Restoration conception of the comedia.

Among the Cavalier dramatists who turned to the comedia was a Scot, Thomas Sydserf (or St. Serfe, as he spelled it in the dedication to his play), the son of a bishop and for a time after the Restoration the manager of a theater in Edinburgh.[36] He had served under Montrose on the Continent as well as in Scotland; perhaps, like other Royalists, he had learned Spanish in the Netherlands. Whatever the source or extent of his knowledge of the language, his one play, *Tarugo's Wiles; Or, The Coffee House,* acted by the Duke's Company in October, 1667, is an adaptation of Moreto's *No puede ser el guardar una mujer* (itself an adaptation of Lope's *El mayor imposible*),[37] the same Spanish play which in 1685 King Charles recommended to John Crowne, who based on it his masterpiece, *Sir*

35. *DNB,* s.v. Thomas Porter.

36. A biographical account of Sydserf, along with records of judicial proceedings in which he is mentioned, is included in *Miscellany of the Abbotsford Club,* 1 (Edinburgh, 1837) : 85–95. Little is known about his life. In bibliographies of the drama, he is sometimes referred to as a knight, but solely on the basis of a reference by Lord Buckhurst (later the earl of Dorset) in commendatory verses on *Tarugo's Wiles.* Neither Langbaine nor Downes, though they mention him, allude to a knighthood.

37. Cf. Adolf Schaeffer, *Geschichte des spanischen Nationaldramas* (Leipzig, 1890), 1 : 164; 2 : 166.

Courtly Nice. If *Tarugo's Wiles* is inferior to *Sir Courtly Nice,* it is nevertheless a closer rendering of the Spanish original, retaining, unlike the later play, Spanish characters and locale and including stretches of dialogue that are loose translations from Moreto.

Even so, *Tarugo's Wiles* is not so close an adaptation of its Spanish original as are *The Adventures of Five Hours* and *Elvira,* and it differs from them in tone. Moreto and, after him, Sydserf have plots that turn on suspicious brothers guarding their sisters, in fact guarding them so closely that they are in effect imprisoned. Yet Moreto, and even more Sydserf, exploits this classic Spanish situation not so much for its manifest possibilities of dangerous intrigue as for its humorous potential. Although both dramatists retain the restrictive conception of family honor as the propelling force for the episodic complications, they shift attention from the hot-blooded antagonists, brothers and suitors of the ladies, to a clever friend of lower rank—Tarugo by name in both versions, though with the important difference that in the Spanish he is a servant and in the English, an impoverished kinsman of one of the suitors. This is a curious change for Sydserf to have made, and perhaps reflects the customary English underestimation of and dislike for the stage type of the gracioso. Despite the difference in his status, Tarugo dominates the action in both the Spanish and English versions, and in much the way that the clever servant often does in Roman comedy, Italian *commedia dell'arte,* French imitations of that Italian form, and such an English derivative of it as the Duke of Newcastle and Dryden's *Sir Martin Mar-all.*[38]

This last play preceded *Tarugo's Wiles* so closely in time, and in its central comic resource resembles Sydserf's so markedly, as to suggest that the later play may owe something to the earlier as well as to *No puede ser. Sir Martin Mar-all* was acted for the first time by the Duke's Company in August 1667 with great success; it was performed the following autumn, once in an interval of the initial run of *Tarugo's Wiles* in the same theater, *Sir Martin* on October 14 and *Tarugo* on October 15.[39] We do not know who had the title role in Sydserf's play, but it would be a reasonable guess that it was Henry Harris, who played Warner, the clever servant and manipu-

38. Dryden, *Works,* 9 : 365–66.
39. *The London Stage,* pt. 1, p. 120.

lator in Newcastle and Dryden's play. The stratagems devised by Tarugo and Warner for aiding their masters to gain access to a closely guarded lady have more than a casual resemblance, extending in one instance to an attempt to beguile the suspicious guardian by an impersonation of a friend or relative supposedly just arrived from a sea voyage. Sydserf's source, even in this episode, was Moreto rather than the earlier English play, but his interest in the Spanish play may have been quickened by the similarity between it and *Sir Martin Mar-all,* and he may have accentuated the resemblances between the two central situations.

The similarity to *Sir Martin,* a farcical comedy of situation with ancestry by way of French intermediaries in commedia dell'arte, suggests a quality in *Tarugo's Wiles* that differentiates it from some of the other Spanish plots. It is recognizably akin to them in locale, characters, episodes, and above all in conception of personal and family honor as motivating forces, and yet its ironical wit results in a difference of tone. Sydserf's Tarugo, an impoverished younger brother of good family, has recently returned to Spain from England, and he has brought home with him an uninhibited mode of speech. His kinsman Don Horatio predicts in the first act that he will "soon recover the gravity of our Spanish conversation, which I perceive you have altogether cast off for the English way of freedom." But the change does not come in the play, in which Tarugo takes the lead in a bantering and satirical review of the irrationalities in Spanish manners; and his recent visit to England leads to remarks on English customs. A controlling sanity appears even on the subject of family honor in the English as earlier in the Spanish play. Not until the brother who keeps his sister immured moderates his excessive suspicion will his own sweetheart accept him.

Less tightly and gracefully organized than *No puede ser, Tarugo's Wiles* nevertheless resembles the Spanish play closely. Apart from Tarugo, the characters have different names, but the important characters have parallel roles, and—always excepting the clever contriver of stratagems, Tarugo—their personalities are similar. Certain minor differences appear; in Moreto but not in Sydserf, for example, the two young gentlewomen are cousins. The sequence of events is not always the same. But the resemblances of detail, and frequently of language, reveal that Sydserf wrote with Moreto's play open before him, paraphrasing the Spanish with a less exuberant imagination. The dialogue of the two plays is so unequal in quality as not to support comparison, and this is to be expected. Moreto was one of the principal Spanish dramatists of the seventeenth century; Sydserf, not a professional dramatist at all, was the author of a single moderately successful comedy, one justly described by Langbaine as "not equal with those of the first Rank," though it "yet exceeds several which pretend to the second; especially the *third* Act, which discovers the several Humours of a *Coffee-house*." [40]

Langbaine isolates the best, and the best-known, scene in the play, one comprising the entire third act, in which Sydserf depicts a coffee-house, obviously an English coffee-house with a representative English clientele, and this despite the nominal setting in Spain. This scene provided Sydserf's subtitle, and to judge from John Downes's reference to "*The Coffee-house,* by Mr. *Sincerf*" [41] the subtitle was customarily used. The scene has no counterpart in *No puede ser,* though it has a thematic resemblance to, and may have been suggested by, Moreto's depiction of a literary salon in a scene (act 1, scene 2), which, like it, satirizes intellectual pretension. Sydserf's characters, who are portrayed with a repertorial honesty and in an antirhetorical idiom reminiscent of Ben Jonson, are thoroughly English in their attitudes and preoccupations.

It is as though Sydserf in his third act put aside his text of the Spanish play and reverted to the native comic tradition deriving from Jonson. The ironical review of manners, apparent throughout the play though elsewhere tempered by the demands of busy intrigue, becomes dominant in this scene, which has little connection with the organizing principle of the play, the stratagems of Tarugo to assist his friend in his courtship. The patrons of the coffee-house carry on conversations about topics that in 1667 were timely and important. If the scene in its discontinuity with the rest of the play represents a structural fault, we can scarcely regret its presence, so convincing is the rendering of conversation. Even in October 1667 the scene attracted comment. Lord Fountainhall wrote that

> heir is the Dukes playhouse, wheir we saw Tom Sydserfes Spanish Comedie Tarugo's Wiles, or the Coffee House, acted. . . . He could not forget himselfe: was very satyricall sneering at the

40. *An Account of the English Dramatick Poets,* p. 434.
41. *Roscius Anglicanus,* p. 31.

> Greshamers for their late invention of the transfusion of blood, as also at our covenant, making the witch of Geneva to wy [sic] it and La Sainte Lingue de France togither.[42]

Much of the dialogue turns on the contemporary experiments of the virtuosi, and the early date of the play, in the first decade of the Royal Society, gives a special interest to talk about such topics as the transfusion of blood. Sydserf anticipates by nearly a decade Shadwell's dramatic satire on the new science, in *The Virtuoso* (1676).[43]

The coffee-house scene is in conversational subject and satirical tone at a distance from cape and sword intrigue, and if the other scenes (focused on problems of young lovers arising from the family pride and suspicious nature of the Spaniards) are less far removed, the play yet provides a reminder that almost from their beginnings in the Restoration the Spanish plots were compatible with the witty observation of social relationships that was in process of emerging as a principal resource of the comedy of manners. Dryden had already written *The Rival Ladies,* in which along with a cape and sword plot he had provided a foretaste of the conversational duel of wit he was soon to bring to perfection; Wycherley was perhaps already at work on one of his first two comedies, in which the matter of the comedia would be anglicized and in the process transmuted into comedy of manners. Sydserf chose as his source a play in which urbane satire was already prominent, and if in his adaptation he could not equal Moreto's stylistic grace, he accentuated the satirical strain of his original and intermittently reconciled it with English comic tradition.

Davenant's *The Man's the Master* resembles *Tarugo's Wiles* in its assimilation within a Spanish plot of broadly comic scenes, though this time the modification of the Spanish original had already been made in a French adaptation that was Davenant's source. Much more successful than *Tarugo's Wiles, The Man's the Master,* with a stage history extending over a century,[44] proved to be the last play in

42. Quoted from *The London Stage,* pt. 1, p. 119.

43. On the later play, see Marjorie Hope Nicolson and David Rodes, eds., *The Virtuoso* (Lincoln, Neb., 1966), pp. xv–xxvi.

44. Alfred Harbage, *Sir William Davenant, Poet-Venturer, 1606–1668* (Philadelphia, 1935), p. 257.

Davenant's long career: it was first acted in March 1668, less than a month before his death. Ultimately based on Francisco de Rojas Zorrilla's *Donde hay agravios no hay celos,* which Davenant seems not to have consulted (though the point has been disputed),[45] the English play is so close an adaptation of Paul Scarron's *Jodelet, ou le maître valet* as to be little more than a translation. Pepys in fact called it a translation. As often in seventeenth-century drama, the French served as intermediaries between the Spanish and the English.

Davenant's choice of his source suggests yet again the importance of the royal exile in determining the nature of Restoration drama and, more specifically, in establishing the vogue of the Spanish plots. Scarron's play was first performed about 1643 and was published in 1645.[46] From late in 1645 until early in 1650, Davenant lived in France, spending much of his time in the circle surrounding Queen Henrietta Maria.[47] He moved in court society at a time when Scarron, a man of social prominence himself, was in full career, writing spirited and popular comedies. Presumably, Davenant became acquainted with his work, and not improbably with him personally; and it could scarcely have escaped a man of Davenant's turn of mind that most of Scarron's plays (eight out of nine, according to an authoritative estimate) [48] derive from Spanish plays, by Calderón and Tirso, among others, as well as Rojas. Scarron adapted the Spanish plays freely, interpolating original material; but he nevertheless retained much from his originals. The dates of his dramatic career are significant: *Jodelet, ou le maître valet* of about 1643 was his first play; he died in 1660. His adaptations from the Spanish were appearing precisely at the time the royalist exiles were in France to see them.

Although Davenant adds a load of farcical stage business and occasionally omits or rearranges scenes, he retains Scarron's characters and follows his sequence of events. Pepys, who attended the première on March 26, commented on the literary origins of the play as well as on the farcical scenes:

45. By James U. Rundle, "D'Avenant's *The Man's the Master* and the Spanish Source," *Modern Language Notes,* 65 (1950): 194–96.

46. Henry Carrington Lancaster, *A History of French Dramatic Literature in the Seventeenth Century,* pt. 2, 2 : 453 n.

47. Harbage, *Sir William Davenant,* pp. 102–10.

48. Lancaster, *French Dramatic Literature in the Seventeenth Century,* 2 : 453.

> To the Duke of York's house, to see the new play, called "The Man is Master," where the house was, it not being above one o'clock, very full. . . . By and by the King come; and we sat just under him, so that I durst not turn my back all the play. The play is a translation out of French, and the plot is Spanish, but not anything extraordinary at all in it, though translated by Sir W. Davenant, and so I found the King and his company did think meanly of it, though there was here and there something pretty: but the most of the mirth was sorry, poor stuffe, of eating of sack posset and slabbering themselves, and mirth fit for clownes.

Pepys's judgment is severe, more so than the subsequent history of the play in repertory would seem to warrant, though we can understand well enough what in the farcical scenes he found objectionable. Davenant follows Scarron in developing much more fully than Rojas the comical aspects of the reversal of roles between master and servant. The situation in the Spanish evokes only such restrained and intermittent humor as is customary in the appearance of a gracioso, here one impersonating his master in order that the master may resolve doubts about his intended wife's honor. In the Spanish play, that is to say, the reversal of roles is a function of an intrigue plot turning on a point of honor; in the French and the English plays, it is that also but becomes, with the added embellishments, a major source of dramatic interest, to the extent that the change in titles is appropriate.

Yet in *The Man's the Master* (as in *Jodelet, ou le maître valet*) the plot is, as Pepys said, "Spanish," and that in the specialized Restoration sense of nocturnal intrigue in and about a house in Madrid, with confusion of identity, scheming to determine relationships between other persons, and threatened duels. Davenant's play opens with Don John, accompanied by his servant Jodelet, arriving by night at the house of his contracted bride, Isabella—the master full of eagerness and love, ignoring like Don Quijote the simple claims of hunger, the servant complaining like Sancho Panza about his "empty stomach." When Don John sees a strange man secretly leaving the house, he becomes suspicious of Isabella, whom he knows only by her picture, the match having been arranged by his father.

Concerned for his honor, he reverses roles with Jodelet when they present themselves at the house, a stratagem he conceives when he learns that his bumbling servant had earlier sent his own portrait rather than his master's to the lady.

Isabella, who is innocent, is reluctant to receive as her intended husband the man she takes to be Don John, understandably so, since Jodelet conducts himself with the extravagant awkwardness that evoked Pepys's description of "mirth fit for clownes." Embarrassed by his servant's antics, Don John finds his predicament complicated by the discovery that his sister, Lucilla, has taken refuge in the house. She has been betrayed by a young man, Don Lewis, who proves to be the stranger who had left the house secretly. When Don John reveals his true identity, he comes to the brink of duels with Don Lewis and with Isabella's father, who is affronted that the loutish Jodelet should have been presented as a suitor for his daughter. Yet matters are quickly and conventionally resolved when Don Lewis makes amends to Lucilla by an offer of marriage, and Don John wins forgiveness and the hand of Isabella.

Even this brief summary will reveal that, Jodelet's farcical "eating of sack posset" notwithstanding, we are confronted with a Spanish plot. In its carefully controlled plot line, the comedy, despite the farcical scenes derived from Scarron in which Jodelet is central, is different in organization from the contemporary comedies of Molière. This is the more notable because of the resemblance between the master-servant relationship in *The Man's the Master* and that in Molière's *L'Étourdi,* the source of the second half of Newcastle and Dryden's *Sir Martin Mar-all,* presented by Davenant's company the year before. In the latter play the master is stupid and the servant clever; in Davenant's play the reverse is true, but the episodical results are much the same. The earlier play, like other adaptations from Molière that were beginning to appear in England, is disjunctive in its emphasis on separate episodes, a structural pattern that was reinforced by the continuing admiration for Ben Jonson, who in this as in much else anticipated Molière. The subordination of episode to plot in *The Man's the Master* reminds us that, its source in Scarron notwithstanding, Davenant's play retains much of the comedia about it.

Did Davenant borrow directly from the Spanish play? That Scarron was his primary source is indisputable, but did he also consult Rojas? James U. Rundle, citing resemblances—including verbal ones—between *The Man's the Master* and *Donde hay agravios,* believes that he did.[49] I find Rundle's evidence less than conclusive. Even the verbal similarities between the English and Spanish plays, some of them commonplace modes of expression, could arise from the shared plots. More particularized and significant resemblances between the English and Spanish than Rundle cites are required, I think, for Davenant's direct indebtedness to Rojas to be demonstrated; and I do not think that they exist. The problem can scarcely be resolved without biographical evidence, which seems not to be available. Yet if Davenant drew only on the French version, he nevertheless produced a Spanish plot, which in its lasting popularity helped to perpetuate the subgenre on the Restoration stage.

Leaving Dryden for separate consideration, here are the plays of the first eight years of the Restoration that are, or in the case of Porter probably are, traceable to the comedia, either directly or through a French intermediary: *The Adventures of Five Hours, Elvira,* Bristol's two lost adaptations from Calderón, *The Carnival, Tarugo's Wiles,* and *The Man's the Master*—intrigue plays, all of them, about family-proud Spaniards. It was these plays that, for the Restoration, gave the Spanish plot definition. And it was on the pattern established by these plays that the more inventive dramatists worked their variations, using cape and sword conventions as a point of origin for plays that approximate comedy of manners.

Except for Davenant and Dryden, the authors of the early Spanish plots were essentially amateurs, men of limited experience and limited talent, and if their plays nevertheless attracted attention and can still be read with interest, no small amount of the credit for them should be transferred to the Spaniards who wrote the originals: Calderón, Coello, Moreto, and Rojas. The early Spanish plots are, always excepting Dryden, essentially translations, in which there is an accommodation to the conventions of the English stage. The plays, new importations from Spain, are a dramatic consequence of

49. Rundle, "D'Avenant's *The Man's the Master,*" pp. 194–96.

IV: DRYDEN AND WYCHERLEY
"Spanish Plot" to Comedy of Manners

"I hate your *Spanish* honor," says Wildblood in *An Evening's Love* (act 5, scene 1) of 1668, and surely he speaks for Dryden, "ever since it spoyl'd our *English* Playes." The previous year Dryden had written even more severely, in the epilogue to his and Davenant's adaptation of *The Tempest,* about the current borrowings from the comedia:

> *Among the Muses there's a gen'ral rot,*
> *The Rhyming* Mounsieur *and the* Spanish *Plot:*
> *Defie or Court, all's one, they go to Pot.*

These pronouncements notwithstanding, Dryden in *The Rival Ladies* and *An Evening's Love* wrote approximations to the Spanish plot, though he did not allow Spanish honor to spoil his plays. And neither did Wycherley, who in his first two plays, both of them comedies of London life, borrowed from Calderón at about the time Dryden was imitating at a distance the dramatic conventions made popular by Tuke and Bristol and the other Cavaliers. Writing when the initial vogue of the Spanish plot had not yet passed, Dryden and Wycherley, in different fashions, experimented with the matter and form of the comedia, producing plays that bear resemblances to the Spanish plot even while they anticipate much that is best and distinctive in their own later work. In their innovative use of Spanish materials, they reveal an intermediate stage between the plays of the Cavaliers and the fully developed comedy of manners of the mid-1670s.

Wycherley's first two plays are satirical comedies, and in fact the

Spanish borrowings in one of them, *Love in a Wood,* though extensive and even decisive in establishing its impact, are so thoroughly assimilated into a view of contemporary London that they were not identified until the middle of the present century.[1] Dryden's *The Rival Ladies* and *An Evening's Love* retain the Spanish characters and settings and at least a residue of the ethos of the Spanish plots, and yet they approximate the critical tone of the comedy of manners. Dryden's *The Assignation,* despite its important borrowings from Calderón, is in site, characters, organization of episodes, and moral assumptions very different from the Cavaliers' Spanish plots; in this instance Italianate sensuality accompanies a locale in Rome. If something of the Spanish narrative line remains, it is subordinated, as in the comedies of manners, to conversational exchanges in sharply realized episodes.

Dryden's *The Rival Ladies* came in 1664, little more than a year after Tuke's *The Adventures of Five Hours* and at about the time of Lord Bristol's adaptations from Calderón; his *An Evening's Love; Or, The Mock Astrologer,* which in its second title carries an acknowledgment of indebtedness to Calderón's *El astrólogo fingido,* came in 1668; and his *The Assignation; Or, Love in a Nunnery,* partially based on Calderón's *Con quien vengo vengo,* came in 1672. Wycherley's first two plays, *Love in a Wood; Or, St. James's Park* and *The Gentlemen Dancing-Master,* both of which include borrowings from Calderón, from *Mañanas de abril y mayo* and *El maestro de danzar* respectively, were first acted in 1671 and 1672, though they may well have been written earlier. All these plays thus originated in the early years of Restoration comedy, soon after the Cavaliers returned from the Continent and before the major dramatic achievements of the mid-1670s.

The dates are significant. The Spanish strain in Dryden's and Wycherley's early comedies is more consequential than that in their later comedies. The sequence of their plays, as of Dryden's critical essays, would seem to reflect the growing preoccupation with French drama and criticism that in the later years of the seventeenth century inhibited Englishmen's relish for the comedia. Wycherley's *The Country Wife* and *The Plain Dealer* include important borrowings from

1. James Urvin Rundle, "Wycherley and Calderón: A Source for *Love in a Wood,*" *PMLA* 64 (1949): 701–07.

Molière and none at all from the Spanish dramatists. If Dryden's neoclassical prejudice against the comedia appears as early as *Of Dramatick Poesie,* his more unqualified criticism of it comes later, as in the preface to *The Parallel betwixt Painting and Poetry,* in which his brief remarks are not inconsistent with the opinions on the subject held by his younger contemporaries, Rymer and Dennis.

To be sure, Dryden wrote two later tragicomedies with Spanish locales and characters, *The Spanish Friar; Or, The Double Discovery* of 1680 and *Love Triumphant; Or, Nature Will Prevail* of 1694, but neither play would seem to have any meaningful relationship to Spanish history, Spanish drama, or the English convention of the Spanish plot. Unlike the settings of *The Rival Ladies* and *An Evening's Love,* the Spain of these plays would seem to be no more functional, no more relevant to form or theme, than the Sicily of Dryden's *Secret Love* and *Marriage à la Mode.* The Spanish setting provides emotional distance, as does the Sicilian one in the two earlier plays; it helps to diminish the impact of voluptuous sexual intrigue and to lend credibility to implausible event. But little is specifically Spanish about either play, apart from background action of warfare and, in *The Spanish Friar,* of Catholicism—hypocritical Catholicism in Dryden's English view.

The Rival Ladies belongs chronologically to the years when Cavalier dramatists were writing the adaptations from the comedia that were the subject of the last chapter. In locale, characters, and episodical detail, Dryden's play resembles them. In outline its plot is quintessentially Spanish: the two maidens of the title, both disguised as men, have separately taken to the road in pursuit of a man whom they both love. Yet if this is a Spanish plot, it is so, not only with the greater inventiveness that differentiates Dryden's work from that of other men who employed currently popular dramatic formulae, but also with a modification of ethical structure, a partial replacement of personal and family honor as the motivating and blocking force with more prudential English concerns.

The modification can be seen if we look at the motives of two of the male characters in their principal actions. Although one of the young men, Don Rhodorigo, attempts to frustrate his sister's marriage, a situation not uncommon in Spanish drama, his motive is a curious blend of self-seeking and a desire for revenge, and not at all preoccupation with family honor. He and Don Manuel have agreed to marry one another's sister. Yet when Don Manuel arrives with his sister Julia for the double wedding ceremony, Don Rhodorigo treacherously attempts to outwit him, insisting that his own sister, Angellina, delay her marriage by a feigned illness, and attempting meanwhile to proceed with his desired marriage to Julia. The stratagem fails when Don Manuel becomes suspicious of him. Love for Julia and prudent considerations of property influence Don Rhodorigo, and yet his principal motive in his attempted betrayal of Don Manuel is, as he carefully explains to a servant, resentment of an earlier frustration (act 4, scene 2):

> Would God the meanest Man in *Alicante*
> Had *Angellina* rather than *Don Manuel:*
> I never can forgive, much less forget
> How he (the younger Souldier) was preferr'd
> To that Command of Horse which was my due—

—an explanation that would seem to be more appropriate to the Italian Iago than to a Spanish *galán*. That Don Rhodorigo is not to be dismissed as a contemptible figure, as merely the villainous antagonist of the honorable young couples, is implied by the denouement, in which, after determining to reform himself, he wins the lovely Julia.

The object of his hate, Don Manuel, conducts his family's affairs with a concern for property settlements more consonant with Restoration comedy of manners than with the comedia. After he understands Don Rhodorigo's treachery, he commands his sister to marry another man, using a financial threat not unlike that at the disposal of Lady Wishfort at the end of the century, when she attempts to influence her niece Millamant's choice of a husband. "You see your Bridegroom," Don Manuel says to his sister (act 2, scene 2):

> and you know
> My Fathers will, who with his Dying breath
> Commanded, you should pay as strict Obedience
> To me, as formerly to him: if not,
> Your Dowry is at my dispose.

This is a practical appeal reinforced by a threat, in the English manner common to Restoration drama, in which the relatives of young lovers never forget the property settlement, but different from the argument that would be used by a family-proud galán of the comedia. The relaxed, practical, and prudential tone of the more admirable characters, in the conversational exchanges of courtship as well as in choosing a proper course of action amid extravagant dangers, links this play, which moves on something like a Spanish plot, with the emerging comedy of manners.

If *The Rival Ladies* is not fully successful even within the limits of its tragicomic form, it is rich in suggestions of what was to come later, in Restoration drama as well as in Dryden's own work. Dryden's promise appears abundantly: his wit, his variety of styles and easy modulations from one to another, his skill in the dialectic of love and honor,[2] his range of allusion in imagery. His dramatic verse is uneven, and he reveals a willingness to exploit absurd situations. But the exploitation of absurdity is not altogether a liability. It may have been calculated and, more to the point, it has a certain usefulness in this drama of Spanish adventure. Dryden, as well as every intelligent man who saw the play, would have recognized the implausibility of the chance encounters of the principal characters and the absence of psychological accuracy in characterization (a quality difficult to achieve amid such redundancy of incident), and he may have indulged in a certain amount of self-burlesque.

For all its Spanish form, *The Rival Ladies* is, in its characterization and dialogue, in a line of development that led to the next plays Dryden wrote, *The Indian Queen* (with Sir Robert Howard), *The Indian Emperour,* and *Secret Love*. The young gentleman whom the disguised ladies pursue, Gonsalvo, is in his moral compunctions a less inhibited version of the Cortes of *The Indian Emperour;* and the disguised ladies themselves, Honoria and Angellina, different in height but alike in sprightliness, resemble in their banter and in their frank pursuit of their beloved the tall and short sisters of *Secret Love,* Olinda and Sabina. (We may guess that the success of the actresses in the play, combining a playful rivalry in love with a striking difference in height, led Dryden to introduce the similar characters in *Secret Love*.) The banter itself, the counterthrusts of rival con-

2. Cf. Arthur C. Kirsch, *Dryden's Heroic Drama* (Princeton, 1965), pp. 75–76.

versationalists, provides a foretaste of triumphs ahead. There is not much of it in this play, and the short stretches of it appear amid analyses of points of honor in a different tone, but the banter nevertheless implies the presence of a critical spirit surveying the delightful absurdities of Spanish adventure.

Its Spanish setting and subject notwithstanding, the dialogue of the play—the banter as well as the serious debates of the lovers—frequently reminds us of mid-seventeenth-century French literature.[3] The scruples of Gonsalvo, the much-pursued youth schematically at the center of the action, recall those of characters in *Le Grand Cyrus* (a famous romance by Mlle. de Scudéry that Dryden was reading at about the time he wrote this play); [4] and Gonsalvo's attention to distinctions of honor in his courtship of Julia, as well as his magnanimous resignation of her to his rival Rhodorigo, recalls the conduct of Corneille's protagonists. Dryden's characters are arranged in a pattern of emotional frustration, and the resolution of their problems comes with a rearrangement of affections that permits the pairing of the three couples. One of the young men, Manuel, alludes to their neatly structured difficulties (act 5, scene 3):

> Wee'r now a chain of Lovers linck'd in Death;
> *Julia* goes first, *Gonsalvo* hangs on her,
> And *Angellina* holds upon *Gonsalvo*,
> As I on *Angellina*.

All this suggests that at the time Dryden was using Spanish intrigue in *The Rival Ladies,* he was preoccupied with the theory of the heroic play; indeed his next two works would be heroic plays, in which symmetrical orderings of characters by attraction and repulsion are prominent.

As nearly always with Dryden, we must speak tentatively about the literary sources of *The Rival Ladies,* recalling the subtlety and unpredictability of his mind, and also the range of his reading. In this instance we have the more reason for caution because Dryden himself, in his dedicatory epistle to the earl of Orrery, alludes to the flow of ideas in the creative act, describing in an almost Coleridgean manner the unconscious mental processes of his imagina-

3. Cf. Dryden, *Works,* 8, 266–67.

4. As he explains in the preface to *Secret Love* (1667), Dryden drew the serious plot of that play from *Le Grand Cyrus*.

tion while writing the play. "This worthless Present was design'd you," he writes to Lord Orrery—and it is worth noting that he is more than conventionally depreciatory of his play throughout the epistle—"long before it was a Play; When it was only a confus'd Mass of Thoughts, tumbling over one another in the Dark: when the Fancy was yet in its first Work, moving the Sleeping Images of things towards the Light, there to be Distinguish'd, and then either chosen or rejected by the Judgment." A passage to be remembered, I think, as we examine the history of the story of the "two damsels" which is the central component of this plot.

Although he demonstrably took the outline of his plot and even suggestions for episodes from his predecessors, Dryden's variations on the several earlier versions of the story—Spanish, English, and French—are as extensive as he implies they are, extensive enough, in any theory of literary property except such a narrow one as Gerard Langbaine's, to constitute transference of ownership. Dryden usually tells the truth—if not the whole and exhaustive truth—in his preliminary essays, and he certainly implies in the dedication to this play that it is largely original. Unless some now unknown source play is discovered, as I think unlikely, we should conclude that *The Rival Ladies* differs from most of the Spanish plots contemporary with it, in that it is not an adaptation of an earlier play.

The story of *The Rival Ladies* ultimately goes back to Cervantes's novel *Las dos doncellas,* from which Fletcher's *Love's Pilgrimage* derives, as do two French plays: Rotrou's *Les Deux Pucelles* (1636) and, through Rotrou's play, Quinault's *Les Rivales* (1653) [5] Dryden may have borrowed from all these works. He was reading widely at the time and in *Of Dramatick Poesie* alludes to Fletcher and Quinault. His title could be regarded as a translation of Quinault's (which emphasizes the *rivalry* of the ladies), though it is obvious enough, and close enough to Cervantes's title and that of James Mabbe's translation of Cervantes, *A Storie of Two Damsells,* to be independent of the French.[6] The most influential of the earlier versions in shaping Dryden's play was Fletcher's *Love's Pilgrimage*—a fact that merits emphasis. As I have explained in previous chapters, the Restoration

5. Dryden, *Works,* 8 : 265. H. C. Lancaster, *French Dramatic Literature in the Seventeenth Century,* pt. 3, 1 : 92–93.

6. On Mabbe's translation, see Randall, *The Golden Tapestry,* pp. 138–39.

Spanish plot was largely a new development, new in the sense of independence from the Spanish studies of Jacobean and Caroline times. *The Rival Ladies,* perhaps alone among the plays of Spanish intrigue of the 1660s, represents a modification of Spanish materials made English in an earlier age, a circumstance that helps to account for its approximation to the pattern of Fletcherian tragicomedy and its difference from the plays of Tuke, Bristol, and the others.

Love's Pilgrimage, first written about 1616 though later revised before publication,[7] illustrates what Dryden had in mind when he said that Beaumont and Fletcher took their plots from Spanish novels. The play is closely and systematically based on Cervantes's *Las dos doncellas,*[8] even to the use of some of the same names and, with variations of detail, many of the same episodes. The play and the novel resemble one another so closely that it would be impossible to demonstrate, with respect to many particulars, whether Dryden borrowed from the one or the other. The novel is one of the least remarkable, for clear and unexpected judgments on human relationships, in Cervantes's *Novelas ejemplares. Love's Pilgrimage* retains the liabilities as well as the assets of its original. It is a brisk and entertaining adventure story, revealing little subtlety of interpretation though it includes stretches of dialogue that have a convincing ring.

The movement of its plot, with the young women dressed as men in pursuit of a faithless sweetheart, provides scope for the depiction of life on Spanish highways and for scenes of romantic love to the accompaniment of swordplay. Improbabilities and coincidences are frequent, as the two young women, deceived by the same man, encounter one another on the road. One of them, traveling with her brother, rescues the other who has been robbed and tied to a tree by bandits. Both of them have received written promises of marriage from their lover, though neither has been compromised; and thus, within the conventions of seventeenth-century literature, they can both be rewarded with husbands: the one with the truant lover and the other with the brother of her rival. Fletcher follows Cervantes's expository mode of understatement, avoiding emotional amplifica-

7. Gerald Eades Bentley, *The Jacobean and Caroline Stage* (Oxford, 1941–68), 367–68.

8. Gerard Langbaine, *An Account of the English Dramatick Poets,* p. 211 (hereafter cited as Langbaine, *Account*).

tion even in situations of potential or actual pathos; like the Spaniard he emphasizes rapidity of movement rather than the characters' response to events. In the play as in the novel, but not in the two French plays on the subject, there are suggestions for the nautical action which Dryden later developed more fully.

Perhaps Fletcher's play in isolation, or Fletcher's play together with Mabbe's translation of Cervantes's novel, provided Dryden with his plot. *The Rival Ladies* does not resemble either of the French plays closely, though details may have come from them. Dryden at the time was reading French drama, and in at least two other plays of the decade, *Sir Martin Mar-all* and *An Evening's Love,* he borrowed from French plays—in the former, in fact, from Quinault.[9] The French renderings of *Las dos doncellas,* Rotrou's and Quinault's, are freer versions of the original story than Fletcher's differing in emphasis as well as in the inclusion of more episodes not anticipated in the Spanish. The French give greater attention to the emotional conflicts engendered by the plight of the two young women, less to dangerous adventure on the road. Quinault's play is a reworking of Rotrou's, a tidying up of the earlier comedy in the interest of neoclassical regularity as well as dramatic intensity.[10] Both the French plays, though Quinault's more than Rotrou's, provide apt illustrations of Dryden's remarks in *Of Dramatick Poesie* on French dramatic construction as it differed from Spanish. Yet Dryden retains in *The Rival Ladies* much of the Spanish—and Fletcherian—extravagance and inclusiveness. *The Rival Ladies* is less closely focused than *Les Rivales* on the moral choices of the principal characters.

The apprentice work of a man of genius, *The Rival Ladies* is properly regarded as an experimental play in the Spanish form so fashionable in the wake of *The Adventures of Five Hours.*[11] Dryden made use of the trappings of Spanish intrigue, perhaps not without a subdued intention of parodying them; and he made use of the Spanish mobility of place, extending it even to scenes aboard a ship

9. Dryden, *Works,* 9 : 364–67.

10. Cf. Lancaster, *A History of French Dramatic Literature in the Seventeenth Century,* pt. 2, 1 : 86; pt. 3, 1 : 92–93.

11. Cf. Allison Gaw, "Tuke's *Adventure of Five Hours* in Relation to the 'Spanish Plot' and to John Dryden," pp. 17–18, 29, 32; Ned B. Allen, *The Sources of John Dryden's Comedies* (Ann Arbor, Mich., 1935), pp. 55–65; F. H. Moore, *The Nobler Pleasure,* pp. 24–27.

at sea. He used physical action, such as an attempted escape from the ship, that is at once exciting and comic. He did not write a tightly constructed drama about family honor. In following Cervantes and Fletcher rather than the comedia, he produced a rambling, loosely plotted adventure story in which the notion of Spanish honor, though not absent, is secondary as a motivating force.

Between *The Rival Ladies* of 1664 and *An Evening's Love; Or, The Mock Astrologer* of 1668, Dryden moved from a position of promising newcomer in the theaters to that of England's leading dramatist, a position recognized, in the same year as *An Evening's Love,* by his appointment as poet laureate. In the interval he wrote, or wrote part of, five plays: two heroic dramas, *The Indian Queen* and *The Indian Emperour,* the latter including striking resemblances to Calderón's *El príncipe constante,* which we must later examine; and three comedies, *Secret Love, Sir Martin Mar-all,* and an adaptation of *The Tempest.* Of these five, it is *Secret Love,* one of the most graceful and successful plays he ever wrote, that most closely anticipates the structural pattern of *An Evening's Love.*[12] The Calderonian background of the latter play notwithstanding, it has a double plot of the kind Dryden had employed in *Secret Love* and defended in *Of Dramatick Poesie.* After *The Rival Ladies,* Dryden wrote no more tragicomedies in the Fletcherian mold of a single if complex action of narrowly averted catastrophe, not even when he wrote plays of Spanish adventure.

An Evening's Love follows at a distance the form of the Spanish plot, which by 1668 had become a well-established convention of the Restoration stage. Having a nocturnal setting in Spain for the tricks and intrigues of young lovers, it still includes dialogue in the vein Dryden had so successfully exploited in the comic scenes of *Secret Love.* His Wildblood and Jacintha of *An Evening's Love* are just such another couple as Celadon and Florimel in the earlier play.[13] Jacintha has no more inhibitions, despite her Spanish origin, than Florimel. To be sure, the Spanish setting, unlike the Sicilian one of *Secret Love,* is more than nominal. For all their gaiety, the Spanish ladies are watched over by vigilant elders and courted by

12. Cf. Moore, pp. 75–78.
13. Ibid., p. 77.

punctilious Spanish gallants, who provide a contrast to the insouciant Englishmen who are their rivals; and the Madrid evening, the long extension of the day, provides an appropriate backdrop for the adventures of the lovers.

Dryden is curiously precise in specifying the time and place of his action: "The Scene *Madrid,* in the Year 1665. The Time, the last Evening of the Carnival"—so precise that I would guess he had something special in mind, perhaps a humorous allusion to the amorous adventures of young Englishmen who had recently been in Spain on diplomatic assignments. Wildblood and Bellamy are, as Jacintha puts it, "feathers of the *English* Embassador's Train" (act 1, scene 1), and in the small London world of the fashionable, everyone would have known that Sir Richard Fanshawe had been the ambassador in 1665 [14] and many would have known the young gentlemen who had accompanied him. (Their names are recorded in Lady Fanshawe's *Memoirs,* see below, p. 121.) Such exact specification of time and place is rare in Restoration comedy and perhaps had meaning to Dryden's first audiences.

The sources of *An Evening's Love* have been discussed and debated from the times of Pepys and Langbaine to the present, and for good reason, since the nature of Dryden's debt to his predecessors poses a theoretical problem in the meaning of literary property. Dryden's extended comments, in his preface, on his sources, as well as on the practices of other dramatists in using borrowed materials, imply that in the interval between the play's first performance in 1668 and its publication in 1671 he had been accused of plagiarism. "There is another crime with which I am charg'd," he writes, adding that he is not much concerned with it. "I am tax'd with stealing all my Playes, and that by some who should be the last men from whom I would steal any part of 'em." His remarks tell much about his theory of literary property as well as about the literary sources of this play:

> *'Tis true, that where ever I have lik'd any story in a Romance, Novel, or forreign Play, I have made no difficulty, nor ever shall, to take the foundation of it, to build it up, and to make it proper for the* English *Stage. And I will be so vain to say it has*

14. Cf. Dryden, *Works,* 10 : 467.

> *lost nothing in my hands: But it alwayes cost me so much trouble to heighten it for our Theatre (which is incomparably more curious in all the ornaments of Dramatick Poesie, than the* French *or* Spanish) *that when I had finish'd my Play, it was like the Hulk of Sir* Francis Drake, *so strangely alter'd, that there scarce remain'd any Plank of the Timber which first built it. To witness this I need go no farther than this Play: It was first* Spanish, *and call'd* El Astrologo fingido; *then made* French *by the younger* Corneille: *and is now translated into* English, *and in print, under the name of the* Feign'd Astrologer. *What I have performed in this will best appear by comparing it with those: you will see that I have rejected some adventures which I judg'd were not divertising: that I have heightned those which I have chosen, and that I have added others which were neither in the* French *nor* Spanish.

In his epilogue he returns to the subject of plagiarism. His protestations to the contrary, the charge obviously rankled. The critics in the pit, he writes,

> *kept a fearfull stir,*
> *In whisp'ring that he stole th'*Astrologer;
> *And said, betwixt a* French *and* English *Plot*
> *He eas'd his half-tir'd Muse, on pace and trot.*

To all of which the author pleaded guilty,

> *Yet said, he us'd the* French *like Enemies,*
> *And did not steal their Plots, but made 'em prize.*

There is a defensive tone in these remarks, more so it would seem in retrospect than was necessary, for Dryden was justified in claiming that he made whatever he borrowed his own. We have no reason, I think, to doubt the essential accuracy of what he says. He might have been more comprehensive and specific: he borrowed, for episodical detail, from other dramatists besides Calderón and Thomas Corneille, notably from Molière; and he borrowed also from Madeleine de Scudéry. But to doubt that he at least consulted the two Continental plays he names, Calderón's as well as Corneille's (though, as the epilogue implies, the latter is the more important source), amounts to accusing him of deception, and unnecessary deception at that.[15]

Pepys provides a hint of the kind of criticism that prompted Dryden's defense of himself. He wrote in his diary, after he saw the play on June 20, 1668, that his wife (who was French and read the romances of Madeleine de Scudéry) told him it was "wholly (which he [Dryden] confesses a little in the epilogue) taken out of the 'Illustre Bassa.'" Pepys misrepresents the epilogue (at least in the form in which it has been preserved), which alludes specifically to Thomas Corneille's "feint Astrologue," and his wife was wrong in thinking that Mlle. de Scudéry was Dryden's single or perhaps even principal source. She referred to "The History of the feigned Astrologer" (to use the English of the translation by Henry Cogan [1652]), which appears at the beginning of the second book of the second part of *Ibrahim: Or The Illustrious Bassa,* a story, like Thomas Corneille's *Le Feint Astrologue,* based on Calderón's play.

In considering Dryden's borrowings for *An Evening's Love,* it is necessary to emphasize how much Calderón's, Corneille's, and Dryden's plays and Mlle. de Scudéry's narrative, in "the Stories of them" (to use Dryden's phrase), have in common. (*The Feign'd Astrologer,* to which Dryden refers in his preface, is a translation of Corneille, a moderately close, often literal translation, though with English locale and characters, one of whom, Bellamy, has the name of a character in Dryden's play.) Dryden's second title, "The Mock Astrologer," translated from the titles of the other two plays, constitutes a form of acknowledgment of literary debt, which exists, however, only in the Bellamy-Theodosia part of his play. The most striking aspect of *An Evening's Love,* the courtship of Wildblood and Jacintha, though in detail indebted to Molière and other writers, is Dryden's extension of the comic resource he had employed in the

15. For comprehensive studies of Dryden's sources in *An Evening's Love,* see Dryden, *Works,* 10 : 433–44, and Salvatore Fiorino, *John Dryden: The Mock Astrologer, Fonti e Pseudo-Fonti* (Palermo, 1959). See also, in addition to Langbaine's full discussion of the subject (*Account,* pp. 163–64), Ned B. Allen, *Sources of Dryden's Comedies,* pp. 154–69; James Urvin Rundle, "The Source of Dryden's 'Comic Plot' in *The Assignation,*" *Modern Philology* 45 (1947) : 111 n.; Max Oppenheimer, "Supplementary Data on the French and English Adaptations of Calderón's *El astrólogo fingido,*" *Revue de Littérature Comparée* 24 (1948) : 547–60; and Ned B. Allen, "The Sources of Dryden's *The Mock Astrologer,*" *Philological Quarterly* 36 (1957) : 453–64.

Celadon-Florimel plot of *Secret Love,* the conversational duel of amorous, uninhibited, and inconstant lovers. In describing the parallels between the English, French, and Spanish plays and the French romance, we leave this, the most delightful part of *An Evening's Love,* out of account. Wildblood functions in the "astrologer" plot merely as the confidant of Bellamy.

How closely the plots of all four versions resemble one another may be noted in the similar roles of the corresponding characters, despite their different names. Even in personality the corresponding characters are alike, with the difference that in Dryden's play, the deceitful lover, Don Melchor, is less amiable and thus can finally be denied either of the ladies he has courted. Dryden's principal departures from the earlier plots are the consequence of his reinterpretation of this character, and they are most notable in the final act, in which, though he retains the garden scene for the denouement, he rearranges events so that Theodosia can be awarded to the mock astrologer.

This requires a substantial amount of Dryden's own invention: much of his fifth act has no parallel in the other versions. Earlier in the play he follows them closely (always excepting the scenes devoted to Wildblood's courtship of Jacintha), if not so closely as Mlle. de Scudéry and Corneille follow Calderón. Scudéry provides a faithful prose summary of *El astrólogo fingido,* though with the setting changed from Spain to Italy, departing from Calderón in little more than is required by the narrative conventions of her romance.[16] Corneille is more inventive, particularly in his interpretation of the character of the mock astrologer. Unlike his predecessors (and Dryden), he does not unmask the character's pretensions to astrology, allowing him to retain his audacious impertinence to the end. Corneille's astrologer does not win the lady, whom, as he explains, he has courted merely out of pique at having been denied; on the contrary, he magnanimously employs his fake art to induce her father to allow his rival (the deceitful lover) to marry the girl.

Unlike Scudéry and Corneille, Dryden omits a slender plot employed by Calderón as a farcical variation on the mock astrologer's intrigues—one in which, as often in the comedia, the gracioso imitates his master. Dryden's Maskall is very different from Calderón's

16. *Ibrahim,* trans. Henry Cogan (London, 1652), pt. 2, bk. 2, pp. 24–25.

Morón, more the clever manipulator deriving from Roman comedy and commedia dell'arte and less the clowning buffoon. In Calderón and his French imitators, the gracioso tries his hand at astrology, more precisely at conjuration, duping a gullible fool into believing that he has been miraculously transported to distant mountains. In the Spanish, the farcical scenes depicting this stage business, having no relationship to the main line of action except as thematic parallel, follow rapidly on more serious scenes. Working within the stricter conventions of English neoclassicism, Dryden rejects the farcical scenes; and he substitutes a slender plot line of his own, as conventional in English drama as Calderón's is in Spanish, that in which Maskall courts and wins Beatrix, his female accomplice, who has supplied him with the information that made possible his master's feats of astrology. The additional marriage reinforces the symmetry of the plot.

Though Dryden reshapes Calderón's gracioso on more English and more consequential lines, his play is in the main gayer than the Spanish. This is partly because of his elaboration of Wildblood's courtship of Jacintha. But it is also the result of Dryden's studied refusal to take the Spanish preoccupation with honor seriously. Such pointed criticism of honor as Wildblood makes, coming from a clearheaded character late in a decade that had seen the importation of the Spanish plot, represents a considered authorial judgment. With the Englishmen present to provide standards of good sense, even the Spanish gentlemen cannot take their reputations as seriously as usual, and the Spanish ladies are easily converted to English habits of thought. This is not to imply that Calderón's characters are somber or preoccupied with thoughts of revenge. The astrological tricks produce merriment throughout his comedy. Yet, like everything else that Calderón wrote, the play treats relationships between lovers with a fundamental seriousness, never approaching the conversational liberty on sexual subjects comparable to that in *An Evening's Love,* which in its duels of wit is uninhibited even by Restoration standards.

Dryden implies in his epilogue that he borrowed most freely from the French, and there is reason enough to believe him. But did he also, as he implies in his preface, borrow directly from Calderón? The subject has been much investigated, and even so there is no clear answer—and perhaps there cannot be, in view of the number of derivatives of Calderón's play to which Dryden had access: Mlle. de Scudéry, Antoine Le Métel D'Ouville (in a comedy *Jodelet astrologue* [1646], to which neither Dryden nor Langbaine refers), and Thomas Corneille, whose play had been translated into English with minor changes as *The Feign'd Astrologer.* A recent Italian critic, Salvatore Fiorino, has found internal evidence, though something less than conclusive, that Dryden did borrow directly from the Spanish.[17] I find his argument, supported as it is by Dryden's own statement in his preface, a strong one, though it is scarcely of a nature to remove doubt on the subject. The resemblances between the Spanish and English plays, which Fiorino describes as differing from the other renderings, are ones of detail which could result from independent composition. I have repeatedly looked at parallel episodes in the Spanish and English plays, hoping to find echoes of Calderón in Dryden's phrasing, only to be disappointed. The difficulty in adducing evidence of Dryden's direct borrowing would suggest that he did not systematically refer to *El astrólogo fingido.* But that is not to impugn his veracity when he implies that he had looked over the play with some undeterminable degree of thoroughness.

It seems curious in retrospect that Dryden should have been charged with plagiarism in *An Evening's Love.* As he observed in his preface, English dramatists, including those held in highest critical esteem, had long been borrowing plots: "*Most of* Shakespear's *Playes, I mean the Stories of them, are to be found in the* Hecatommithi, *or hundred Novels of* Cinthio"—not quite accurate in detail, but Dryden was justified in making the point. He made a similar one in *Of Dramatick Poesie,* when he compared Ben Jonson's borrowings to the conquests of an invading monarch; and he reaffirmed his opinion on the subject much later, in the preliminaries to *Don Sebastian* (1690), when he replied defensively to Langbaine's attack on him in *A New Catalogue of English Plays.* Dryden's attitude toward literary property would seem to have been similar to Pope's later pronouncement in *An Essay on Criticism,* the couplet about true wit being familiar thoughts given superlative expression. Yet if Langbaine, in his obsession with plagiarism, lacked generosity of spirit and critical

17. *John Dryden: The Mock Astrologer.*

perceptiveness, his concept of literary property, much more sharply defined than the one customarily held earlier, became widespread in late seventeenth- and early eighteenth-century England, and in fact received expression from Pope himself in *The Dunciad.* Dryden, as the leading dramatist of the Restoration, came under attack even though his guilt was less than that of others, certainly much less than that of the Cavalier authors of Spanish plots. His *An Evening's Love* seems to have occasioned the first skirmish in what later became a literary war.

An Evening's Love derives from *El astrólogo fingido,* of course, and we have Dryden's word for it that he knew the Spanish play but his major sources were French renderings of Calderón's plot. His *The Assignation; Or, Love in a Nunnery* (1672), on the other hand, has a more direct relationship to a play of Calderón's, *Con quien vengo vengo,* from which, as Rundle has demonstrated, Dryden's "comic plot" is partly taken.[18] *The Assignation* provides the least equivocal instance of Dryden's use of the comedia. Prior to Rundle's discovery, it was assumed that the borrowing from Calderón came by way of Paul Scarron's *Roman comique;*[19] this would now seem improbable because the correspondences between the French novel and Dryden's play are less detailed and extensive than those between the Spanish and English plays. The existence of some other intermediary story or play in French or English is of course a possibility. Yet no French adaptation of *Con quien vengo vengo* is cited by H. C. Lancaster, nor is any English adaptation known.[20] Dryden, as always, borrows inventively, and his habitual freedom in reworking material is reinforced by the pronounced differences between Spanish and English conventions of dramatic dialogue. We can rarely detect verbal echoes of the Spanish play. Rundle cites some possible echoes. I note the use, not in parallel situations, of the same proper name: *Ursino* in Calderón, *Ursini* (act 3, scene 2) in Dryden. (The name also occurs in Calderón's *Peor está que estaba;* probably it occurred in Bristol's lost *Worse and Worse.*) But it is in similarities of

18. Rundle, "Source of Dryden's 'Comic Plot' in *The Assignation,*" pp. 104–11.
19. Langbaine, *Account,* p. 155; Allen, *Sources of Dryden's Comedies,* pp. 184–86.
20. Congreve later borrowed from *The Assignation* for his novel, *Incognita:* Montague Summers, ed., *The Complete Works of William Congreve* (London, 1924), 1 : 4–5.

characters and plots that the strongest evidence of a relationship between the plays is to be found.

The Assignation, like *Secret Love* and *Marriage à la Mode,* has two fully developed plots, of approximately equal importance, concerned with the affairs of two separate groups of characters. Yet unlike those of the earlier plays, the plot of *The Assignation* with characters of higher station, far from having a heroic dimension, provides the pretext for the audacious second title, *Love in a Nunnery.* For this action, drawn from a story in an anonymous collection of prose fiction,[21] there is no precedent in *Con quien vengo vengo;* the resemblances to the Spanish play are confined to the second plot, which involves the courtship of two young couples. The significant parallels are in the earlier parts of the two plays.

In the opening scenes of both plays, a young gentleman, Camillo in the English and Don Juan in the Spanish, is courting, or attempting to court, a young woman who is closely guarded by a suspicious relative—an uncle, Mario, in *The Assignation,* whose motive in his unreasonable conduct is mercenary; and a brother, Don Sancho, in *Con quien vengo vengo,* whose motive is protection of the family honor. The difference is more than one of detail. The English concern for property evident in Dryden's play, a more pressing concern of the characters than propriety in sexual relationships, is incompatible with the taut sensitivity to points of honor in the Spanish. The gallant in both plays has a friend who determines to accompany him, in the guise of a servant, to a nighttime rendezvous with the lady in her garden. The rendezvous is arranged by letter, and in both plays, in scenes that are strikingly alike, the sister of the recipient intercepts the letter and, in turn, soon decides to accompany her in the guise of a maidservant.[22] Dryden did not translate, to be sure; he had no need to do so; but he certainly seems to have taken his idea for the scene from Calderón. The fact that the scene is the opening one in the Spanish suggests that it may have caught his eye and led him to use the play as a whole.

In both plays there are two successive meetings of the two couples, in the dark, in gardens, each member of the one couple thinking

21. *The Annals of Love, Containing Select Histories of the Amours of Divers Princes Courts* (London, 1672), pp. 81 ff. Cf. Langbaine, *Account,* p. 155; Allen, *Sources of Dryden's Comedies,* pp. 177–83.

22. Rundle, "Source of Dryden's 'Comic Plot' in *The Assignation.*"

that the other is a servant and experiencing surprise that a servant should have such a ready wit. In both plays the confusion of identity is complicated by a real servant, a vain and maladroit coxcomb, the sight of whom by day leads one of the young women to lament her infatuation with him. Dryden makes much more of the servant than Calderón. The latter's character is a gracioso; the former's a redaction of the character type with which he had scored in *Sir Martin Mar-all,* the stupid and clumsy bungler, in this case servant rather than master, who inadvertently betrays clever stratagems to win a lady.[23] Yet if Dryden turned in his elaboration of the character to his own earlier work, he would have found in Calderón the basis for the character and his role.[24]

Con quien vengo vengo is just such a play as shaped the conception of Spanish drama held by the interlocutors in *Of Dramatick Poesie.* It abounds in the sharp and frequent changes in the direction of dramatic action, to which Dryden's spokesmen allude as typical of the comedia, and it reveals the customary subordination of characterization to plot. Calderón's characters are scarcely differentiated from others in similar roles in other plays, and yet their lack of individuality does not interfere with their dramatic function as agents in the conduct of a complex and neatly contrived plot that conveys a summary theme and judgment, here as often in Calderón expressed epigrammatically in the title.

It is in the last act that Calderón's theme, *"con quien vengo vengo,"* reaches its clearest expression, in a situation where father and son are driven by the compulsions of honor to engage one another in a duel—mercifully broken off by the arrival of the governor before either is injured. "With whom I come, I come": that is to say, when I engage my honor to support a friend in a difficult situation—in this instance as a second in a duel—I must fulfill my obligation no matter with whom it brings me into conflict. Ursino, the father of Juan, has accompanied Sancho, the jealous brother of the young women whom Juan and Octavio have courted. At the outset of the duel Ursino is paired against Octavio, but in the abrupt and violent course of the fighting, he finds himself facing his own son, who asks pardon even as he fights. The governor's interruption soon comes,

23. Cf. Moore, *Nobler Pleasure,* p. 114.
24. Rundle, "Source of *The Assignation,*" p. 107.

and offenses to family honor are remedied by marriage rather than bloodshed. The authorial judgment on a code of honor that could bring such a cruel confrontation is merely implicit in the situation itself; it remains a suspended judgment to be interpreted, and differently interpreted, by individual spectators.[25]

Neither the events of Calderón's last act, nor the theme of honor that emerges from them, have a parallel in Dryden's play. The two sisters are confined to a "nunnery" in which a highborn lady who is courted by a duke's son, as well as by his own father, the duke, is also confined. The principal obstacle to be overcome before all the young couples can be married turns out to be the rivalry between the duke and his son for the same young woman, the son having matrimony in view, the father, seduction. And thus there is a curious kind of parallel with the father-son duel at the close of *Con quien vengo vengo*—an opposition between father and son, but in circumstances that are radically different, and different in an illuminating way. The theme, and to some extent the tone, of Calderón's play is suggested by its title; the tone, though not the theme, of Dryden's is well conveyed by its title.

Dryden avoids some of the implications of his title by revealing that the lady courted by the father and son has not taken her final vows, but he does not convey this information until late in the play (act 4, scene 4). He exploits his audiences' prurient interest in forbidden love even while finally escaping from the difficulties of the audacious subject. Dryden presumably took the Roman setting and nationality of his characters from the story, in the anonymous *The Annals of Love,* that provided his source for this plot. In any event, Spanish nationality would have been incongruous in *The Assignation,* with its frequent approaches to blasphemy as well as its sexually suggestive dialogue and episodes.

The Assignation and *Con quien vengo vengo* are strikingly different in their moral attitudes. The characters in the Spanish play, even the high-spirited young ones engaged in audacious courtships, are scrupulous about their personal honor, to such an extent that the climactic event of the play, as I have already noted, represents a

25. For a recent analysis of the critical problem presented by the conception of honor in the comedia, see C. A. Jones, "Spanish Honour as Historical Phenomenon, Convention and Artistic Motive," *Hispanic Review* 33 (1965) : 32–39.

final refinement in observance of the code of honor. Calderón's dialogue is chaste and free of the sexual innuendo so prominent in the English play. *The Assignation* represents Dryden in his more relaxed comic vein, repeating formulae that he had successfully used before—the love banter of young wits, the farcical absurdities of a conceited bungler—and his two plot lines, only loosely brought together at play's end, can scarcely be said to embody a controlling theme in the sense of thesis.

Con quien vengo vengo is much more closely ordered. All the episodes, however numerous and complex their interrelationships, advance a single line of action. It may have been to this typical neatness of organization, as well as to the division into three acts, that Dryden referred when he wrote in the preface to *Albion and Albanius* that "even Aristotle himself is contented to say simply, that in all actions there is a beginning, a middle, and an end; after which model all the Spanish plays are built." [26] In any event, *Con quien vengo vengo* has in a specialized sense a well-defined beginning, middle, and end.

The conception of unity of action embodied in the play must be explained. The hazardous courtship of the two young couples, complicated by mistaken identities and the brother's jealousy, does indeed start at the beginning of the play, reach a middle stage of confusion and obstacle, and a final stage, after mounting confusion and obstacle, of resolution in marriage. Yet encompassing this single, dramatized plot, there is a background plot related by Octavio, the suitor in the guise of a servant, and by Sancho, the jealous brother. Making use of the Spanish convention of the long narrative speech, the two characters can, not together but separately, tell from their differing points of view their related experiences of frustrated courtship. Each believes the other responsible for his disappointment.

In the first act Octavio recounts to his friend Juan his adventures since the time the two of them were fellow students at Bologna. When Juan's father summoned him home to Verona, Octavio, on his own father's instructions, entered the army. During his military service he won the love of a lady in Milan. In the fullness of his heart he confided his love and his hopes to a friend—Sancho, as we subsequently learn. Suddenly ordered away with his regiment, he was not

26. *Essays*, 1 : 279.

able to return to Milan until an accident of war sent him there on a mission for his commander. This much we learn in his narration of the first act, before he is interrupted by the entrance of Juan's father.

Early in the second act comes the beginning of the complementary narration by Sancho, who speaks to one of his sisters, partly to explain the severity of his guardianship. In Milan, ignorant of Octavio's courtship, he had fallen in love with the same lady Octavio loved. After giving him preliminary encouragement, the lady left him for his unknown rival. From her servant he learned that she planned to admit a gallant to her house by night. Bribing the servant, he arranged to be admitted himself. On the same day Octavio, not knowing of Sancho's interest in the lady, confided his love for her to him. Yet, as Sancho explains to his sister in a bit of casuistry, since he had known in advance of the planned rendezvous of that night, he was not bound in honor to protect Octavio's confidence. Sancho's rationalization of his action turns on the nature of a man's obligation to a friend who has trusted him, the theme which prompted the title, *Con quien vengo vengo*. Having squared matters with his conscience, Sancho explains, he entered the lady's house that night, with the servant's assistance, and went to the lady's room. Surprised and frightened at seeing him, she shouted in alarm and people came to her assistance. In the fighting which ensued, Sancho reports, some were injured.

Only a little later Octavio, when he finds himself alone with Juan, resumes his narrative. Upon first arriving in Milan, he fulfilled his assignment from his commander, returning a lost portrait of a lady to a captured nobleman and giving the nobleman his freedom. Then, full of expectation, he went to the house of his beloved. Far from experiencing the happy reunion he anticipated, he found the house abandoned and desolate; and from a passerby he learned the melancholy reason. On the evening after his regiment departed, Sancho entered the house and, in the turmoil which followed the lady's shouts for help, killed a man. The lady herself, disconsolate at these events, entered a monastery. Sancho disappeared from Milan, and, so Octavio has heard, made his way to Verona. And it is for this reason that Octavio, who assumes that Sancho violated his confidence, has also come to Verona.

All this is narrative background to the dramatized action. Octavio and Sancho meet in the latter's garden when he surprises the gallants courting his sisters. Again the obligations of friendship are recalled, this time in a soliloquy of Octavio, who fears that he must either endanger a lady's reputation or betray his friend, who has managed to escape from the garden. He resolves his problem by telling Sancho he has come to kill him for the old wrong, and in the duel which ensues he wounds Sancho, though not fatally, before making his escape.

The final act of the play, which as I have said has no parallel in *The Assignation,* redoubles the complications and confusions arising from mistakes in identity and comes to a climax in the duel between father and son. No more is said about the earlier enmity between Octavio and Sancho, who, in the marriages that are to terminate the hostilities, will become brothers-in-law.

If *Con quien vengo vengo* possesses unity of action, the unity is in the dramatized events, exclusive of the retrospective narrative speeches. The earlier rivalry between Octavio and Sancho has only a tangential relationship to Octavio's and Juan's courtships of the young women. It helps to explain Sancho's vigilance in watching over his sisters, and it intensifies his hostility to Octavio when he encounters him, but all this is scarcely necessary to make Sancho's motives credible, given the conventions of the Spanish stage. Yet if we shift attention from events to theme, we may see the narrative passages as superbly relevant, presenting as they do a problem in the obligations of friendship supplementary to that posed by the dramatized courtships and duels.

We can only infer the authorial judgment on Sancho for his secret entry into the lady's house after having heard in confidence from Octavio about his love for her, but the judgment is scarcely ambiguous. Sancho's rationalization—that he was breaking no confidence since Octavio had told him something he already knew—is not convincing; he acted treacherously, and the results of his action were grave. His treachery to his friend is placed in relief by Ursino's loyalty in the climactic duel. The two episodes, the narrated one of betrayal of friendship and the dramatized one of loyalty in friendship, may indeed be isolated as the principal vehicles for the theme enunciated in the title.

English dramatic tradition did not permit extensive narration. The amplitude and the thematic reinforcement gained in Spanish by narrative passages had to be sought in another fashion. In *The Assignation,* the amplitude comes from the presence of two distinct and largely independent plots. It is difficult to speak of the one plot reinforcing the theme of the other; it is indeed difficult to speak of a serious theme in the play at all. The two plots are alike in tone, rather than complementary in the manner of *Secret Love,* in which a heroic plot about the problems of young lovers contrasts with a comic one on the same subject. To be sure, the title plot of *The Assignation* shows occasional signs of heroic intention in diction and in intermittent blank verse, but that intention is not sustained.[27] Such authorial judgments as are to be found in the play are to be sought in the attitudes toward courtship and the social decorums.

The play had a limited success when it was new—because of faults in the acting, Dryden wrote in his dedication [28]—and it has been one of the least favored of Dryden's comedies by later generations. It is perhaps too patently a manipulation of dramatic formulae with which he had succeeded in earlier plays. Benito may owe something to the gracioso, Celio, of Calderón, but he owes much more to Dryden's own Sir Martin Mar-all. Just so, Laura and Violetta resemble Dryden's earlier witty ladies more closely than they do Calderón's Lisarda and Leonor. The play is competent, steadily intelligent, and entertaining, but it is hard to feel warmth for it.

And in part because of the subject. "Love in a nunnery" is, after all, calculated to repel many readers—more so now, perhaps, than in the climate of hostility to Catholicism in which Dryden wrote. His evasive maneuver in revealing that the young woman is not "professed" comes late in the play, and in any event scarcely palliates the audacity of the young man's courtship of an immured and costumed nun. So also the complication in his courtship, the rivalry of his own father, whose motives are unambiguously sensual and methods, gross. This is coarse material from which to construct a play, and the coarseness is intensified by stretches of dialogue that approach the

27. Cf. Frank H. Moore, "Heroic Comedy: A New Interpretation of Dryden's *Assignation,*" *Studies in Philology* 51 (1954) : 585–98.

28. Yet John Downes lists it among the "most taking" plays of the Restoration: *Roscius Anglicanus,* pp. 12, 15.

blasphemous. All this is partially relieved by Dryden's ever surprising wit. Yet in comparison with *Con quien vengo vengo, The Assignation* conveys an impression of loose improvisation, in moral control as well as in dramatic structure.

Perhaps the most intriguing uncertainty in the study of Anglo-Spanish dramatic relations turns on the identity of the "Mr. Wycherly" mentioned by Lady Fanshawe in her memoirs as a gentleman attendant on Sir Richard Fanshawe when he went to Spain in 1664 as English ambassador.[29] Was he William Wycherley, whose *Love in a Wood* (ca. 1671) and *The Gentleman Dancing-Master* (ca. 1672) reveal borrowings from plays by Calderón? The surviving records of Fanshawe's embassy are insistently silent on the subject,[30] and the notoriously meager biographical records of the dramatist provide no help. Barring some unexpected discovery, we must remain in doubt. Yet the known facts establish a likelihood, I think, that he was indeed the man to whom Lady Fanshawe refers. He would have been of suitable rank, appearance, and age—in his twenties—for such an assignment, and, more to the point, he later displayed an interest in and knowledge of Spanish literature and manners. The debt to Calderón in *Love in a Wood* is extensive, and if that in *The Gentleman Dancing-Master* is less so, Wycherley alludes in the play to foibles of the Spanish character, implying familiarity with them. In the earlier play he includes an esoteric allusion (act 4) to the pomposity of Spanish titles as they appear in dedicatory epistles. We have it on the authority of an anecdote Pope told Joseph Spence that Gracián was among Wycherley's favorite authors,[31] though he could have read Gracián, but not Calderón's plays, in an English translation.

Whether as an attendant on Fanshawe or not, Wycherley must have learned to read Spanish: neither of the source plays had been translated into English or French.[32] *The Gentleman Dancing-Master*

29. *Memoirs*, p. 146.

30. I am indebted to my colleague Professor David Harris for a thorough search of the records.

31. Cited in Thomas H. Fujimura, *The Restoration Comedy of Wit* (Princeton, N. J., 1952), p. 122.

32. Neither is listed in the indexes of H. C. Lancaster's *French Dramatic Literature in the Seventeenth Century*, pts. 1, 2, and 3 (terminal date covered: 1672).

carries its acknowledgment to Calderón in its title, which is a loose rendering of *El maestro de danzar*. *Love in a Wood* does not, and in fact was not known to have a Spanish source until Rundle's discovery in 1949 of its relationship to *Mañanas de abril y mayo*.[33] In both instances Wycherley used his borrowed material boldly, reworking it and transforming its tone. His plays, far from being adaptations from the comedia, are vigorous comedies of manners, shaped by and helping to shape the emerging pattern of Restoration comedy. I would hazard a guess that the ambitious young playwright, in his search for episodic detail to carry the satirical conversation that came to him so readily, turned to two plays of Calderón which he remembered from his diplomatic mission.

The deflated and astringent tone of *Love in a Wood* expressed in the critical assessment of motive—frequently financial motive—represents an identifying quality of Restoration comedy of manners. My Lady Flippant's opening, and characterizing, remark, "Not a Husband to be had for mony," establishes the familiar sensual atmosphere. Lady Flippant and her brother, Alderman Gripe, in their separate efforts to serve their lusts and to preserve their reputations, reveal the hypocrisy that is the principal satiric target of Wycherley's comedies. If he found in *The Country Wife* a more perfect vehicle for his satiric vision of human bestiality hiding beneath the decorums, already in *Love in a Wood* that vision determines the judgments on characters.

The savagery with which Gripe is depicted, exposed as he is in a futile and costly attempt at lechery and deprived by a vain young fortune hunter of his daughter, provides a reminder that *Love in a Wood* is a Cavalier's play, bristling with the remembered resentments of the Civil Wars, when nonconformist merchants of London took Parliament's side against the king. The antagonism between Gripe, "seemingly precise, but a covetous, leacherous, old Usurer of the City," and Mr. Dapperwit, "a brisk conceited, half-witted fellow of the Town," derives from the conflict between social classes as well as between generations: the rich mercantile class under assault by the gentry, stronger in wit—real or, as in this case, pretended—than in ready money. Gripe is served, in his covert attempt to quench his lust, by Mrs. Joyner, "a Match-maker, or precise City Bawd,"

33. James Urvin Rundle, "Wycherley and Calderón."

like himself a caricature of merchant-class calculation and hypocrisy. She is as carnivorous, and rather more successful, than he, and like him carries the burden of royalist hatred of dissenters.

Yet the play also includes a plot turning on the fortunes of two young and romantic couples whose problems arise from mistaken identity in courtships carried on by night. It is this plot, the "love in a wood" of the title, that Wycherley took from *Mañanas de abril y mayo*. The resemblances between the two plays are specific and extended. The *parque del palacio de Madrid* has become St. James's Park (the "wood" of the title); it may well have been the current popularity of St. James's Park that gave Wycherley the idea of reworking the Spanish play about youthful merriment in a park. In any event, despite the authentic English personality and conversational idiom of his characters, he approximates the Spanish dramatist's manner of complicating the plot by heaping successive confusions of identity one on another.

Each play includes two pairs of young lovers, one couple more serious in temperament and beset with more serious problems than the other. The contrast in styles of courtship in the Spanish approximates a contrast that had been a convention of English comedy at least since *Much Ado About Nothing*. The serious couple in each play had been separated when the young man, following a duel with an adversary whom he took to be a rival, fled to avoid arrest. In the Spanish the adversary was killed; in the English, seriously but not fatally wounded. At play's opening, the young man has secretly returned, despite fear of retribution from the public authorities and revenge from the adversary's kinsmen, out of jealous concern for his beloved; and he takes refuge in the lodgings of a trusted friend. His effort to ascertain the faithfulness of his lady is complicated by the masqueradings of the more sprightly young woman; and, ironically, by his own lady's effort to seek him out, an audacious act that he first misinterprets as an intrigue with another man.

All this is in the pattern of the cape and sword play: a jealous lover, quick to draw his sword; a rapid sequence of turns in a plot kept moving by mistakes of identity. As is customary in the Restoration, Wycherley ignores the contrasting figure of the gracioso in his original. Presumably he had in mind, as he borrowed from *Mañanas de abril y mayo* (so extensively that he must have had the Spanish play before him as he wrote), the adaptations from the comedia so prominent on the English stage during the preceding decade. And yet he produced a play that in its total impact is altogether unlike the Spanish plots.[34]

Wycherley's several lines of action—the duping of the old merchant Gripe, the mercenary courtship of the fatuous Dapperwit, and the romantic courtships in the park—are strikingly different in tone. The contrasts in the play are studied and effective. Even the modes of speech of the separate groups of characters, as Rose A. Zimbardo has explained, are carefully differentiated.[35] The calculating and even sordid animality of the scenes in which Gripe and his associates appear gives way to the idle prattle of Dapperwit, and that in turn to the imaginative gaiety of the young couples. Yet even the love affairs of the young couples are scarcely in the romantic mood of Calderón's play.

As often, Calderón's title provides an interpretative key—*Mañanas de abril y mayo,* mornings of youth and springtime, as we may paraphrase and expand it—in which the beauty of the dawn in a Spanish park provides an emblematic backdrop. A song sung offstage early in the first act articulates the mood,

> Mañanicas floridas
> de abril y mayo,
> despertad a mi niña,
> no duerma tanto,

a song that will remind an English-speaking reader of Herrick rather than Wycherley. The distance in moods between the two plays is just one mark of the originality of *Love in a Wood.*[36]

The differences in the dramatic conventions controlling Wycherley's and Calderón's plays will suggest, I think, why discriminating

34. P. F. Vernon has written a perceptive comparison of the two plays, to which I am indebted in the following paragraphs: "Wycherley's First Comedy and Its Spanish Source," *Comparative Literature* 18 (1966) : 132–44.

35. Zimbardo, *Wycherley's Drama* (New Haven, 1965), pp. 33–48.

36. I find unconvincing the argument of Rose A. Zimbardo that in *Love in a Wood* Wycherley was indebted in a substantial way to Fletcher's dramatic pastoral *The Faithful Shepherdess.* Although Wycherley's play does indeed resemble Fletcher's in its pastoral qualities and in certain details of plot such as confusions of identity of young women, it resembles in these respects Calderón's play much more specifically. Mrs. Zimbardo does not allude to Rundle's discovery of the source in *Mañanas de abril y mayo.* Cf. Zimbardo, *Wycherley's Drama,* pp. 21–33.

students of Restoration comedy of manners have been reluctant to admit any substantial contribution to it from the comedia.[37] Certainly the contribution to English conventions of dialogue is slight. To turn from the one play to the other, even in those scenes in which Wycherley follows Calderón most closely, is to be strikingly reminded of Spanish and English differences in expository manner. In *Mañanas de abril y mayo* the extensive use of long monologues permits rapid narratives of past events; in *Love in a Wood* the approximation, or seeming approximation, of casual conversation enforces a slower revelation of what has gone before.

In Calderón, rapidity of movement, made possible by conversational summaries of events and expectations, contributes to the neatness of an intricate design that is itself a principal source of aesthetic pleasure. There are distinctly realized characters, notably the voluble pair of half-reluctant lovers Hipólito and Clara, the former not unlike Dryden's Celadon of *Secret Love,* the latter resembling Florimel. But the consecutive and harmonious playing out of the narrative line does not permit the episodic interruption so prominent in *Love in a Wood.* Wycherley's gallery of well-defined characters, and the astringency of the commentary they provide on London life, remind us that Ben Jonson was his master. He made liberal use of his source in Calderón, and he played variations on the English convention of the Spanish plot, but he was altogether his own man, using Spanish intrigue merely as an ingredient in what is finally a satirical comedy of manners.

The relationship of Wycherley's next play, *The Gentleman Dancing-Master,* to the comedia is at once more overt and less consequential than that of *Love in a Wood:* more overt because the title derives from Calderón's *El maestro de danzar* and because Spanish manners and the conventional intrigue of the Spanish plot provide butts of satire; less consequential in that much less of the dramatic action follows Calderón.

In one of its dimensions *The Gentleman Dancing-Master* is a parody of the Spanish plots—of their intrigues originating in the

37. Cf. Kathleen Lynch, *The Social Mode of Restoration Comedy* (New York, 1926), pp. 164–66; Charlotte Bradford Hughes, ed., *John Crowne's Sir Courtly Nice* (The Hague, 1966), Introduction, pp. 28–41.

close confinement of young women, of their code of honor, of at least one of their character types, the suspicious father. Mr. James Formal—or, as he prefers to be called, Don Diego—who has the conventional function in Restoration comedy of the father to be outwitted by the young couple bent on matrimony, is "An old rich *Spanish* Merchant newly returned home, . . . much affected with the Habit and Customs of *Spain*." An English caricature of a suspicious and family-proud Spanish father, he has immured his daughter Hippolita as closely as if she lived in Madrid. "Have you had a *Spanish* care of the Honour of my Family?" (act 2), he asks his sister upon his return to London. In explanation he tells her that he has passed some fifteen years in Spain: "Now in *Spain* he is wise enough that is grave, politick enough, that says little; and honourable enough that is jealous; and though I say it that shou'd not say it, I am as grave, grum, and jealous, as any *Spaniard* breathing." His references to his clothing and his beard suggest that on the stage his physical appearance would have recalled characters in the Spanish plots with whom Restoration audiences were familiar. As often in the comedia, the father's "honor" provides a blocking force to the schemes of the young, though with the difference that results from Wycherley's burlesque intention.

The daughter, as vivacious as Calderón's heroines and less inhibited by national custom, has been attracted by a young man who courts her as best he can despite physical separation. "You know," she tells her foppish cousin whom her father has chosen as her intended husband (act 1),

> my Chamber is backward, and has a door into the Gallery, which looks into the back-yard of a Tavern, whence Mr. *Gerrard* once spying me at the Window, has often since attempted to come in at that Window by the help of the Leads of a low Building adjoyning, and indeed 'twas as much as my Maid and I cou'd do to keep him out—

Her resistance does not preclude affection for him, and she is driven to assume the initiative by her father's eagerness to marry her off to her cousin, Mr. Parris—or Monsieur de Paris as he styles himself—who is as addicted to the manners of France as her father is to those of Spain. By way of her obtuse cousin, she conveys a message to

Mr. Gerrard. When in response he comes to her house, they are surprised together by her father, who is as prompt to draw his sword as any *viejo* of the comedia. To save themselves, they pretend Mr. Gerrard is a "gentleman-dancing-master"—a stratagem Wycherley borrowed from Calderón's play. Although the father is not wholly convinced, the couple gain time—enough time for them to contrive a secret marriage, with the unwitting assistance of the stupid cousin. The father is reconciled by his recognition that Gerrard is a man of honor and spirit and that Parris is not. The latter consoles himself by making an agreement with a woman of the town, in a clever parody of the Restoration proviso scenes, to take her into keeping.

Parris is a Frenchified fop, an earlier and cruder version of the character type exemplified by Etherege's Sir Fopling Flutter, and like him he embodies a judgment on the imitation of French manners in that age of *le grand roi* (to whom Parris refers). In the juxtaposition of Monsieur de Paris and Don Diego, the satirical commentary includes a comparative evaluation of French and Spanish mannerisms. (The Dutch national character, if not English imitation of the manners of that nation, comes in for conversational abuse.) Remembering Wycherley's preoccupation with the London scene around him, we may surmise that in Don Diego's affectations he had a particular target in view.

The mockery of Spanish customs is a function of the parodic intention of the play, burlesque of the Spanish plots. But more is involved, and we can get some notion of what it is by remembering the careers of prominent Restoration courtiers. Wycherley would scarcely have glanced directly at men of such high rank as the earl of Arlington, known for his affectation of Spanish manners, or Sir William Godolphin, ambassador to Spain at the time the play was first performed, whose devotion to the country as well as his religion led him to remain there even after he was recalled, in 1678, from his diplomatic mission (see above, pp. 43–44; 62). Wycherley would rather have had in view lesser men, merchants perhaps like Mr. James Formal himself. But biographical records of the great survive as those of men of lower rank do not, and they can suggest the social reality underlying the satirical superstructure of the play.

The borrowings from *El maestro de danzar,* though specific and even in passages detailed, are isolated. They are of such a nature that they could derive from an old memory of a performance of the play, perhaps reinforced by reference to the printed text. Not verbal or consecutive, they are rather situational, of a kind that the young dramatist searching for episodes to carry his satirical comment on the London life about him (and on the English cape and sword plays) might recall from a performance of some years earlier. Don Diego, the name taken by Mr. James Formal, is that of his counterpart in the Spanish play, though the correspondence may be owing merely to the conventional and contemptuous English use of that name. Calderón's play has a much busier plot, with more closely organized intrigue, including two major lines of action, only one of which has a counterpart in Wycherley's play. Yet in outline the correspondences in the relevant portions are rather close.

In an expository speech at the beginning of *El maestro de danzar,* the servant of Don Enrique, the *galán,* recalls that a rich merchant, Don Diego, while on a long voyage overseas, left his daughter Leonor under the tutelage of his brother. Don Enrique lived next door, and from his adjacent balcony secretly courted Leonor on her own balcony. The situation reappears in *The Gentleman Dancing-Master,* as we learn in retrospective conversation in the first act, with an aunt being substituted for an uncle as the girl's guardian and with the difference that the girl has been less overtly receptive to her suitor's advances. In both plays the father's return not long before has precipitated a change of strategy in the couple's intrigues. All this Wycherley could have learned from the servant's opening speech in the Spanish play.

About midway in each play, after differing episodic detail, comes the situation that justifies the two titles, and here Wycherley obviously—and after all admittedly—borrowed from Calderón. The scene is superbly comic in both plays, as the young lover, having contrived a meeting with the young woman, is suddenly interrupted by the suspicious father. In both instances a maidservant aids the deception; and in both her quick-witted mistress thinks of the stratagem, introducing the slowly comprehending gallant as her dancing-master. The deception almost miscarries in both plays because the young man does not know how to dance—and we can imagine how a clever actor, Spanish or English, would have conveyed his perplexity. The couple gains time for further stratagems, which differ in the two plays except for their successful outcome.

El maestro de danzar has the Spanish gravity about it notwithstanding the disillusioned chatter of the gracioso and the absurdity of the situation that provides the title. As often in the comedia, the galán and his servant the gracioso have something of a Don Quijote and Sancho Panza relationship, one alluded to here in a literary expostulation of the servant (act 1), who compares his master, not precisely to Don Quijote, but to the chivalric heroes whose adventures had turned his head. When a moment later the master rushes to the aid of a distressed lady, the servant is confirmed in his opinion:

> Sólo esto
> le faltaba a tu fortuna,
> para ser hecho y derecho
> caballero andante.

Yet this is the customary undertone of the cape and sword play, the critical grip on reality that lends plausibility to the heroic assumptions of the gallant, in his impetuous rush into hazardous adventure. The play is far indeed from burlesque of the conventions of honor, of which the gracioso may have intellectual but not emotional understanding. Not one, as in Wycherley, but two young couples play a dangerous nocturnal game against the threat of a father or a brother's sword to win marriage to the desired partner; and the complicated but closely controlled plot moves rapidly to the denouement. Calderón's verse can be witty and yet lyrical, and his long speeches are typically economical in exposition.

The Gentleman Dancing-Master is of course an English comedy of manners, its dialogue taken up with commentary on the preoccupations of its London audience, including in this instance the fondness for Spanish customs and for Spanish comedies of intrigue. Satirically delineated characters and realistically conceived conversation, in prose, provide the focus of attention. The plot is loosely contrived, its Spanish ancestry notwithstanding; vivid and to some extent disjunctive episodes receive emphasis. In its permissive sexual attitudes, apparent in innuendo and flagrant in scenes in which ladies of pleasure appear on stage, the play differs markedly from the chaste tone of Calderón. Wycherley had found his own style, with an English ancestry in Jonson, Dryden, and Etherege; and he turned his borrowings from Calderón to his own English uses.[38]

Wycherley made the leap to satirical comedy of contemporary London life as Dryden never did, and this notwithstanding the fact that he made more direct and extensive use of the comedia than Dryden. However critical Dryden was of the Spanish code of honor, in his comedies of Spanish locale and characters he remained on the middle ground of Fletcherian romance and Jonsonian comedy of humors [39]—his characters are individualized as Calderón's rarely are, but are kept at a distance, as Wycherley's are not, from the ordinary circumstances of English life. His comedies remind us of the importance of setting. Though his characters talk like King Charles's courtiers, they are equipped with an insulating shield of Spanish decorum. Neither Dryden's nor Wycherley's plays are, in any strict sense, Spanish plots; and yet they derive from the Cavaliers' adaptations and translations. These two great dramatists, even in their irreverence toward the comedia, paid tribute to it by using it as a point of departure for splendidly original plays.

38. In a forthcoming article, David Stuart Rodes examines the literary background of *The Gentleman Dancing-Master* more comprehensively.

39. Cf. Moore, *Nobler Pleasure,* passim.

V: THE LEGACY OF THE CAVALIERS
Varieties of Spanish Romance

IT is curious that in an age of such pronounced Hispanic interests as the Restoration, the English should have concentrated so heavily on a single category of the comedia, and one not representing the highest accomplishment of the Spaniards in drama at that. If the Spanish drama lacks the easily recognizable, formal division into tragedy and comedy (and tragicomedy, history, and pastoral, as Polonius would put it), it nevertheless does have superb tragedies, and comedies that do not conform to the cape and sword pattern; it also has a broad range of characters, plots, tones, and forms of dramatic language. Restoration dramatists could have found tragedies and history plays to adapt as readily as cape and sword plays. Yet when they wrote plays in the Spanish manner, they followed, if sometimes at an amused distance, the intrigue form popularized by Tuke, Bristol, and the others.

With very few exceptions Restoration Englishmen, even after the early experimental years, ignored the plays that are now considered to be the Spanish masterpieces. The exceptions or possible exceptions are quickly listed—apart from *El príncipe constante,* only Tirso's *El Burlador de Sevilla* and Calderón's *La vida es sueño.* Tirso's *El Burlador* made an indirect contribution to an English play, Shadwell's tragedy *The Libertine.* Shadwell refers to the Spanish original in his preface but implies that he has not read it. His primary sources are French, though he follows many of the conventions of the Spanish plot. *La vida es sueño,* either directly or through an intermediary, provided the subplot of Aphra Behn's *The Young*

King; in this instance the connection between Spanish original and English derivative may be closer than in *The Libertine.*

Few ambiguous instances of direct borrowing from the comedia exist after the first decade of the Restoration, and several of these few appear in plays that are not, in the Restoration sense, Spanish plots: Wycherley's *Love in a Wood* and *The Gentleman Dancing-Master* and Crowne's *Sir Courtly Nice.* Only John Leanerd's *The Counterfeits* seems to have the kind of close relationship to a Spanish original we have noted in Tuke's, Bristol's, and Sydserf's adaptations. Yet the Spanish plots—or comedies of Spanish romance—continued to appear. Their literary ancestry is often obscure. On grounds of probability, we must assume that some have sources in the comedia which have not yet been discovered; and we must also assume that some of the sources we think we have found—for Cibber's *She Would and She Would Not,* to cite a possible example—are not the right ones, or at least not the direct ones. Several of the closest approximations to the conventions of the Spanish plot, Ravenscroft's *The Wrangling Lovers,* for example, have sources in prose fiction rather than in the comedia. Tradition had become a force in the English imitations of the cape and sword plays, and it was often more influential in shaping the English plays than the sources from which the dramatists took their materials. The Spanish contribution to Restoration drama was formal as well as substantive.

As the years passed, French dramatic example and critical precept, as well as French renderings of Spanish drama and prose fiction, increasingly conditioned the English interpretation of Spanish literature. The author of a prologue spoken at Drury Lane in 1717 described epigrammatically his countrymen's borrowings from the two countries: "*Theirs are the Rules of* France, *the Plots of* Spain / . . . / *They pall* Moliere's *and* Lopez *sprightly strain, / And teach dull* Harlequins *to grin in vain.*"[1] "The Rules of France, the Plots of Spain": a difficult combination, productive of tensions. Dryden's reservations about Spanish honor notwithstanding, he had a considerable knowledge at least of the cape and sword plays, and he recognized their lively charm, even though he found it difficult to reconcile his admiration for them with neoclassical principles. The

1. Prologue to Gay, Pope, and Arbuthnot, *Three Hours after Marriage* (London, 1717).

other two major literary theorists of the later seventeenth century, Thomas Rymer and John Dennis, both of them younger men, were less tolerant of the comedia.[2] Dennis's remarks about the Spanish source of Crowne's *Sir Courtly Nice* reveal in fact a patronizing condescension, as he commiserates with Crowne about the difficulty of the task, imposed on him by Charles II, of basing an English comedy on such an insubstantial foundation as *No puede ser*. In this hostile critical atmosphere, the English derivatives from the comedia usually embodied radical departures from the Spanish originals.

Aphra Behn, one of the most capable of the dramatists to turn to Spanish materials, began her prolific career in the theater at the end of the first decade of the Restoration. Her work illustrates the later phase of the Spanish plots, in which Spanish themes, character types, and situations are assimilated in plays within the rapidly evolving patterns of Restoration drama. Her work also illustrates the continuing impact on the drama of the royal exile—in her case not of the experience itself (the best guess would place her age at about twenty in 1660),[3] but of the literary experience transmitted by the plays, and no doubt also by the conversation, of the Cavaliers who had shared King Charles's wanderings on the Continent. Her best play, *The Rover,* with the very appropriate subtitle *The Banished Cavaliers,* had as its principal source Thomas Killigrew's semiautobiographical *Thomaso; Or, The Wanderer,* his unacted and unactable rendering, nominally in dramatic form, of his own and his friends' experiences during the exile, in Spain and elsewhere. Of the four Spanish plays from which (if we may accept Floriana T. Hogan's convincing analysis) [4] she borrowed, three had been adapted by Lord Bristol and performed in the decade before she began writing. This

2. Cf. Rymer, "Preface to Rapin," in *Critical Works.* ed. Curt A. Zimansky (New Haven, Conn., 1956), pp. 1–2; "Short View of Tragedy," in ibid., p. 118; Dennis, Letter of June 23, 1719, in *Critical Works of John Dennis,* ed. E. N. Hooker (Baltimore, 1939–43), 2 : 405–06.

3. For a chronology of Mrs. Behn's career, see Behn, *The Rover,* ed. Frederick M. Link (Lincoln, Neb., 1967), Appendix B.

4. Hogan, "Notes on Thirty-One English Plays and Their Spanish Sources," *Restoration and Eighteenth-Century Theatre Research* 6 (1967): 56–59. I am deeply indebted to Dr. Hogan's analysis of the source problem in Mrs. Behn's plays. However, as I shall explain, I differ from Dr. Hogan's conclusions in certain details. I think it likely that at least some of the borrowings from the Spanish plays came through intermediary plays or prose narratives rather than directly.

could scarcely be coincidence. If she did not make use of Bristol's adaptations, she must at least have had her attention drawn to those Spanish plays by Bristol's English versions of them. Thorough professional that she was, she had an eye to the taste for Spanish intrigue engendered by such plays as Bristol's, Tuke's, and Dryden's.

The internal evidence of her writings, though not conclusive, would suggest that she had some knowledge of Spanish. Three of the four comedias from which she apparently borrowed, as I have said, had appeared in English; and the fourth, Calderón's *La vida es sueño,* was already so famous that we need not assume she read it in Spanish.[5] If no English translation had yet appeared, the play had been translated into Dutch and performed both in Amsterdam and Brussels (see above, pp. 36–37), cities Mrs. Behn visited. Although she seems not to have made use of it, a French novel, Le Métel de Boisrobert's *La Vie n'est qu'un songe* (1657), had been based on the play.[6] The strongest argument for her use of an untranslated Spanish source has been adduced by Ernst Garland Mathews, who traces a principal episode of her *The False Count* to a novela included in Alonso Castillo de Solórzano's *Noches de placer* (1631).[7] Yet remembering the extraordinarily complex relationships between plots in the seventeenth century, we may regard the argument as less than conclusive. In the preface to her translation (1688) of Fontenelle's *Entretiens sur la pluralité des mondes,* she implies an acquaintance with the language when she asserts that Spanish and Italian are easier to translate than French because they are closer to Latin.[8]

Her travels provide a clue to her obvious interest in Spanish subjects and apparent knowledge of the language. Any inferences from her travels must be used with caution, however, because the records

5. It should be noted, however, that Mrs. Behn's editor, Montague Summers, asserts that she borrowed directly from Calderón: "Mrs. Behn has undoubtedly taken the whole episode of Orsames directly from Calderon's great philosophic and symbolical comedia, *La Vida es Sueño* (1633). That Mrs. Behn had a good knowledge of Spanish is certain, and she has copied with the closest fidelity minute but telling details of her original." Montague Summers, ed., *The Works of Aphra Behn* (London, 1915), 2 : 102–03.

6. Cf. Cioranescu, "Calderón y el teatro clásico francés," in *Estudios de literatura española y comparada* (Laguna, Canary Islands, 1954), p. 152.

7. Mathews, "Studies in Anglo-Spanish Cultural and Literary Relations, 1598–1700," in Harvard University, Graduate School of Arts and Sciences, *Summaries of Theses, 1938* (Cambridge, Mass., 1940), p. 313.

8. I am indebted to Frederick M. Link for calling her statement to my attention.

concerning her life provide a classic case of the difficulty in separating truth from fiction—in determining how much is true in the autobiographical statements embedded in her work, how much literary artifice. Some order has been brought to the subject by Robert Adams Day, who uses bibliographical analysis, and by W. J. Cameron, who collates her own statements with contemporary documents, principally governmental records.[9] Cameron concludes that she went to Surinam, as she asserts in *Oroonoko,* and that she was indeed a secret agent in Flanders, as she asserts in *The Fair Jilt.* Public records, in fact, leave no doubt that she went to Antwerp in 1666 as a spy and they would suggest, though not prove, that she had gone three years earlier to Surinam with her father, who died on the outward voyage.

Of these two adventurous episodes, the residence in Flanders is the more relevant to Mrs. Behn's knowledge of Spanish. She apparently remained only a few months in Surinam, which in any event was an English colony at the time and would have provided little exposure to Spanish (though rather more to Indian culture: she brought back wreaths of feathers that were used in staging Dryden and Howard's *The Indian Queen*).[10] Flanders was still under Spanish rule. Having literary interests and aptitudes, she would have noted the Spanish plays then appearing in Brussels, both in translation and sometimes in the original language.

In any event, she would have observed the wanderings of expatriated Englishmen and would have remembered them during the following decade when, in *The Rover,* she provided a spirited rendering of the adventures of Cavaliers in exile. (It may be significant that Thomas Killigrew, the author of *Thomaso; Or, the Wanderer,* her principal source for *The Rover,* was an intermediary between her and the English ministers who sponsored her expedition as a spy.)[11] Whatever her linguistic accomplishments, by the time her first play was produced in 1670 she had an experience of the world uncommon in the seventeenth or in any other century.

9. Day, "Aphra Behn's First Biography," *Studies in Bibliography* 22 (1969) : 227–40. Cameron, *New Light on Aphra Behn: An Investigation into the Facts and Fictions Surrounding Her Journey to Surinam in 1663 and Her Activities as a Spy in Flanders in 1666* (Auckland, New Zealand, 1961).

10. Dryden, *Works,* 8 : 282.

11. Cameron, *New Light on Aphra Behn,* p. 20.

Mrs. Behn's use in *The Young King* of *La vida es sueño* acquires interest by reason of the excellence of the Spanish original, not in this instance a cape and sword play, but a subtle philosophical and religious drama that is one of the supreme masterpieces of Spanish literature. The fact of her borrowing is scarcely disputable, though her means of access to the Spanish play, whether in print or on the stage or through the French novel, must probably remain unknown. Companies of Spanish actors sometimes performed in the Netherlands and may have presented it. Flemish actors presented it in Brussels at about the time she was there (see above, pp. 36–37). The nature of the resemblances to Calderón, situational and not verbal, is compatible with her use of a translation or a free prose rendering. Although her play was not performed until 1679, it was, on the cryptic evidence of her dedicatory epistle, written much earlier, perhaps before the first of her plays reached the stage in 1670, and its origin may well be related to her sojourn in the Netherlands.

Not necessarily, of course. The fact that she drew from a French novel, La Calprenède's *Cléopâtra,* for her main plot [12] might suggest that she drew for her subplot from the French novel based on *La vida es sueño,* which is included in Le Métel de Boisrobert's collection *Nouvelles héroïques et amoureuses,* published in Paris in 1657. Yet one crucial detail argues against Mrs. Behn's use of Boisrobert. Although his French redaction of Calderón's story follows the original closely, it omits the episode in which Rosaura accidentally encounters Segismundo in his prison before he is first taken to court. In *The Young King* (act 2, scene 1), on the other hand, the episode is included.

The resemblances between *La vida es sueño* and *The Young King,* I have said, are situational and not verbal—except for the several allusions in the English play to the difficulty in discriminating between waking and sleeping, the problem—part epistemological and part theological—that provides an organizational metaphor in the Spanish play. We search in vain for passages in *The Young King* in which the parallels are close enough to demonstrate that Mrs. Behn was writing with Calderón's play open before her. Yet the resemblances are striking enough, both in the opening situation from which the successive action derives and even a series of episodes, to show that the

12. Langbaine, *Account,* p. 22.

relationship between the two plays is closer than that of merely cognate expressions of the folk motif of the sleeper awakened. Mrs. Behn may have known this motif in its most famous English version, the Christopher Sly episode in *The Taming of the Shrew*. She may have taken suggestions from other English plays, from the Davenant-Dryden adaptation of *The Tempest,* for example, where she would have found a precedent for a young man's first meeting with a young woman.[13] She changed names and locale, presumably as a means to bring the subplot into a coherent relationship with the main plot borrowed from La Calprenède. But she followed *La vida es sueño* closely enough to imply familiarity, not necessarily with the language of the original, but with the sequence of its action.

In both plays, *La vida es sueño* and *The Young King,* the prince-king (Segismundo-Orsames) has since infancy been secretly confined in a remote castle, without knowledge of his own identity, in the custody of an elderly guardian (Clotaldo-Geron), because of one parent's (Basilio, King of Poland; the Queen of Dacia) fear of a prognostication that his succession to the sovereignty which is his inheritance would lead to disaster. Although the young man has been carefully educated by his guardian, the conditions of his life have given him a rough and violent disposition, an impatience with the constraint he has always known. In both plays the young man's first encounter with someone from the outside world comes in his chance meeting with a young woman (Rosaura-Urania), who inadvertently discovers his place of confinement. The emotional dimensions of the encounters are parallel: from despondency the young man is aroused by the young woman to delighted animation, extended in the English though not in the Spanish version to a frank if unwitting sexual response. The meeting is soon interrupted—by the guardian in the Spanish, by the young woman's lover in the English—and the young man returns to his former isolation.

The isolation is broken in each play by a test period of sovereignty so that the parent may determine whether or not the predictions of disaster were soundly based. The parent is troubled in conscience by his repressive treatment of the legitimate heir, even while fearing the outcome of experiment—and hence the decision to arrange a test that can be easily terminated, with the explanation given to the

13. Cf. Summers, ed., John Dryden, *Dramatic Works* (London, 1931–32), 2 : 102.

young man that his experience of grandeur was but a dream. The awakening scenes are similar, and so are the demonstrations of the young man's inability to rule, though with a predictable difference in emphasis: in Calderón, a more probing examination of the validity of human knowledge and a more comprehensive attention to the duties of kingship; in Mrs. Behn, a more sensual interest in the sexual excitement latent in the situation (including an approach to incest, when the untutored young man expresses improper interest in his own mother). Yet even Calderón's Segismundo is so unrestrained in his advances to Rosaura that he precipitates a duel. The young man in both plays, deemed to have failed his test, is put to sleep and returned to isolated captivity; his guardian explains that all that has happened was merely a dream.

The resolutions are again parallel, though Mrs. Behn's is complicated by her main plot. An armed revolt on behalf of the young man restores him to his rank, this time not to the appearance but to the substance of it; and this time, having learned decorum and restraint from earlier frustrations, he conducts himself properly. He forgives his parent for the cruelty of his confinement, and the parent laments his misplaced belief in auguries. In neither play does the young man marry the young woman (Rosaura-Urania) to whom he had earlier been so strongly attracted. Rather, he marries a first cousin (Estrella-Olympia), a suitable match for a sovereign or prospective sovereign.

It is not profitable to compare at length plays so dissimilar as *La vida es sueño* and *The Young King*. Apart from the parallels I have described, they have little in common. Even the similar plots occupy different positions: primary and emphatic in the Spanish, secondary in the English. The authorial evaluations of the common experience are not alike beyond the most superficial level. Implicit in the folktale of the awakened sleeper, in Mrs. Behn as in Calderón, there is, to be sure, the problem of the validity of knowledge. But in *The Young King* the problem remains implicit; it is not, beyond the use of the fable itself and references to waking and dreaming, formulated or explored. Furthermore, the effect of the fable is muted by its relationship to the extravagant main plot, derived in mood as well as in values celebrated and in episodes from Calprenède's *Cléo-*

patre. Mrs. Behn's play is alternately courtly and sensual. She depicts characters committed to a chivalric ideal of behavior and yet she introduces scenes that are sexually provocative. Calderón's seriousness is lightened by his gracioso Clarín, a fully developed character, important to the elucidation of the Spanish play's meaning; and perhaps the seriousness is also modified by the naïve fervor of Segismundo's initial response to the great world; but the play remains somber, even pessimistic, in its total impact.

The Young King is not a Spanish plot but rather a two-plot tragicomedy, having formal resemblances to such plays of Dryden's as *Secret Love* and *Marriage à la Mode.* Like Dryden in those plays, Mrs. Behn drew from French romance, and it is her borrowings from La Calprenède rather than those from the Spanish dramatist that are decisive in establishing her tone of romantic and improbable adventure. Her conception of *La vida es sueño* seems to have been different from ours, as different, say, as Davenant and Dryden's conception of *The Tempest* was from ours. Because in the seventeenth century Calderón's and Shakespeare's plays did not have the prescriptive claim to greatness established by subsequent analytical criticism, they were vulnerable to changes and exaggerations of emphasis that altered the original design. We may recognize Mrs. Behn's failure to respect the integrity of Calderón's theme, her employment of his fable of human conversion and regeneration as merely a tale of exotic adventure. But it would be as much of an anachronism to censure her for failing to perceive Calderón's subtlety as it would be to censure the Restoration adapters of Shakespeare for failing to comprehend his achievement.

Four of Mrs. Behn's comedies take place in Spain or in a part of Italy controlled by Spain, and as usual in Restoration drama a Spanish setting has a functional relationship to theme and plot. It is in these plays, *The Dutch Lover, The False Count,* and the two independent parts of *The Rover,* that she experimented with the Spanish plot, the conventions of which she handled almost as freely as Dryden.

The Rover; Or, The Banished Cavaliers, part 1 (1677) and part 2 (1680), derives from Thomas Killigrew's very long closet drama *Thomaso; Or, The Wanderer,* written (if we may trust a statement prefixed to the published play) in Madrid in 1654.[14] I have already alluded to *Thomaso* as a record of experiences that contributed to the Spanish plays of the Restoration—a record not, of course, to be accepted in literal detail, and yet perhaps conveying more of the quality of life experienced in exile than factual records such as letters and legal documents do. Mrs. Behn retains, in her greatly altered adaptations from *Thomaso,* a sense of the Cavaliers' devotion to pleasure and adventure based partly on the desperation engendered by poverty. Her Cavaliers have the spur of want as well as sexual passion to drive them forward in their escapades, and they have the freedom from inhibition that residence abroad and lack of responsibility provide.

The two parts of *The Rover* have little continuity between them; the second and inferior part was apparently an afterthought, written to take advantage of the success of the first. Part 1 is located in Naples, the Naples of Spanish rule, and part 2 in Madrid, the change of place signaling the introduction of a new and unrelated series of intrigues. The Neapolitan setting of part 1 notwithstanding, most of the characters, apart from the exiled English, are Spanish, and their social code and manners are Spanish. Yet if this is a Spanish plot, it is one in which the conventions are reinterpreted.

Mrs. Behn's formal model would seem to be Dryden's *Secret Love,* French and not Spanish in its foreign antecedents, and *An Evening's Love.* The latter play, we recall, has a time and place of action specified with precision: "*Madrid,* in the Year 1665. The Time, the last Evening of the Carnival", a circumstance that may have suggested Mrs. Behn's "Naples, in Carnival time" for part 1. The carnival intensifies the gaiety of her young lovers and provides an occasion for high jinks that complicate her plot. Like Dryden in *An Evening's Love,* Mrs. Behn juxtaposes English and Spanish characters, using relaxed though honorable Englishmen to provide contrast to the intense and suspicious Spanish gallants. The Englishmen, in Mrs. Behn as in Dryden, are gifted conversationalists, and they find fit antagonists in young Spanish ladies, who are more articulate than their fellow countrymen. The exchanges of Willmore ("the Rover") and Hellena include just such wit, and just such an uneasy combina-

14. *The Rover,* ed., F. M. Link, pp. xi–xii. Cf. Alfred Harbage, *Cavalier Drama,* pp. 181–83. Langbaine alludes to Killigrew's travels in Spain in *Account,* p. 311.

tion of affection and reluctance, as Dryden had made famous in the banter between Wildblood and Jacintha in *An Evening's Love* and between Celadon and Florimel in *Secret Love*. The Rover, like Celadon, is a notorious inconstant, and Hellena, like Florimel, must witness his pursuit of other women before she can bring him to heel. In the Rover's remarks about Hellena (act 1, scene 2), Mrs. Behn seems even to recall the famous passage in *Secret Love* (act 1, scene 2), in which Celadon describes Florimel.

If Mrs. Behn's formal model was Dryden, she nevertheless seems to have taken suggestions for *The Rover,* as Dr. Hogan has pointed out, from Calderón's *Mejor está que estaba* [15]—I would guess, on grounds of probability, through Lord Bristol's rendering of it as *'Tis Better than It Was,* performed sometime between 1662 and 1665.[16] In *The Rover* as in *Mejor está* (and in Dryden's *An Evening's Love*) the adventures are played out in carnival time, the masking and freedom of association of the carnival helping to set them in motion. This is a generalized resemblance. Much more specific is the resemblance between the intrigue in *The Rover* in which Belville, a royalist colonel in exile, pursues and wins Florinda, and that in *Mejor está* in which Carlos Colona pursues and wins Flora (a name perhaps significantly similar to Florinda).

With a few changes and substitutions, the persons and the events of the parallel plots are alike. Carlos Colona, like Belville a stranger from afar, is the son of a man who had earlier, in battle, saved the life and honor of Flora's father (act 2). With a change of generations, the relationships reappear in *The Rover*. Florinda had known Belville when Pamplona was under siege, she explains to Hellena in the first scene: "he was then a Colonel of *French* Horse, who when the Town was Ransack't, Nobly treated my Brother and my self, preserving us from all Insolences". Subsequent events in Mrs. Behn's plot follow Calderón. Flora-Florinda disdains a choice of husband, Licio-Antonio, made for her by her father-brother, preferring the gallant stranger Carlos-Belville. In both plays the stranger's readiness with his sword in carnival time leads to his arrest and imprisonment; and in both he eventually appeases the lady's family—makes amends for seeming offenses against their honor—by marrying her. He is

15. Hogan, "Notes on Thirty-One English Plays," p. 57.
16. John Downes, *Roscius Anglicanus,* p. 26.

aided in doing so by the father-brother's remembered gratitude to him. In elaborating her wholesale borrowings from *Thomaso,* Mrs. Behn perhaps remembered Bristol's *'Tis Better than It Was*—perhaps merely remembered seeing performances of it, for the apparent borrowings are of a generalized, situational kind.

Since *Thomaso* had not been performed, Mrs. Behn must have worked with the written text of it. Her defensive postscript to her first edition implies that she had been accused of plagiarism in making such free use of Killigrew's play, and it implies also, by silence, that she had not secured Killigrew's permission. This might be assumed, in any event, from the fact that *The Rover* was performed by the Duke's rather than the King's Company, of which Killigrew was the patentee. The postcript includes no reference to Calderón or Lord Bristol, something less than an adequate acknowledgment to Killigrew, and, perhaps as compensation, something more than an adequate acknowledgment to the Jacobean dramatist Richard Brome, from whose *The Novella* she took suggestions for two episodes.[17] "That I have stoln some hints from it [*Thomaso*]," she writes,

> *may be a proof, that I valu'd it more than to pretend to alter it, had I had the Dexterity of some Poets, who are not more Expert in stealing than in the Art of Concealing. . . . I will only say the Plot and Bus'ness (not to boast on't) is my own: as for the Words and Characters, I leave the Reader to judge and compare 'em with* Thomaso, *to whom I recommend the great Entertainment of reading it.*

This last clause carries justifiable irony. Few but research students now, and perhaps not many more in the seventeenth century, could find even mild entertainment in reading the massive *Thomaso.* It would seem to have been written rather more for the author's than for the reader's pleasure.

Resemblances of character and plot between *The Rover* and *Mejor está* notwithstanding, Mrs. Behn's play is much more loosely constructed than Calderón's. It is more a construction of heterogeneous elements—of the duel of wit, as Dryden had developed it, in the exchanges between Hellena and Willmore; of situational

17. *The Rover,* ed. Link, p. 130 n.

farce in the episodes in which Blunt, "An *English* Country Gentleman," no more sophisticated than booby squires in Restoration comedy usually are, is duped and humiliated by Lucetta, "A jilting Wench"; as well as of the conventional matter of the cape and sword play. Yet if we leave out of account the anglicized adaptations from the comedia such as Wycherley's, perhaps no Restoration plays except Dryden's reveal a more creative employment of Spanish materials.

The English dramatists could not retain the poetry of the comedia, the lyrical and expository monologues and the modulations from one verse form to another. Lacking these resources, they could not sustain the Spanish intensity of preoccupation with one or two love intrigues. The diffuseness of *The Rover,* the discontinuous action and the variations in tone from one episode to the next, may be seen as a necessary compromise, not merely with English taste, but even more with the resources of English dramatic dialogue. Mrs. Behn's dialogue is at its best, not in the occasional passages of loose blank verse, but in the exchanges, in prose, between Willmore and Hellena. She had to adapt her Spanish materials to the stage for which she wrote and offer compensation for the qualities impossible to retain in English.

She does not burlesque the Spanish sensitivity to honor even though she would seem to offer, in the characters of the English Cavaliers, a corrective contrast with it. She could not disparage the Spanish—and English—concern for reputation and the point of honor without destroying a major premise of her intrigue plot; but she could and did show Colonel Belville moving rapidly and easily from insouciance to sensitive response to a just claim on him, as at the beginning of act 4, when Belville, out of gratitude to the viceroy's son Antonio, who has saved him from prison, agrees to fight a duel in the place of Antonio, then disabled by a wound. The Cavalier deflation of mood could give way on fit occasion to a chivalric response to an obligation. Drawing on the writings of Cavaliers—certainly Killigrew and probably Lord Bristol—Mrs. Behn, in her best play, gave expression to an aspect of the exile beyond the reach of those who had personally known it.

The Rover, part 2, first performed three years after the earlier play and after Mrs. Behn had written three other plays, represents an effort to recapture the earlier success. This time the "banished cavaliers"—a new group of them except for Willmore and the gullible country gentleman Blunt—are in Madrid. Their adventures and mischances are much the same. Mrs. Behn dedicated the play, appropriately, to the duke of York, recalling in her epistle his own military service under the king of Spain: "allow him," she writes, referring to her title character, "a shelter and protection, who was driven from his Native Country with You, forc'd as You were, to fight for his Bread in a strange Land, and suffer'd with You all the Ills of Poverty, War and Banishment." She alludes to the duke's liking for the earlier play, and we may guess that her calculated allusions in dialogue to the remembered experiences of royalist officers contributed to the success of both parts. The duke and his brother the king would have understood well enough Willmore's reference (act 1, scene 1) to "*Bruxels* that inchanted Court . . . where our Hero's Act *Tantalus* better than ever *Ovid* describ'd him, condemn'd daily to see an Apparition of Meat, food in Vision only."

The setting in Madrid notwithstanding, the second part takes the cape and sword pattern less seriously than the first. Here there are no Spanish gallants or Spanish gentlewomen, and the mistaken identities and the sword fights are rendered broadly. The English characters fit the Restoration pattern of true wits and would-be wits: the socially accomplished gentlemen Willmore and Beaumond ("the *English* Ambassadors Nephew") and the maladroit country squires, Blunt and Fetherfool, both of the latter aspiring to adventures they lack the finesse to accomplish. Beaumond's role is analogous to that of Colonel Belville in the earlier play. Like Belville before him, he comes off successfully in the matrimonial dance, though he encounters no such hazardous adventures along the way as had the colonel. His principal rival, in fact, is Willmore himself, now a widower, who, as in the earlier play, pursues simultaneously an honorable young woman, "the *English* Ambassadors Daughter-in-law," and the beautiful courtesan La Nuche, whose role is similar to that of Angellica Bianca in part 1. This time Fetherfool experiences the kind of farcical disappointment in love to which Blunt had been subjected in Naples. In place of the beautiful woman he expected, he finds himself in bed with a lustful old grandee. The play is often farcical, never solemn, and sometimes luxuriantly sexual. In returning to the adventures of the exiled Cavaliers, Mrs. Behn included little, apart from her setting and the shape of some of her episodes, that is Spanish.

Her *The False Count: Or, A New Way to Play an Old Game* (1682) has an even broader farcical strain, though one that turns on an intrigue plot. "*'Tis a slight Farce, five Days brought forth with ease*," goes a disclaimer in the epilogue, and so unstudied and conventional is it in character relationships and exposition that we have little trouble in believing that it was written in less than a week. Yet it is entertaining, obviously the work of a seasoned professional, and it merits attention as a comedy with a narrative line apparently derived from Spanish fiction. For as Mathews pointed out, the climactic action of the play, in which a young Spanish nobleman and his friends posing as Turks capture a ship bearing a beautiful young woman and her old and jealous husband and subsequently induce the cowardly husband to surrender his wife, has so many parallels with a story of Castillo Solórzano as to imply a literary debt.[18] So far as is known, there had been no previous translation, in either French or English, of the novela, *El celoso hasta la muerte,* which appears in the collection *Noches de placer,* published in 1631. I am less firmly convinced than Mathews that Mrs. Behn worked directly from the Spanish. The interrelationships of seventeenth-century plots, nondramatic and dramatic, are so complex as to leave doubt except where there are close verbal similarities, and I find the verbal similarities he cites unconvincing. The plots have situational differences. (In the English but not in the Spanish, for example, the objective of the piracy is to win the lady from her unworthy husband for a rejected suitor.) Yet the case for direct borrowing is strong.

Whatever its source, *The False Count* resembles the Spanish plots in its narrative line, characters, and setting. Still, it is not in the usual sense a cape and sword play but a farcical comedy of outwitting—of the impotent old husband by the rejected suitor and of the old man's affected and vain daughter by the "false count," a chimney sweep in disguise, who marries and humiliates her. (This latter action was suggested by Molière's *Les Précieuses ridicules.*)[19] The mold of

18. Mathews, "Studies in Anglo-Spanish Cultural and Literary Relations," p. 313. See also Mathews's unpublished thesis, pp. 529–36.

19. Langbaine, *Account,* p. 20; Behn, *Works,* ed. Summers, 3 : 97.

Restoration comedy shapes the dialogue and defines the antagonism between generations and between true wits and would-be wits. The Spanish ingredients are assimilated into an English pattern.

Mrs. Behn's *The Dutch Lover* (1673) has a more direct connection with the comedia. The extraordinary complexity of plot, a greater complexity than that of any Restoration play we have yet considered, implies that Mrs. Behn freely drew suggestions for it from earlier writers; and several sources have in fact been identified.[20] Of immediate interest, Dr. Hogan suggests "*direct* borrowings" from Calderón's *No siempre lo peor es cierto* and *Peor está que estaba*.[21] These plays are two of the three Lord Bristol translated or adapted in the early 1660s (see above, pp. 79–80). I would guess that Mrs. Behn drew on Bristol's English versions rather than on the original Spanish. In any event, both of Calderón's plays had been adapted by French dramatists,[22] and she may have referred to the French versions as well as to the English or Spanish.

Mrs. Behn keeps some four distinct lines of love intrigue going simultaneously in *The Dutch Lover:* that of Marcel, son of Ambrosio, to win Clarinda; of Silvio, "Supposed bastard Son" of Ambrosio, to win the presumably incestuous love of Cleonte, the daughter of Ambrosio; of Antonio, a villain, until his repentance in act 4 to win revenge on Marcel by the cruel exploitation of his sister Hippolyta, whom Antonio has seduced; of Alonzo, a colonel just returned from Flanders, to win Enphemia. All these characters have important roles, and so has the title character, Haunce van Ezel, "A Dutch Fop contracted to *Euphemia,* newly arrived at *Madrid,*" who provides an obstacle, easily overcome, to Alonzo's courtship of his lady. With such a crowded stage, character development must

20. Langbaine, *Account,* p. 19, identified an important source: "The Plot of this Play is founded on a Spanish Romance, written by the ingenious *Don Francisco de las Coveras* stiled *Don Fenise,* see the Stories of *Eufemie,* and *Theodore, Don Jame,* and *Frederick.*" "Francisco de Las Coveras" is apparently a garbled form of the pseudonym "Las Cuevas" employed by Francisco de Quintana. Cf. Dale B. J. Randall, *The Golden Tapestry,* pp. 118–20.

21. Hogan, "Thirty-One English Plays," p. 57.

22. *No siempre lo peor es cierto* had been adapted by Paul Scarron as *La Fausse Apparence,* published in 1663: Lancaster, *French Dramatic Literature in the Seventeenth Century, pt. 3, 1 : 85. Peor está que estaba* had been adapted twice, by the elder Brosse as *Les Innocens coupables,* published in 1645, and by Le Métel de Boisrobert as *Les Apparences trompeuses,* published in 1656: Lancaster, ibid., pt. 2, 2 : 472–73; pt. 3, 1 : 65–66.

be subordinated to contrivance of dramatic action. The denouement is tidy enough, in a final sequence of marriages, though it is accomplished by manipulation of plot unrelated to the dramatized nature of the characters involved. Alonzo, we learn, is in fact the wealthy brother of Clarinda, and can provide her with a dowry; and Silvio is not the son of Ambrosio but of the famous Count of Olivarez, and thus he can marry Cleonte.

If in outline the plot seems absurdly complex, fairness to Mrs. Behn requires an acknowledgment that she manipulated the strands of intrigue skillfully. The attentive reader has little trouble in moving from one plot line to another, and he can take pleasure in the resolution of carefully developed suspense. This is Restoration comedy of Spanish romance in one of its most highly developed forms, graceful and entertaining—and yet remote from the serious concerns of life or honest portrayal of human relationships.

The resemblances of *The Dutch Lover* to the two plays of Calderón are intermittent rather than sustained, of a kind that are more likely to have resulted from Mrs. Behn's seeing Bristol's adaptations of them performed than from her reference to the Spanish texts of the original plays. In a preceding chapter I have described *Elvira,* a free translation of *No siempre lo peor es cierto,* made to conform in dialogue and act division to the conventions of the English stage, a play about the intrigues of two young women to win their gallants (see above, pp. 80–81). When one of the young women left her father's house following a misadventure in which her beloved had discovered and wounded a man he unexpectedly found there, the other received her into her house. This situation appears with variations in *Peor está que estaba,* and presumably it also appeared in Bristol's lost *Worse and Worse.*

The circumstances of the misadventure in *Peor está,* as they are recounted by the distressed young woman to the one who takes her in, resemble more closely than those in *No siempre* the circumstances in *The Dutch Lover.* In *Peor está,* Flérida tells Lisarda how a young man, a stranger to her, had admired her without any encouragement from her. He discovered that she had a lover, and one night, while she was awaiting a secret visit, he entered her garden. When her lover came a duel ensued (act 1). In *Peor está* the stranger was wounded; in *The Dutch Lover* (and, as we shall see, in Thomas

Durfey's later *The Banditti,* in a similar situation), the young woman's lover. In both the Spanish and English plays, as also in the parallel situation in *No siempre lo peor es cierto* and *Elvira,* the lover believed that his sweetheart had betrayed him. In *Peor está* and *The Dutch Lover,* the couple separated as they fled, the young woman leaving the house out of fear of a parent's wrath; in *No siempre* and *Elvira* they fled together. In both Spanish and both English plays the distressed woman finds refuge with another woman who has love problems of her own but who nevertheless helps the first to clear her honor and regain her estranged lover. Before this is accomplished in *The Dutch Lover,* however, much transpires that is without parallel in either Spanish play.

All this is complicated enough. Yet a summary account, even though it does not exhaust the possible similarities and relationships among the plays, is somewhat misleading because it leaves out of account the strands of Mrs. Behn's plot without parallel in the Spanish—and even more important, the difference between Calderón's dramatic judgments on his material and her own.

The most obvious and the most consequential difference lies in the contrast between the chaste reticence and consistent moral structure in the Spanish, and the lasciviousness and manipulation of event in the English. Consider Mrs. Behn's portrayal of the Silvio-Cleonte and the Antonio-Hippolyta relationships. In the former she explores the voluptuous possibilities of incest. In the second act (scene 6), Cleonte *"is discover'd in her night-gown, at a Table, as undressing,* Francisca *by her,"* and following a brief exchange about Silvio, Francisca sings to her mistress an erotic song.

After this musical aphrodisiac comes a stage direction: *"enter* Silvio *all undrest, gazing wildly on* Cleonte," and for the first time his courtship becomes so passionate that she cannot misunderstand him—and indeed she has little desire to do so. Here is dramatized eroticism as bold perhaps as we find in Restoration drama. The fact that the dialogue is largely free from sexual innuendo does not diminish the voluptuous impact of the scene, intensified as it is by the titillation provided by the assumption that the love is incestuous. The tragic potential of all this is avoided in subsequent events. Finally repelled by his criminal love, Silvio in his passion determines to kill Cleonte. Yet a disclosure in the last act that the couple are not brother and sister provides an easy resolution, with an evasion of judgment on their conduct.

Similar manipulation of event and suspension of judgment appear in the bizarre relationship between Antonio and Silvio's other supposed sister, Hippolyta, whom Antonio has seduced. Hippolyta's degradation is symbolized by her appearance (act 2, scene 2) in a bawdy house, *"drest like a Curtizan,"* an extremity to which she has been driven by Antonio's treachery. His motive, he explains, was a desire to avenge himself on her brother Marcel. Yet Antonio, when he sees her life threatened by the humiliated Marcel, undergoes a change of heart and promises to marry her, which he does in the final act. His acquisition of a sense of honorable obligation is as abrupt and unconvincing as that of characters in the sentimental dramas of the eighteenth century.

Calderón's plays are different in moral impact as in formal conventions.[23] Although both *Peor está* and *No siempre* turn on fear of or regret for illicit sexual relations, they are never erotically stimulating, either in episode or innuendo. In the former, to be sure, Lisarda imprudently meets a young man, Don César Ursino at an inn, but she does so veiled and in the company of her servant Celia; and the conversational duel with Don César that ensues is sublimated and metaphorical in its expression of emotion. The meeting does not lead to an illicit relationship but rather to a dangerous situation, when her father, the governor, comes to the inn seeking Don César. Because Lisarda is veiled, her father does not recognize her. Assuming that she is the lost Flérida, he takes her to her own house, where unknown to him Flérida is hiding. Emphasis falls on the cleverness with which Lisarda escapes detection and manages to present Flérida to her father as the young woman who was at the inn. Neither she nor Flérida nor the gallants, Don Juan and Don César, is guilty of more than indiscretion; they can be paired off in the final act without violating the poetic justice to which Calderón consistently adhered.[24] The chaste tone of the romantic intrigue—and the same could be said of *No siempre lo peor*

23. On the chaste tone of Calderón's theater, see Margaret Wilson, *Spanish Drama of the Golden Age* (Oxford, 1969), p. 37.

24. Cf. A. A. Parker, *The Approach to the Spanish Drama of the Golden Age* (London, 1957).

es cierto—differs radically from the eroticism of *The Dutch Lover,* typified by such scenes as that in which Hippolyta appears in a brothel and that in which Silvio makes love to his supposed sister.

As often in Calderón, elaboration of plot takes precedence over characterization. The two pairs of young lovers in *Peor está* and *No siempre* are largely interchangeable, as they are with other characters in similar plays. If we approach *Peor está* and *No siempre* with expectations founded on seventeenth-century English comedy, in which the precedents of Shakespeare and Jonson were decisive in influencing characterization, we will underestimate them. Yet this is, to use Pope's phrase about Shakespeare, "like trying a man by the laws of one country, who acted under those of another." [25] Calderón's cape and sword plays, like the other forms assumed by the comedia, require an acceptance of the formal conventions that shaped them.

Calderón's *Peor está que estaba* provided suggestions, I think, for still another Restoration comedy, Thomas Durfey's *The Banditti* (1686), one of the Spanish plots that can be traced to a suggestion of Charles II. "*The distress of the* Story," Durfey writes in his preface, "*was hinted to me by the* Late Blessed King *of ever-glorious Memory, from a* Spanish Translation." Durfey does not identify the translation, but in the remarks that follow he includes a reference to a locale that enables us to venture a guess:

> *and tho' I was advis'd to call the* Play *the* Banditti, *or* Sbanditti, *because of the Newnesse of the* Title, *and lay the* Scene *in* Spain *instead of the Kingdom of* Naples, *yet the more proper Title wou'd ha' been the* Spanish Out-laws, *tho' in such a Case as this, in* Dramatick-Poetry, *I think any* Poet *may do as he pleases, Especially since* Naples *is Substitute to the* King *of* Spain *as well as* Madrid.

Presumably, the Spanish translation to which the king called Durfey's attention was set near Naples. Now *Peor está,* of which Bristol's lost *Worse and Worse* was an adaptation, is set in Gaeta, then in the Kingdom of Naples. Bristol's adaptation, which if it corresponded to his *Elvira* could be considered a translation, was performed at court

25. Pope, Preface to Shakespeare, in *Works,* ed. W. Elwin and W. J. Courthope, (London, 1871–89), 10 : 537.

on November 6, 1666,[26] having been performed earlier by the Duke's Company in their public theater. Remembering the king's long friendship with Bristol, we may assume that he knew the play. To judge from its source, *Worse and Worse* included a situation that would have provided the "distress" of Durfey's plot—though Durfey drew on other sources as well, notably from a prose narrative translated from the Spanish of Francisco de Quintana,[27] and perhaps from Bristol's *Elvira* and Mrs. Behn's *The Dutch Lover*.

The "distress" of Durfey's play, that of two young lovers, Don Antonio and Lawra, arises when an unknown man is accidentally admitted to Lawra's house while she is waiting for Antonio, a situation that leads to a violent encounter when Antonio subsequently enters and then to the separation of the lovers, as Lawra flees, fearing the disclosure of her relationship with Antonio. Now with differences of detail, in which *The Banditti* corresponds to Quintana's prose narrative, Lawra's plight is that of Flérida in *Peor está que estaba*. As I have explained, in *Peor está* a stranger was accidentally admitted as Flérida awaited her lover—significantly also named Antonio—and when the latter subsequently arrived, a fight ensued. In Calderón, it is the stranger who is wounded; in Durfey, the woman's lover. In both plays the lover believes that the woman has betrayed him, and in both the woman promptly flees out of fear of one parent's (father in the Spanish, mother in the English) anger at the disclosure of the affair. When we remember that Durfey specified a translation from the Spanish with a locale in the Kingdom of Naples recommended by Charles II, we may reasonably, though not certainly, conclude that he drew from Bristol's version of Calderón's

26. *The London Stage,* pt. 1, p. 97.

27. Langbaine (*Account,* p. 179) cites as a source of the play *The History of Don Fenise:* "The chief Plot of this Play is founded on a Romance . . . call'd *Don Fenise* translated into English. . . . See the History of *Don Antonio,* Book 4, p. 250" (cf. note 20 above). The plot of the story has a generic resemblance to those of the three plays adapted from Calderón by Lord Bristol; and Durfey's use of proper names as well as episodical details found in the story suggests that he consulted it. But because the story has a setting in Spain rather than in the kingdom of Naples, it can scarcely be the translation recommended to him by King Charles.

Durfey may, of course, have borrowed from Mrs. Behn's *The Dutch Lover* as well as from the translation to which he referred. On his sources, see also Robert Stanley Forsythe, *A Study of the Plays of Thomas D'Urfey* (Cleveland, 1916), pp. 62–63. Hogan, "Thirty-One English Plays," pp. 56–59, does not list *The Banditti* among the plays with borrowings from the comedia, but her analysis of the sources of *The Dutch Lover* provides an aid in the approach to Durfey's play.

play. The difficulties of the young lovers in *The Banditti* have analogues in many Spanish works other than *Peor está que estaba,* to be sure, and yet few of them have settings near Naples, and fewer still would have been known to the king in English translation.

Durfey wrote *The Banditti* in mid-career, turning at the king's suggestion to the form of the Spanish plot, observing its conventions rather fully though not to the exclusion of farcical incident. It is a competent drama, enhanced by Durfey's graceful songs. A comedy of romantic love, with night rendezvous against the wishes of a watchful parent and fighting between young men, it takes Spanish honor seriously, though it includes more of the broadly comic than Calderón's plays. Durfey reaches to the Restoration ideal of wit but not so intensely and consistently as to undermine the credibility of the code of honor. His farcical episodes are largely confined to a plot line separate from the affairs of the lovers. A father (or, as it turns out, supposed father) tries to educate his unwilling son to the accomplishments and conduct appropriate to his station. The young man, who is as maladroit in his efforts to improve himself as Molière's *bourgeois gentilhomme,* rebels and runs away to join a group of bandits. In the adventures on the road that occupy the latter part of the play, Lawra is captured by the bandits, though she is promptly rescued and the bandits themselves are captured, and a disclosure of unknown family identities occurs that assist Lawra and Antonio to their final reunion. Even as Durfey drew dialogue, comical character type, and episode from Restoration tradition, he conformed to the English pattern of the Spanish plot.

Several years after *The Banditti,* Durfey turned again to a translation from Spanish, this time to Shelton's translation of the most famous work of all; and he achieved such popular success with the first two parts of *The Comical History of Don Quixote* (1694) that he was encouraged to write a third part (1696). It is easy to imagine the effectiveness in the theater of Durfey's broadly conceived portrayal of the knight and his squire, whose wanderings were presented, to the accompaniment of songs, against a backdrop of scenes painted to represent places in the Spanish countryside. Yet the plays now come as a disappointment to those who read them.

The disappointment is partly a result of the expectations we take to them. Durfey's plays are the earliest surviving adaptations to the

English stage of Cervantes's central characters, and we expect them to be better than they are. (An earlier dramatic rendering, "The History of Donquixot, or the Knight of the ill favored face: a Comedy," was advertised as forthcoming between 1658 and 1662, though it seems never to have appeared.)[28] Since the time of Fletcher, dramatists had drawn on the *Novelas ejemplares,* and they had also drawn on the intercalated stories in *Don Quijote;* but with the possible exception of Beaumont in *The Knight of the Burning Pestle,* they had ignored the central themes and literary strategies of the famous novel. That Beaumont's play, despite its greater distance from the literal subject of the novel, approximates more closely than Durfey's *The Comical History* the achievement of Cervantes, helps to explain the deficiencies of *The Comical History.*

Like *Don Quijote, The Knight of the Burning Pestle* is a calculated though benign and witty literary satire, having well defined satirical objectives and including an analytical assessment of perennial qualities of personality. If *The Knight of the Burning Pestle* does not approach in comprehensiveness or subtlety Cervantes's analysis of the human mind, the play is still more than an entertaining stage romp. The same can scarcely be said for *The Comical History*—and hence our disappointment. In Durfey's defense it can be said that Henry Fielding fared little better a generation later. *Don Quixote in England* (1734) may be more entertaining to read, by reason of its commentary on English political life, than Durfey's closer adaptation of the novel, but it failed to achieve a success in the theater comparable to that of *The Comical History.*

Durfey's plays lend support to the opinion expressed by E. M. Wilson, P. E. Russell, and others that seventeenth-century Englishmen, notwithstanding their liking for Cervantes's novel, missed its thematic subtleties and thought of it primarily as a work of fun.[29] Nearly everyone who read anything knew about the novel. Allusions to it in Restoration literature, including comedy, are of such frequency as almost to attain the status of cliché. The novel had contributed to the most famous political satire of the 1660s, Samuel But-

28. W. W. Greg, "Gerard Langbaine the Younger and Nicholas Cox," *Library,* 4th ser., 25 (1944–45) : 68 n.

29. Wilson, "Cervantes and English Literature of the Seventeenth Century," *Bulletin Hispanique,* 50 (1948) : 27–52; Russell, "'Don Quixote' as a Funny Book," *Modern Language Review* 64 (1969) : 312.

ler's *Hudibras*.[30] The popularity notwithstanding, Englishmen underestimated *Don Quijote,* just as they underestimated the comedia, regarding the knight and his squire as absurd caricatures of contrasting personalities, and their adventures as a succession of farcical episodes—a critical attitude that would seem to have controlled Durfey's adaptations.

The first two parts of *The Comical History,* both produced in the spring of 1694, were probably planned and largely written in a single stretch of time; the third part came a year and a half later, presumably having been written at a different time, to make further profit from the earlier successes.[31] More of it than of the first two parts is original with Durfey,[32] a circumstance again suggesting that it did not form part of his original design; and for this or some other reason (in his preface Durfey alleges a hostile clique in the audience), it did not succeed.

Has the dramatization of the novel, we may ask, any meaningful connection with the comedies of Spanish romance that have been under consideration? How closely has Durfey approached the conventions of the Restoration Spanish plot, a subgenre that even in the 1690s was not extinct, though it had lost much of its earlier popularity? Audiences would have retained a set of expectations about comedies with Spanish characters and a Spanish setting, even if the comedies bore the title of a famous comic novel. The expectations—of love intrigue, resort to the sword, sensitive conception of honor—were not disappointed. In Durfey's plays, to be sure, the comic and deflationary episode takes precedence over the romantic, rather than the reverse, as usual, but the romantic is not absent. The episodic and disjunctive scenes in which Don Quixote and Sancho appear notwithstanding, part 1 and to a lesser extent the other two plays have lines of tightly plotted action with excitement and suspense in the idiom of the Spanish plot. Less than a decade before, Durfey had written *The Banditti,* and he knew the resources of the form.

Part 1 depicts the adventures in love of two couples, one of the men having abandoned his betrothed for the beloved of the other.

30. Wilson, "Cervantes and English Literature."

31. See Forsythe, *Plays of Thomas D'Urfey,* pp. 101, 105, 110, for a tabular analysis of Durfey's use of the separate portions of Cervantes's novel.

32. Forsythe, *Plays of Thomas D'Urfey,* p. 109.

The woman who has been betrayed, like so many of her sisters in the comedia, has fled her home protectively disguised as a boy; and the other man, deprived of his mistress, has gone mad with grief. A confrontation between the two gallants brings the threat of a duel, as the frustrated Cardenio "offers to fight." But by play's end, the couples have been resorted and the lover's madness cured, in a sequence of events neatly joined to the adventures of Don Quixote and Sancho.

In parts 2 and 3 the romantic intrigue is neither so prominent nor so conventional, but again it provides contrast with the absurdities of Don Quixote, and again it is cleverly related to the knight's fortunes. In Part 2, Durfey introduces a romantic heroine, Marcella, whom he describes in the dramatis personae as "A young beautiful Shepherdess of *Codova,* extreamly coy, and Averse to men at first, but afterwards passionately in Love with *Ambrosio.*" Ambrosio, remembering her earlier scorn of his friend Chrysostome, rejects her, and she, with Spanish intensity of passion, goes mad. In part 3 a young couple, thwarted by the greed of the girl's father, who insists that she marry a rich man, succeed, with Don Quixote's assistance even at the wedding feast itself, in outwitting the unloved man and the avaricious father and accomplishing the marriage they desire. Durfey has modified the Spanish plot by elevating to primacy the comic scenes presided over by the gracioso, here Sancho, and reducing to secondary position the intrigues and passionate sufferings of the young lovers.

Sancho is indeed a rare gracioso, perhaps the most fully developed of the English renderings of that famous character type. Few Restoration dramatists felt comfortable with the character: the neoclassical sensitivity to inconsistencies of tone made it difficult for them to introduce, in romantic plays of intense emotion, a contrasting character from lowlife who could observe and describe with earthbound common sense the indifference of his betters to prudential behavior. The absence of fully developed graciosos, with their validating clarity of vision, must be reckoned a liability in most of the Spanish plots. But a dramatization of *Don Quijote* without Sancho Panza would be unthinkable, and Durfey's reversal of the customary relationship between the romantic and the comic enables him to develop at length Cervantes's novelistic parallel to the gracioso of the comedia. With a folk wisdom to which proverbs come readily, Sancho functions as a choral figure, interpreting and explaining the gratuitous and often unwarranted assumptions of other characters—above all his master—who are in the grip of ideals of behavior that would deny the claims of the flesh. So accomplished a comic actor as Thomas Dogget (described by John Downes as "very Aspectabund"),[33] who had the role in part 1, would have excelled as Sancho.

The preface to the second part includes a boast about the faithfulness of the rendering of the two main characters as well as about the success of the plays. Durfey will content himself, he writes:

> *with the good Opinion and kind Censure of the Judicious, who unanimously declare, that I have not lessened my self in the great undertaking, of drawing two Plays out of that Ingenious History, in which if I had flagg'd either in Stile or Character, it must have been very obvious to all Eyes; but on the contrary, I have had the honour to have it judg'd that I have done both* Don Quixote *and* Sancho *Justice, making as good a Copy of the first as possible, and furnishing the last with newer and better Proverbs of my own than he before diverted ye with,*

—a boast implying that the audience knew the translation of the novel well and expected fidelity in the dramatization. Within limits they got it. If Don Quixote appears in farcical and humiliating circumstances, so does he also in Cervantes; and the dramatic character, like the original, has—despite all—a persevering dignity. Durfey did not transform him into a stupid clown, and as the prefatory remark about faithfulness in the rendering of style suggests, Don Quixote retains something of his original manner of speaking. Shelton in his translation had imitated the rotundity of the Spanish prose, and Durfey preserved this quality, frequently rising to dialogue that verges on the mock heroic. (His success in capturing Cervantes's stylistic tricks is such that in reading the plays we are occasionally reminded of Fielding's prose in *Joseph Andrews,* a novel, so the title page affirms, "Written in Imitation of the *Manner* of Cervantes.")

Yet the plays disappoint us. We cannot see them performed with

33. Downes, *Roscius Anglicanus,* p. 52.

the painted scenery and superb comic actors of the 1690s, nor hear Durfey's tuneful songs. The selectivity imposed by the dramatic form forced concentration on a few striking episodes—the tilting at windmills, the use of a barber's basin as helmet, the freeing of convicts. It did not permit the extensive elaboration of motive required to bring into view the thematic subtleties of the novel, even if, as seems unlikely, Durfey had possessed a more comprehensive understanding of those subtleties than other Englishmen of his time.

John Crowne's *Sir Courtly Nice; Or, It Cannot Be* (1685), like Durfey's *The Banditti,* resulted from a suggestion of Charles II's and, like *The Comical History of Don Quixote,* has a prominent satirical strain. Closely based on a Spanish play, it is still no more a Spanish plot than are Wycherleys' first two comedies. Just as in *Love in a Wood* and *The Gentleman Dancing-Master,* a shifting of locale to London is accompanied by an abandonment of the cape and sword conventions.

Sir Courtly Nice had its origin in a request Crowne made to the king for patronage. Crowne, John Dennis writes,

> desir'd his Majesty to establish him in some Office, that might be a Security to him for Life. The King had the Goodness to assure him, he should have an Office, but added that he would first see another Comedy. Mr. *Crown* endeavouring to excuse himself, by telling the King, that he plotted slowly and awkwardly; the King replyed, that he would help him to a Plot, and so put into his Hands the Spanish Comedy called *Non pued Esser.*[34]

Crowne had reason enough to be grateful, for the suggestion resulted in his most successful play. In his dedicatory epistle written after the king's death, he tells with pride of the royal command: "The greatest pleasure he [the King] had from the Stage was in Comedy, and he often Commanded me to Write it, and lately gave me a *Spanish* Play called *No puedeser: Or, It cannot Be.* out of which I took part o' the Name, and design o' this." Whether the king remembered the earlier comedy based on the same source, Sydserf's *Tarugo's Wiles,* we cannot know; Crowne himself did not learn of the existence of the earlier play, according to Dennis, until he had written three acts

34. Dennis, *Critical Works,* 2 : 405.

of his own.[35] He completed his play, making no apparent use of Sydserf's,[36] though he was disappointed of the reward he expected from the king, who died before it was performed. Following the king's death in February, the play was necessarily postponed until May 9, when it was the first new comedy acted in King James's reign.[37]

Crowne in his dedication and Dennis in his later critical essay emphasize the differentness of *Sir Courtly Nice* from its Spanish original and its conformity with English dramatic tradition, both of them referring slightingly to Moreto's play. "I received the Employment as a great Honour," Crowne writes of the royal command, "because it was difficult; requiring no ordinary skill and pains to build a little Shallop, fit only for the *Spanish* South Seas, into an *English* Ship Royal." The metaphor does not inspire confidence that Crowne knew much about Spanish drama, though it is accurate enough in its implication that his play, except in plot, is unlike Moreto's. Neither he nor Dennis alludes to his transformation of Moreto's graceful verse into prose—vigorous satirical prose, to be sure, but different from and not necessarily superior to the language of the original.

Dennis praises *Sir Courtly Nice,* at least all in the play, "that is of *English* Growth." He is inclined to attribute what he regards as faults to the Spanish: "For tho' there is something in the part of *Crack* which borders upon Farce, the *Spanish* Author alone must answer for that. For Mr. *Crown* could not omit the Part of *Crack,* that is of *Tarugo,* and the *Spanish* Farce depending upon it, without a downright Affront to the King, who had given him that Play for his Groundwork." Dennis could no more appreciate even a modified version of the gracioso than could other critics of the time. Dennis's praise of the play is consistently neoclassical, and in all its specifics implies that Crowne has anglicized the comedia, making of it a satirical rendering of distinctly English characters.[38] To Dennis the Spanish element in *Sir Courtly Nice* was intractable material forced on a dramatist by the command of a king.

35. Ibid.

36. Arthur Franklin White, *John Crowne: His Life and Dramatic Works* (Cleveland, 1922), pp. 137 38; Charlotte Bradford Hughes, ed., *Crowne's Sir Courtly Nice,* Introduction, p. 20.

37. *The London Stage,* pt. 1, p. 336.

38. Dennis, *Critical Works,* 2 : 405–06.

The originality of its dialogue notwithstanding, *Sir Courtly Nice* is in plot, even to episodical detail, very much like its source, *No puede ser,* and its analogue, *Tarugo's Wiles.* Although Crowne's characters are Englishmen, they retain the roles they have in the other two plays.[39] The elevation of the rival lover, Sir Courtly Nice, to the position of title character suggests the most notable departure. The role is transformed from one of subordinate status to that of a fully realized English fop, a variation on the type character used by Etherege the decade before in *The Man of Mode.* Crowne's clever manipulator, Crack, is closer in social status to Moreto's Tarugo, a servant, than to Sydserf's, an impoverished gentleman. Even so, Crack, who has studied at Oxford (cf. act 2), is scarcely a gracioso. Crowne's is a freer adaptation than Sydserf's, more independent of the Spanish original in characterization and in dialogue, and much more successful. Despite its detailed borrowings from Moreto, it is a mature comedy of manners controlled by English convention.

In the rough and caustic raillery of the dialogue and in the nature of the characterization, the play resembles the comedies of Ben Jonson. John Dennis praised Crowne's satirically conceived characters in terms reminiscent of Jonsonian humors; [40] and in analytical detail, if not in the warmth of his evaluation, Dennis's is an accurate judgment that emphasizes how English in subjects of satire the play is. Yet there is also precedent for the satire in the Spanish source. Moreto anticipates more closely than his Spanish contemporaries the Restoration pattern of comedy of manners. "He stood apart from the Calderonian current," Ruth Lee Kennedy writes, "rejecting both the extremes of the *pundonor* and the bombastic dialogue that characterize the tragedies of that school, the abuses of disguise and the overcomplication of plot that mar its comedies." [41] No doubt it

39. The principal correspondences of characters in the three plays are the following:

Crowne	Sydserf	Moreto
Lord Bellguard	Don Patricio	Don Pedro
Farewell	Don Horatio	Don Felix
Sir Courtly Nice	Don Rodrigo	Don Diego
Crack	Tarugo	Tarugo
Violante	Sophronia	Doña Ana
Leonora	Livinia	Doña Ines

40. Dennis, *Critical Works,* 2 : 406.

41. Kennedy, *The Dramatic Art of Moreto* (Northampton, Mass., 1932), p. 122. *No puede ser* is a reworking of Lope's *El mayor imposible:* cf. Kennedy, pp. 186–88.

is more than coincidence that the two English plays based on *No puede ser*—*Tarugo's Wiles* and *Sir Courtly Nice*—include caustic reviews of social aberrations. The English elaborated on a quality present in restrained form in Moreto's play.

The vitality of Crowne's abrasive dialogue on the failings of Restoration England represents his major achievement. In bare outline the plot is not unlike that most conventional one of Restoration comedy in which an older relative, who is an obstacle to the marriage of the lovers, is successfully challenged by youthful invention. In Moreto, as in Sydserf, attention is focused on the cleverness of the stratagems by which the outwitting is accomplished. In Crowne, as in Wycherley before him, interest turns from episode to language, from intrigue to satirical dialogue.

Several comedies of Spanish romance, deservedly obscure, are imitations of the comedia rather than adaptations from it; they have sources (so far as I have been able to determine) in prose fiction or in French and English drama. Unlike *Sir Courtly Nice,* they conform loosely to the conventions of the Spanish plot, illustrating the force of a continuing tradition derived from the adaptations by the Cavaliers.

As we study these plays, we become increasingly aware of the importance of French literature in shaping Restoration drama, even that part of it in which locale, characters, and conventions are Spanish. H. C. Lancaster concludes an investigation of the sources of Edward Ravenscroft's *The Wrangling Lovers; Or, The Invisible Mistress* (1676) with a remark to which we might give a generalized application: "one sees France in this business serving as an international clearing-house, not for ideas, but for entertaining situations." [42] Apart from the plays already considered, there are very few late seventeenth-century comedies that would seem to derive directly from the comedia. I can in fact name only one, John Leanerd's *The Counterfeits* (1679). Yet the formal pattern of the cape and sword play persisted.

Ravenscroft's *The Wrangling Lovers* is an intelligent and entertaining comedy, having Spanish characters, a setting in Toledo, and the predictable business of the Spanish plot, though not without

42. Lancaster, "Calderón, Boursault, and Ravenscroft," *Modern Language Notes* 51 (1936) : 528.

burlesque of its conventions. Count de Benevent is a self-important, proud Spanish father, preoccupied with punctilios of honor to such an extent that he seems, intermittently, a parody of the dramatic type. Late in the third act, not one but two lovers appear at night under a lady's window to serenade her; and the complications that arise from mistaken identities seem absurd in their complexity. The extravagance and intermittent burlesque notwithstanding, the play approximates the cape and sword form, reproducing nearly all the customary plot and atmospheric devices as well as the character types. The gracioso appears in Sanco; the jealous brother in Don Ruis. A disguised lady moves about surreptitiously, as in Calderón's *La dama duende* and many another Spanish play. All this is conveyed in a dialogue that is competent and witty if without distinction.

Owing to the researches of Lancaster, the sources of the play are comprehensively known: a French novel immediately, and back of that (apparently not consulted by Ravenscroft) one French and two Spanish plays.[43] Having begun his dramatic career several years earlier with an adaptation of Molière's *Le Bourgeois gentilhomme,* Ravenscroft turned in this, his third play, to a French novel, Boursault's *Ne pas croire ce qu'on voit: histoire espagnole,* published in 1670. Boursault had drawn on Thomas Corneille's *Les Engagements du hazard* as well as on the two plays of Calderón from which Corneille himself had borrowed, *Los empeños de un acaso* and *Casa con dos puertas.* The literary interrelationships are complex indeed, but they lead back to Calderón, who is ultimately responsible for the materials Ravenscroft shaped into *The Wrangling Lovers.*

John Corye's *The Generous Enemies; Or, The Ridiculous Lovers* (1671) provides a similar instance of a Spanish plot drawn from French drama: this time from two French plays,[44] one of which has a source in the comedia. The Spanish setting with its corollaries in dramatic action comes from Thomas Corneille's *Don Bertram de Cigarral* (1650), which in turn derives from Francisco de Rojas's *Entre bobos anda el juego;*[45] much of the love intrigue, including

43. Ibid., pp. 523–28. In *Modern Language Notes,* 62 (1947) and 63 (1948), James U. Rundle and Lancaster carried on an extended debate about the sources of *The Wrangling Lovers.* In my opinion, Lancaster demonstrated the accuracy of his original analysis.

44. Allardyce Nicoll, *A History of English Drama, 1660–1900,* vol. 1: *Restoration Drama* (Cambridge, 1955), p. 190.

45. Gustave Reynier, *Thomas Corneille: sa vie et son théâtre* (Paris, 1892), p. 193.

the oft-repeated motif of a young woman disguised as a man in pursuit of her errant lover, comes from Philippe Quinault's *La Généreuse Ingratitude* (1654), which had been translated into English in 1659 by a royalist in exile, William Lower, as *The Noble Ingratitude*.[46] More skill than Corye possessed was needed to bring such diverse source materials into a harmonious relationship in *The Generous Enemies,* which reveals the maladroit hand of a beginner experimenting with the cape and sword conventions.

Two of the obscure Spanish plots, Lord Orrery's *Guzman* (1669) and Thomas Duffett's *The Spanish Rogue* (1673), would seem on the evidence of their titles to derive from Mateo Alemán's famous novel, *Guzmán de Alfarache,* well known in seventeenth-century England in the masterly translation by James Mabbe entitled *The Rogue.* But the connection between the plays and the novel is either nonexistent or tenuous in the extreme. Apart from the name of his title character, Orrery would seem to have made no use at all of the novel, or indeed, as far as has yet been determined, of any other narrative source.[47] Yet to quote Pepys, April 16, 1669 (who in turn quotes Thomas Shadwell), in "trying what he could do in comedy, since his heroique plays could do no more wonders," he must have had in mind the recent success of the Cavaliers' and Dryden's plays, for he follows, though in the idiom of farce, the Spanish conventions. Thomas Duffett's title points to Mabbe's translation, and it has been suggested that the play derives from the novel. Perhaps so, but the relationship is by no means clear.[48] Although the character Mingo, like Guzmán, is undoubtedly a "Spanish rogue," the novel provides precedent, neither in the picaresque adventures of Guzmán himself nor in the intercalated stories, for episodes in the play. Probably Duffett merely made capital of Mabbe's title, taking his plot of Spanish intrigue from some as yet unidentified work.

A satirical exchange in Farquhar's *The Twin Rivals* (1702; act 3) suggests that to the end of the century and beyond, dramatists continued to regard Spanish drama as a reservoir of plots available for

46. Harbage, *Cavalier Drama,* p. 136.

47. William Smith Clark, ed., *The Dramatic Works of Roger Boyle, Earl of Orrery* (Cambridge, Mass., 1937), 1 : 437–39.

48. Cf. Randall, *The Golden Tapestry,* pp. 183–84, and David W. Maurer, "The Spanish Intrigue Play," p. 101.

use on the English stage. Mr. Comic has come to the levee of a usurping lord, Benjamin Wouldbe, to request patronage:

> MR. COMIC: . . . I have another Play just finish'd, but that I want a Plot for't.
>
> BENJAMIN WOULDBE: A Plot! you shou'd read the *Italian*, and *Spanish* Plays, Mr. *Comick*—I like your Verses here mightily—[49]

The exchange bears more than a casual resemblance to the one between Crowne and King Charles that led to *Sir Courtly Nice*, a play in which little of the Spanish remains except the plot.

The difficulties in tracing some of the Spanish borrowings are extreme. The nature of the problems involved may be illustrated by an examination of John Leanerd's *The Counterfeits* (1678) and Colley Cibber's *She Would and She Would Not* (1702), plays with similarities so strong as to have led to the assumption, I think mistaken, that the later was based on the earlier. Conventional opinion on the connection between the two plays and on their sources is summarized by William M. Peterson:

> *She wou'd, and She wou'd not*, one of Colley Cibber's most successful and least sentimental comedies, is derived directly from *The Counterfeits* (1678), attributed to John Leanerd, and indirectly from "The Trapanner Trapann'd," a story in *La Picara, or the Triumphs of Female Subtilty* (1665) by John Davies of Kidwelly.[50]

49. A couplet in the prologue to Mary Davys's *The Northern Heiress* (1716) conveys a similar impression:

> *Besides, she* [the author] *wants those Helps that some have got,*
> *Who take from* French *or* Spanish *Plays their Plot.*

50. Peterson, "Cibber's *She Wou'd, and She Wou'd Not* and Vanbrugh's *Æsop*," *Philological Quarterly* 35 (1956) : 429. Langbaine, *Account*, p. 528, states that *The Counterfeits* is based on "The Trapanner Trapann'd" and adds that some details of the play are apparently derived from Thomas Corneille's *Dom César d'Avalos.* The similarities he noticed between *The Counterfeits* and *Dom César* are to be accounted for by the fact that the French play derives in part from Tirso's *La villana de Vallecas*, the ultimate source of *The Counterfeits.* Cf. Lancaster, *French Dramatic Literature in the Seventeenth Century*, pt. 4, 1 : 447–48.

DeWitt C. Croissant (*Studies in the Work of Colley Cibber* [Lawrence, Kans., 1912], p. 19) alone of later scholars adds substantially to the customary interpretation of the relationship between the story and the plays: he suggests that the plays are independent adaptations of the story, and cites as analogues to both the plays and the story

In fact, neither *The Counterfeits* nor *She Would and She Would Not* is based on "The Trapanner Trapann'd." Rather, *The Counterfeits* is a close adaptation of Moreto's *La ocasión hace al ladrón,* itself an adaptation of Tirso's *La villana de Vallecas;* and *She Would* appears to derive from Tirso's *Don Gil de las calzas verdes,* probably through some as yet unidentified play or novel. The similarities in plot between all these plays and "The Trapanner Trapann'd" are presumably to be accounted for by the circumstance that Alonso de Castillo Solórzano, the author of the original from which "The Trapanner Trapann'd" is translated (by way of a French intermediary),[51] based his work on a Spanish story similar to those Tirso used in *La villana de Vallecas* and in *Don Gil de las calzas verdes.* The similarities between the Spanish and English plays are far more particularized than those between the English plays and the prose translation of Castillo Solórzano by John Davies.

Although resembling the story in general plan, *The Counterfeits* follows *La ocasión hace al ladrón* in detail. In both plays a young woman has been seduced by a man employing an assumed name who subsequently deserted her, and in both a brother of the young woman learns of her dishonor and determines to avenge her. However, the sister, unknown to her brother, decides to manage her own affairs. Accompanied by a maidservant, she goes to Madrid in pursuit of her seducer. (*The Counterfeits,* in conformity with the unities, begins in Madrid; *La ocasión,* in Valencia, where the young woman resides.)

In an inn the young woman meets a stranger, a young man just arrived in Spain from Mexico, whose true name is identical to the one her seducer had used. This man has come to Spain to marry the daughter of an old friend of his father's. However, he has lost his letters of accreditation to his betrothed through an inadvertent exchange of portmanteaus with a stranger—who is in fact the seducer. The latter, meanwhile, meets by accident the betrothed of the man from Mexico and falls in love with her. When he discovers in the portmanteau letters of accreditation to her father, he presents him-

---

Tirso's *La villana de Vallecas* and Moreto's *La ocasión hace al ladrón.* Croissant provides suggestions needed to account for the relationships among the several plays, but his conclusions are, I think, erroneous.

51. *Cambridge Bibliography of English Literature,* 2 : 69.

self in the guise of the other man and is favorably received. The man from Mexico subsequently comes to the house and is treated with suspicion. In both plays the true young man is put in jail but later released by the impostor's uncle, who mistakes him for his nephew. All are finally brought together and the deceits revealed; the impostor marries the woman he has wronged, moved by fear of her brother, and the other man marries his betrothed.

If nothing else, the proper names the two comedies have in common (not always for parallel characters) provide sufficient evidence of a link between them: Gomez, Luis, Violante, and Crispin appear in both plays, Peralta is the father of the true young man's betrothed in Moreto and of the impostor in Leanerd; the Marquis of Velada is, in both versions, an addressee of a letter in the impostor's portmanteau. The main differences between the plays result from the English author's presentation of much of the early action by way of retrospective conversation in order to observe the unities of time and place.

The relationship of Cibber's *She Would and She Would Not* and Tirso's *Don Gil de las calzas verdes* is not so close as that between the plays just examined. Some other play or novel—Spanish, French, or English—may have intervened between *Don Gil* and *She Would,* perhaps in the manner in which *La ocasión hace al ladrón* intervened between *La villana de Vallencas* and *The Counterfeits.* Certain passages in *She Would* are borrowed from John Fletcher and Sir John Vanbrugh.[52] But the similarities are too considerable to be merely accidental. Cibber's play is much closer to Tirso than it is to "The Trapanner Trapann'd" or to *The Counterfeits.*

The parallels are restricted to the first half of both plays, but here they are striking. In both *She Would* and *Don Gil* a vivacious and resourceful young woman, disguised as a man, goes to Madrid with an old servant (of different sex in the two plays) in pursuit of a former suitor who has left her to court another young woman with whose father his own father has entered into negotiations. Upon arriving in Madrid, the young woman engages a new and garrulous servant, who talks freely of his previous experience in service. The young woman gains possession of the papers of accreditation as well

52. Peterson, "*She Wou'd . . .* and Vanbrugh's *Æsop,*" pp. 429–35; Richard Hindry Barker, *Mr Cibber of Drury Lane* (New York, 1939), pp. 45–46.

as some money of the man she is pursuing. Still disguised as a man, she convinces the father of the other young woman, by means of the papers, that she is the intended husband about whom the father has been in correspondence. She also gains the cooperation of the other young woman. When the stratagem succeeds, the young man in both plays is treated by the father as an impostor. The intrigues are worked out differently in the last half of the two plays.

The Counterfeits and *She Would and She Would Not*—the one little more than a translation of Moreto's play and the other a free adaptation of Tirso's, probably by way of some intermediary version—share the common fate of Spanish plays in neoclassical England. In each instance a Spanish verse comedy has been refashioned into a prose comedy of intrigue, dependent for its effectiveness on the suspense provided by the gradual resolution of dramatic conflict. Tirso, who is ultimately responsible for both *Don Gil* and *La ocasión,* is after all a major dramatist. If he is frequently careless in details of dramatic structure, as he is in *Don Gil* and *La villana de Vallecas,* he provides compensation by elaborating the texture of his plays through modulations of metrical patterns, ingenuity of repartee, and subtlety of characterization. In comparison with the Spanish plays, the English adaptations by Leanerd and Cibber are factual renderings of dramatic action in which the poetry of the originals is lost.

Yet though the poetry is lost, the Spanish plots survive in English form. The neatly contrived intrigue of *La ocasión* gives pleasure even when it is conveyed in the inexpert dialogue of *The Counterfeits.* Gerard Langbaine, a discriminating critic when his passions were not aroused, was reluctant to credit it to Leanerd because of its quality: "This Comedy is ascribed by some to Learnard; but I believe it too good to be his Writing." [53] Langbaine did not know that the play was taken from Moreto. The knowledge would have reinforced the opinion of Leanerd he elsewhere expressed: "A confident Plagiary, whom I disdain to stile an Author." [54] *She Would and She Would Not* is also superior to most of its author's other work, and again, in part at least, by reason of its borrowings from the Spanish. The charm of Tirso's heroine in *Don Gil* reappears in Cib-

53. Langbaine, *Account,* p. 528.
54. Ibid., p. 319.

ber's Hypolita, called by Cibber's biographer (who did not know of the indebtedness to Tirso) "the best of all the parts in the play, and perhaps the best Cibber ever wrote." "In scene after scene," he adds, in terms that recall praise frequently lavished on Tirso, "Hypolita displays her coquetry, her daring, her timidity, her quick-wittedness, and finally, in the big scene of the fourth act, she runs through her whole gamut of emotions, changing from one to another with almost bewildering rapidity." [55] It is only just that this discriminating praise be redirected in part to Tirso.

Cibber, like Leanerd before him, reduced the complexity of the Spanish plot that was his source. Yet though Cibber's dramatic action is more orderly than Tirso's, his moral structure as expressed in the implied evaluation of the characters is less clearly defined than in the Spanish play. Tirso conformed to a code of poetic justice that Cibber apparently found too severe, for he eliminated the events of deeper moral import. In *Don Gil,* the young man has deserted his sweetheart after seducing her with a promise of marriage; in *She Would,* he has deserted her only out of despair of ever winning her in marriage. In Tirso the young man, a vacillating and weak-willed individual, deserves and receives the punishment of severe humiliations. Cibber's young man neither deserves to be, nor is, treated harshly. Unlike Cibber, Tirso insists on a moral judgment: A condemnation of a man's treachery. He is permitted a happy end only after he has been thoroughly punished and presumably reformed. The moral judgment of the Spanish play gives way in the English to a graceful rendering of an adventure story.[56]

Vanbrugh's *The False Friend,* first produced in 1702, the same year as *She Would and She Would Not,* is at once an adaptation of a Spanish play and a subtle perversion of it. Even though based on a French intermediary, it is close enough to be a free translation, and yet it incorporates changes in detail and in tone which alter the

55. Barker, *Mr Cibber,* p. 44–45.

56. In "Spanish Drama in Neoclassical England," *Comparative Literature* 11 (1959): 29–34, I published the substance of this discussion of *The Counterfeits* and *She Would and She Would Not.* After the appearance of my article, I read the unpublished dissertation of James U. Rundle, "The Influence of the Spanish *Comedia* on Restoration Comedy: A First Essay" (University of Cincinnati, 1947), and learned that he had partially anticipated my discoveries concerning the sources of *The Counterfeits.*

emotional impact to the point that, what in Spanish is a tragedy of divine retribution becomes in English a comedy. To be sure, the essential modification of the Spanish had already occurred in the intervening French play; Vanbrugh merely accentuated the modification. Except for topical allusions, a certain boisterousness of wit, and small though important changes in episode, the English play follows the French.

Vanbrugh's source was *Le Traître puni,* which Le Sage (as he notes on his title page) had translated from Rojas Zorrilla's *La traición busca el castigo.* The text from which Vanbrugh worked was apparently in a collection, *Le Theâtre espagnol . . . traduites en françois,* published at The Hague in 1700; Vanbrugh's editors suggest that his friend Tonson brought the collection to him from Amsterdam.[57] In any event, Vanbrugh wrote with the French play before him, at times following it verbally, at times merely in the structure of scenes.

The English play is a strange kind of comedy in which the character who gives the play its title is killed in the final scene; but nevertheless in tone and even in the conduct of action it is more a comedy than a tragedy or even a tragicomedy. How, we may ask, could Vanbrugh—or more strictly, Le Sage, since he first made the decisive changes—follow the comedia so closely and yet produce a play so different from it?

The title of *La traición busca el castigo* states its theme: "Treachery seeks its own punishment," here in the strange and inexorable operation of providence to bring retribution to a man who has violated a solemn obligation placed on him by his friend and who has compounded his guilt by accusing an innocent man. The action is comparatively uncomplicated as it moves, not precisely to a catastrophe, but to its fatal conclusion. The plot turns on the rivalry of three young men, Don Andrés, Don Juan and Don García, for a lady, Leonor, the daughter of Don Félix. García, her neighbor, has long loved her, and she has returned his affection, though chastely and with attention to her father's commands. Because García is an impoverished younger son, he is unacceptable to her father, who has contracted her to Juan.

Andrés, however, has paid court to Leonor, haunting the street ad-

57. Bonamy Dobrée and Geoffrey Webb, eds., *The Complete Works of Sir John Vanbrugh* (London, 1927), 2 : 151.

jacent to her house and attempting to gain admittance, though with no encouragement from her and with no success. As he explains to her servant in an expository conversation at the opening of the play, he desires her but does not love her, nor indeed any other woman. (He bears more than a casual resemblance to Tirso's Don Juan, and it is not coincidental that, like him, he meets punishment through divine intervention.) García goes to Andrés's house, complains about his public courtship of Leonor, and challenges him. The father goes there too and expostulates with Andrés, but because he knows Andrés is rich and well born, he offers him Leonor in marriage. Andrés refuses insultingly, and the father leaves angry. Then Juan, recently arrived from military service in Flanders, goes to see Andrés, his friend and former comrade-in-arms, to tell him about his impending marriage. He does not know that Andrés has pursued Leonor, though he knows that García and some other unknown man have done so. Convinced of the propriety of her conduct, Juan wishes to proceed with the marriage.

These, then, are the relationships among the principal characters as they emerge in conversations at the house of Andrés, who is the pivotal character, the "hero villain," to use a term applied to English Renaissance drama. He accompanies Juan to Leonor's house. There they find García, accompanied by his sister, conversing with Leonor, who inadvertently reveals her love for García. Still, she is a dutiful daughter, and her marriage to Juan follows promptly. The marriage is consummated that night—the fact deserves emphasis, in view of the changes Le Sage and Vanbrugh made—and, as we learn in a conversation of the following morning between Leonor and her maidservant, Juan assured himself of her chastity through physiological evidence; yet he is troubled by the mutual affection between her and García.

When Juan is soon called away by the news that his father is dying, he turns to his friend Andrés, revealing his fears of García and solemnly charging Andrés to guard his wife for him. Andrés accepts the responsibility, and after his friend departs he has misgivings about his intended treachery. But lust overcomes his compunctions, and in the darkness of night he invades Leonor's bedchamber. Her prompt cries for help prevent him from raping her and bring García running from his house nearby. In the darkness Leonor cannot distinguish who is the guilty one and who the protector. At this juncture Juan enters with a candle and, understandably outraged, is bent on vengeace.

The final act is devoted to Juan's effort to determine which of the two is guilty. He discovers reasons to be suspicious of Andrés and meets him with sword drawn, but the latter convinces him that the guilt is García's. Together they plan to kill García, and they go to take him by surprise in his own house. But in the darkness Juan stabs Andrés, who as he is dying confesses his guilt. With the death of the principal character, and the discovery of García's innocence, the play closes.

Even this brief summary will suggest the play's somber tone and emphasis on retribution. The subject of the tragedy is the betrayal of friendship and trust. Andrés and Juan explain their mutual obligations deriving from their earlier companionship in the Flemish wars when they meet in the first act, and Andrés returns to the subject in the second act. The long speeches and soliloquies in the Spanish permitted an exploration of motive and moral significance that was difficult to achieve within the conventions of the French and English stages. The exploration of Andrés's mind keeps him at the center of interest, makes his crimes more despicable, and prevents a diversion of attention to the turns of the intrigue plot.

The fact that Juan's marriage to Leonor is consummated, as it is not in either the French or the English play, intensifies the horror aroused by the treachery. In the French and English versions the marriage might be considered nominal, even potentially reversible, but not so in the Spanish, in which the secrets of the marriage bed are related with an explicitness that might, in another context, be erotic. *La traición busca el castigo* is the more conspicuously somber in references to sexual relations because we approach the play by way of Vanbrugh, known even among Restoration dramatists for the permissiveness of his sexual attitudes. In the Spanish play the attempted rape appears graver than in the English or even than in the French. And thus the death of the treacherous friend, far from seeming a mere preliminary to the resolution of the matrimonial plot, as it does in Vanbrugh, is itself the fulfillment of the action.

I have already suggested the principal differences that separate Le Sage's and Vanbrugh's versions from Rojas's original: less attention to the heinousness of the friend's crime and intensified emphasis on the stages of the love intrigue. In the French and English plays the news of the father's fatal illness arrives before the marriage; immediately after the ceremony the bridegroom departs, having charged his friend to watch over his new wife. The friend in Le Sage's version has brief misgivings about his designs on Léonor, though he quickly rationalizes them (act 2, scene 10): "N'aimois-je pas Léonor avant qu'il songeât à l'épouser? C'est lui qui me trahit, qui me fait une infidélité en m'enlevant une maîtresse." Vanbrugh's title character does not have even momentary misgivings (act 2): "What, let Love direct, for I have nothing else to guide me." Vanbrugh's source notwithstanding, he endows his character with the attitudes of a long line of rake heroes. Within the Restoration tradition, exemplified in Vanbrugh's own *The Relapse* (1696), the betrayal of a friend in an attempt to seduce his wife could scarcely be viewed with Spanish gravity: the final death could not have the impact of a deserved and inevitable retribution.

It is the denouement of *The False Friend* that is its most conspicuous weakness. In the adroit conduct of the love intrigue, in characterization, and above all in dialogue, Vanbrugh's play is more than competent. If we could leave the unsatisfactory denouement out of account, it would be one of the best of the close adaptations from the comedia. Yet its emotional center is off balance, a flaw fully evident in the final scene, which seems a hastily contrived termination rather than a fulfillment of what has gone before. English audiences were accustomed to young lovers, in this case Leonora and her neighbor, finding a way around the barriers put up against them by their older relatives; they were not accustomed to self-sacrificing filial submission. In the earlier acts of the play Vanbrugh seems in a fair way to satisfy their expectations. Yet in the final scene, as in his source, the death of the villain is followed by the reconciliation of husband and wife.

The curtain speech illustrates at once the incongruity of the denouement and the distinctive quality of English comedy Vanbrugh has given his borrowed materials.[58] There is an ambiguity, probably calculated, in the lines spoken by Leonora. Her husband speaks first:

58. Cf. Nicoll, *History of English Drama*, vol. 2: *Early Eighteenth-Century Drama*, pp. 150–51.

JUAN: Come, Madam, my Honour now is satisfied, and if you please my Love may be so too.
LEONORA: If it is not

> *You to your self alone, shall owe your smart,*
> *For where I've given my hand, I'll give my heart.*

These lines are presumably spoken to her husband, and "hand" is a synecdoche for her person. But earlier Leonora had inadvertently given her hand to her neighbor when her prospective husband first met her, a circumstance that had aroused his suspicion. An actress, by a covert glance at the neighbor as she spoke, could have conveyed the meaning that he need not despair. Far indeed from Rojas's tragedy of retribution, this is more in the spirit of *The Relapse* and *The Provoked Wife.*

In their reworkings of the comedia, the English, it will now be apparent, consistently treated sexual ethics more casually than the Spanish did. But there is an exception in one of the most impressive of all the Restoration plays deriving from the comedia, Thomas Shadwell's *The Libertine,* the first important version of the Don Juan legend in English. It was performed in 1675 with such success that it won a place in the repertory.

Here is a Spanish plot interpreted in a radically different manner. Shadwell called it a tragedy (though he referred in his preface to its "Irregularities"), and the term is accurate, at least to the extent that the title character and many other persons die. Yet so distinguished a historian of the drama as Allardyce Nicoll has called it a comedy,[59] a classification one can understand—if not necessarily accept—so different from those customary to tragedy are the emotions evoked by the deaths in which the play abounds.The emotional structure is different both from that of neoclassical tragedy and that of the other Spanish plots. Yet most of the conventions of the cape and sword play, as they were adapted in England, are present: the Spanish setting and characters, the sensitive conception of honor as blocking force in the intrigues of lovers, the mistaken identities and nocturnal rendezvous, the duels, the young woman disguised as a man pursuing

59. Ibid., vol. 1: *Restoration Drama,* p. 431.

her faithless lover, the loquacious and cowardly gracioso, participating unwillingly in his master's dangerous intrigues. The gracioso, in fact, in his evaluating and contrasting relationship to his master, is one of the closest Restoration approximations to the type character of the comedia. Whether or not the term "Spanish plot" is finally appropriate to this remarkable play, it owes much to the conventions popularized during the previous decade in the adaptations of Tuke and Lord Bristol.

Shadwell drew liberally from earlier versions of the Don Juan legend, but he had not read the two greatest, Tirso's *El Burlador de Sevilla* and Molière's *Dom Juan* (the latter, though acted a decade before, had not yet been published). In his preface Shadwell refers to the earlier versions, acknowledging, not without understatement, his indebtedness to them:

> The story from which I took the hint of this Play, is famous all over *Spain, Italy,* and *France:* It was first put into a *Spanish* Play (as I have been told) the *Spaniards* having a Tradition (which they believe) of such a vicious *Spaniard,* as is represented in this Play. From them the *Italian* Comedians took it, and from them the *French* took it, and four several *French* Plays were made upon the Story.
>
> The character of the *Libertine,* and consequently those of his Friends, are borrow'd; but all the Plot, till the latter end of the Fourth Act, is new: And all the rest is very much varied from any thing which has been done upon the Subject.

This is a good summary statement of the earlier history of the legend, and in the main a just description of the relationship of *The Libertine* to the legend, though Shadwell's borrowings from the French in his first four acts are more considerable than he suggests,[60] notably from the play by the actor Claude Rose, Sieur de Rosimond, *Le Nouveau Festin de Pierre, ou l'athée foudroyé* (1669),[61] which must be regarded as Shadwell's principal source.

Although *The Libertine* includes, in its depiction of the insatiable

60. Gendarme de Bévotte, *La Légende de Don Juan* (Paris, 1906), pp. 338–41.

61. Leo Weinstein, *The Metamorphoses of Don Juan* (Stanford, 1959), p. 193. Weinstein (p. 35) notes that the legend had earlier been represented, in fragmentary form, in an English play: Sir Aston Cockain's *The Tragedy of Ovid,* not acted but printed in 1662.

lust of an unprincipled adventurer and in its episodes, much that is familiar from other versions of the story—namely, Don Juan's seduction of a highborn lady in the darkness by pretending to be her lover, his shipwreck and subsequent betrayal of his rescuers, his exchange of hospitality with the marble statue of a man he has killed—Shadwell's stern interpretation of the traditional materials would seem to embody his response to the contemporary English drama. His Don Juan is more vicious, more aggressively evil, than any other well-known exemplar of the tradition; [62] and the extent of his depravity, as well as that of his two constant companions, precludes the ameliorating qualities of grace and style apparent in some Don Juans. Most of them kill only when required to do so by the exigencies of their love intrigues; the English Don John kills for profit and for sadistic pleasure too. The addition of wholesale murder, as well as parricide, incest with his sisters, and calculated robbery, alters the impression conveyed by the character drawn from the familiar figure of legend—that of a man in the grip of lust, driven to violence by necessity, and postponing religious observance for present pleasure—to that of a demon incarnate, who sins out of calculation and rejoices in the extremes of his iniquity. Shadwell's Don John, like Milton's Satan, acts from principle; unlike Satan, he is an atheist, as he carefully and repeatedly explains.

Why, then, the ambiguity of tone to which I have alluded, the uncertainty whether the impact of the play is comic or tragic? Because, I would answer, the multiplicity and gravity of Don John's sins convey an impression that borders on the burlesque. The pace of the action is fast, as one instance of villainy follows hard on another—so fast that the horror that would be the reader's normal response is muted. In its original run the emotional quality of the play must have been conditioned by the actors' interpretations of their roles. The great tragic actor Thomas Betterton played Don John, and we have it on Downes's authority that his performance "Crown'd the Play"; [63] but how he interpreted the role neither Downes nor anyone else tells us.

Some scenes, to be sure, are inescapably comic: the one in act 2, for example, when six different women whom Don John has recently

62. Cf. ibid.
63. Downes, *Roscius Anglicanus,* p. 37.

married appear simultaneously to claim him, each assuming that she alone is his wife and the others but scheming and deluded aspirants to the charming man. There is much grim humor in the play, as when late in act 3 Don John proposes in rapid succession to two sisters, that is reminiscent of Marlowe's *Dr. Faustus*. Farce and tragic event are brought together and produce an uncertain effect. The resemblance to *Dr. Faustus* becomes patent (perhaps merely because the two legends of which the plays are exemplars resemble one another) in the midnight scene of retribution, when hell claims its own, and Don John and his two companions, confronted by the animated statue and surrounded by ghosts and devils, sink into everlasting flames.

Dr. Faustus is a tragedy and so is, according to its author, *The Libertine*—a tragedy in intermittent burlesque, perhaps, but still a play about the destruction of a man who lives by mistaken principles. It is as though Shadwell, the moralist and avowed disciple of Ben Jonson, were fully and schematically dramatizing certain assumptions allegedly present in plays written by his contemporaries, and demonstrating their logical and inevitable consequences. In the absence of seventeenth-century comment on the subject, I must be tentative in offering this interpretation; and yet I think it fits the observable relationship between *The Libertine,* many of the Restoration comedies, and the lives of several of the principal court wits.

For Don John, the atheistical philanderer, is an extreme embodiment, perhaps even a caricature, of amoral qualities periodically revealed by a score of young sparks in Restoration comedy, libertines like him, who are committed to the unscrupulous pursuit of women. We have only to think of the duke of Buckingham and the earl of Rochester to recall that Shadwell might have had targets in contemporary life as well.[64] Just a few years earlier, in the preface to *The Sullen Lovers* (1668), he had complained that in recent comedies "the two chief persons are most commonly a Swearing, Drinking, Whoring, Ruffian for a Lover, and an impudent, ill-bred *tomrig* for a Mistress"; and it is easy enough to find characters from earlier comedies whom he might have had in mind. Don John was perhaps his response to them—his dramatic demonstration of what he re-

64. On the contemporary reputation of Rochester, see David M. Vieth, *Attribution in Restoration Poetry* (New Haven, 1963), pp. 164–203.

garded as the ultimate consequence of that freethinking in religion and libertinism in courtship exhibited in restrained form by the "fine gentlemen" of Restoration comedy. In any event, Etherege's Dorimant of a few months later (like Wycherley's Horner of a few months earlier), if more witty and less vicious than Don John, is not totally unlike him in his relations with women and his freedom from religious inhibition. The small circle around King Charles was not without its critics even among the dramatists.

It is the religious theme of *The Libertine* that is most arresting, the close and causal relationship established between atheism and criminal behavior. Don John and his two companions are men without inner controls—"psychopaths," in modern terminology—and they are so, as Don John explains, because they are free of belief in the supernatural. Even after he has been warned of his danger through a demonstration of supernatural power (when the marble statue invites him to dinner), Don John reaffirms his independence of mind. To the question of his terror-stricken servant, "Will not these Miracles do good upon you?" he responds with his credo (act 4):

> There's nothing happens but by Natural Causes,
> Which in unusual things Fools cannot find,
> And then they stile 'em Miracles. But no Accident
> Can alter me from what I am by Nature.

And so he persists to the end, in the face of death reaffirming his defiance and independence, refusing to repent his crimes. His death speech has in it the kind of nobility of resolution, the refusal to compromise in the face of overwhelming force, that led nineteenth-century critics to admire Milton's Satan.[65] Even after he has seen his two companions swallowed up in thunder, he persists (act 5):

> These things I see with wonder, but no fear.
> Were all the Elements to be confounded,
> And shuffl'd all into their former Chaos;
> Were Seas of Sulphur flaming round about me,
> And all Mankind roaring within those fires,
> I could not fear or feel the least remorse.

65. It is significant that Coleridge admired *The Libertine:* cf. *Biographia Literaria,* ed. J. Shawcross (Oxford, 1907), 2 : 185–86.

To the last instant I would dare thy power.
Here I stand firm, and all thy threats contemn;
Thy Murderer stands here, now do thy worst.

There are echoes of Milton in these lines, and perhaps of Lucretius, so admired by seventeenth-century freethinkers.[66] With characteristic bluntness, Shadwell provides a cautionary fable for some of his contemporaries. The consequence of their convictions and their course of life, he would seem to say, is not comedy at all but tragedy.

Though he had no direct knowledge of *El Burlador de Sevilla,* Shadwell retains much of the framework of Tirso's splendid play; and he also retains the conventions of the Restoration Spanish plot. Yet the theme is his own. Not Tirso's "Qué largo me lo fiaís," the procrastination of a man who has not lost all religious faith but is yet unwilling to forego his pleasures,[67] but calculated philosophical atheism and, in Shadwell's view, its moral consequence: this is the organizing principle of *The Libertine.* And it is this principle that makes the play unique among the Restoration Spanish plots.

66. Shadwell could not have written these lines in 1675—eight years after the publication of *Paradise Lost,* seven years before the publication of Dryden's *Religio Laici* —without knowledge of their relevance to current religious controversy. For discussion of the controversy, see Edward N. Hooker, "Dryden and the Atoms of Epicurus," *ELH, A Journal of English Literary History* 24 (1957) : 177–90; and Dale Underwood, *Etherege and the Seventeenth-Century Comedy of Manners* (New Haven, 1957), pp. 10–40. Underwood writes (p. 11) that "In seventeenth-century drama the Don Juan legend, with which both Shadwell and Rosimond deal, had itself become a locus of libertinism . . . , and had assimilated most of the libertine doctrines and practices reflected in the Restoration comedy of manners."

67. Cf. Weinstein, *Metamorphoses of Don Juan,* p. 16.

VI: HEROIC CONVENTION AND CATHOLIC HISTORY

The Indian Emperour and *El Príncipe Constante*

IN the opening scene of the second part of *The Conquest of Granada,* King Ferdinand and Queen Isabella reflect upon their enterprises of 1492: their campaign to complete the reconquest of Spain and Columbus's voyage of exploration. "At length the time is come," says the king, "when *Spain* shall be / From the long Yoke of Moorish Tyrants free." The prospect delights the queen, she replies, even more than success in the voyage of discovery would. Adventures of epic proportions, the search for gold in the Indies and the campaign against the Moors provided Dryden with subjects for rhymed heroic plays, his experiments in the adaptation of epic matter to dramatic form.

So many of Dryden's serious plays have subjects impinged upon by Spanish or Portuguese history that collectively they are a kind of celebration of Peninsular achievement in the Golden Age. In chronological order of imagined time rather than in sequence of composition, he wrote the two parts of *The Conquest of Granada,* a dramatization of the event that terminated the seven-hundred-year Moorish occupation of Spain; *The Indian Queen* (with Sir Robert Howard), unlike the others in having no historical dimension except in the general sense that it depicts Peru under the Incas a generation before the conquest, and that the portrayal of Incan civilization is remotely, and at second hand, based on the reports of Spanish travelers; its sequel *The Indian Emperour,* a dramatic history of "The Conquest of Mexico by the Spaniards" in 1519; and *Don Sebastian,*

King of Portugal, which takes the calamitous battle of Alcazar-Kebir in 1578 as the starting point for dramatic action that is imaginary. Four out of six of Dryden's rhymed heroic plays and five out of twelve of his serious plays have subjects that have something to do with Spanish or Portuguese history in the era that began in 1492.

This is not to imply that Dryden was a dramatic historian of the Golden Age in the way Shakespeare was of the Wars of the Roses. Dryden celebrates events; he does not chronicle them. The historical component of his plays is much more slender than that of Shakespeare's. Yet there is more use of historical event, and more accurate reporting of it, than may at first appear. Dryden read Spanish and Portuguese history, and in the preliminaries to *The Indian Emperour, The Conquest of Granada,* and *Don Sebastian* alluded to the fact that he had done so. He drew from fiction, often historical fiction, for characters, episodes, and even structural patterns, but he used history to provide an enclosing framework.

The opportunities provided by American and Moorish settings for ceremonial and spectacle had something to do with his choice of subjects. The plays were extravagantly mounted costume pieces. A character in *The Indian Queen,* as already noted, wore wreaths of feathers Aphra Behn had brought to England from Surinam.[1] So effective were the scenes and costumes for that play that the company used them again a year later in *The Indian Emperour. "The Scenes are old,"* Dryden humorously acknowledged in the prologue to the later play; *"the Habits are the same / We wore last year, before the* Spaniards *came."*

Yet any remote civilization could have provided the exoticism needed in heroic plays. There were more fundamental reasons, I think, for Dryden's recurrent interest in Spanish and Portuguese history, and the most important was the magnitude of the peninsular accomplishment in the Renaissance. Like Pierre Corneille, whose plays he admired, and like Madeleine de Scudéry, from whose romances he borrowed, he sought great events in which characters had been caught in situations that tested them to the utmost. The selectivity inherent in the recording of history ensured a concern with the superlatives of experience, with qualities of character demon-

1. Dryden, *Works,* 8 : 282.

strated in momentous action; and the recent history of Spain in Dryden's time, more than that of any other country, provided the superlatives and momentous action.

Four of the plays, as I have said, are in the rhymed heroic form, and the fifth, *Don Sebastian,* though in blank verse, has resemblances to the heroic plays. Dryden's most systematic account of the dramatic form appears in the preface to *The Conquest of Granada,* in which he insists on affinities between the epic and the heroic play, the latter of which is properly, he writes, "an imitation, in little, of an heroic poem." [2] In defending his leading character Almanzor from such detractors as the duke of Buckingham,[3] Dryden traces his literary ancestry to the heroes of Renaissance and classical epics, to those of Tasso and Ariosto, Vergil and Homer. And he cites the precedent of Corneille for the heightening of dramatic character. It followed from his theory that his plays should permit the leading characters to display heroic fortitude in action of epic scope. Hence the special appropriateness of Spanish history. Dryden implied as much when he wrote of Montezuma in the dedication to *The Indian Emperour:* "His story is, perhaps the greatest, which was ever represented in a Poem of this nature; (the action of it including the Discovery and Conquest of a New World.)" The achievements in exploration and conquest of the Spanish, that is to say, made them suitable subjects for the heroic play—the more so since they traveled and fought in exotic places which could justify the introduction on stage of ceremonial and spectacle.

A study of Dryden's serious drama becomes in part a study of his interpretation of Spanish and Portuguese civilization. To Anne T. Barbeau we owe the valuable insight that Dryden's heroic plays are in a specialized sense a drama of ideas embodying a theory of history; [4] and we may add that in the conflict of the Spanish with the American Indians and the Moors he found suitable illustrations of the historical process as conceived to embody a widening territorial expansion of Christendom. "Dryden suggests that the fall of Granada is like the fall of most great kingdoms:" Miss Barbeau writes, "these

2. *Essays,* 1 : 150.

3. Cf. W. S. Clark, "The Sources of the Restoration Heroic Play," *Review of English Studies* 4 (1928) : 52–53.

4. Barbeau, *The Intellectual Design of John Dryden's Heroic Plays* (New Haven, 1970), pp. 3–23.

are torn by rival parties, preyed upon by ambitious, vain courtiers, and governed by dull, sensual tyrants." [5]

True, though we should add the qualification that the historical process she describes is implicit in Dryden's sources, Spanish history and Spanish and French historical romance. The completion of the Reconquest, Miss Barbeau concludes, "has occurred in such a way that justice has prevailed," [6] and we may accept her analysis as it applies to this play, even if reservations suggest themselves if the pattern is extended to *The Indian Emperour:* the Mexicans are scarcely more corrupt than the Spaniards, and the triumph of Roman Catholicism as depicted by Dryden is not unambiguously the triumph of justice. Still, *The Indian Emperour* and *The Conquest of Granada* alike conclude in epic victories for Christian heroes. It is one of the marks of the tragic structure of *Don Sebastian* that the pattern is reversed: the Christian hero can only achieve a personal and moral victory in a life of exile, whereas the Moors are successful politically, even though they are again "torn by rival parties, preyed upon by ambitious, vain courtiers, and governed by dull, sensual tyrants." In North Africa the historical process responsible for the expansion of Christianity had reached its limit.

As already noted, it has been argued that *The Indian Emperour* is based on Calderón's *El príncipe constante*.[7] Whatever our determination on this difficult subject, the fact that striking similarities exist between the English and the Spanish plays suggests resemblances—more important resemblances than have usually been recognized—between the work of Dryden and that of Calderón. There are resemblances as well between *Don Sebastian* and *El príncipe constante*. If Dryden made use of the Spanish play in writing *The Indian Emperour,* we may plausibly consider *El príncipe constante* in examining the literary background of *Don Sebastian,* which, at least in subject, bears closer resemblances to *El príncipe constante* than Dryden's earlier play.

Dryden alluded to the affinity of his heroic plays with Corneille's drama. Certainly Corneille's dramaturgy was influential in shaping the heroic plays—in determining their ethos, their conversational

5. Ibid., p. 126.
6. Ibid.
7. N. D. Shergold and Peter Ure, "Dryden and Calderón: A New Spanish Source for *The Indian Emperour,*" *Modern Language Review* 61 (1966): 369–83.

dialectic, their structure.[8] It counts for something in assessing Dryden's knowledge of the comedia that Corneille's most famous play, *Le Cid,* about the national hero of medieval Spain, is based upon (in certain passages even translated from) a Spanish play, Guillén de Castro's *Las mocedades del Cid.* At the least, Dryden knew the Spanish play through the French intermediary. *Las mocedades del Cid* itself reveals qualities of subject, theme, and style similar to those distinctive of Dryden's heroic plays. Even if it finally proves to be impossible to determine how much Dryden knew about the comedia, a parallel examination of his plays and the Spanish ones they resemble, referring to Corneille as intermediary when appropriate, will suggest a spectrum of shared themes and dramatic strategies.

That Dryden read widely in history and historical fiction about Renaissance Spain and Portugal is beyond question, as his serious plays and critical writings reveal. But did he draw in his serious plays on the comedia? Here we encounter the most difficult and the most important problem of all in assessing Dryden's debt to the Spanish drama: that of the relationship of *The Indian Emperour* to Calderón's *El príncipe constante.* I have already said that Dryden's remarks in his critical writings about Calderón and Spanish drama seem to be inconsistent with the assumption that he had the kind of close knowledge of this somber religious tragedy which his use of it as a source would imply (see above, pp. 6–7). Yet the resemblances between the two plays are striking. If, as Professors Shergold and Ure argue, Dryden studied this superb Spanish play closely and at length in one of the printings of Calderón's *Primera parte,* a collection that included many of Calderón's best plays, the dimensions of our subject are enlarged. We must then consider the comedia as a source of the heroic play; and we may, with reasonable hope of success, search for other borrowings from, or formal imitations of, the comedia among Dryden's serious plays.

Shergold and Ure point to resemblances of both situation and language between *The Indian Emperour* and *El príncipe constante.* The most notable are parallel passages, early in both plays, in which a messenger reports to a sovereign the arrival of foreign ships.

8. Arthur C. Kirsch, *Dryden's Heroic Drama* (Princeton, 1965), pp. 46–65.

Are the resemblances merely the result of two seventeenth-century poets addressing themselves to a common subject, the first sighting of distant ships at sea; or are they so close as to require us to assume that Dryden followed Calderón? In *The Indian Emperour* Guyomar, the younger son of Montezuma, returns from an exploratory mission to report to his father in Mexico City the arrival of Spanish ships, which to him, since he has never seen the like before, seem supernatural creatures.[9] In *El príncipe constante* Muley, a Moorish general, while on a naval reconnaissance expedition, sighted an approaching fleet of hostile ships, as he subsequently reports to the king of Fez. Unlike Guyomar, he had no difficulty in identifying the ships for what they were, as soon as he could see them clearly. Shergold and Ure assert that Muley's report to his sovereign begins with a statement, "Salí, como me mandaste, . . . gran Señor," which is translated by Dryden as: "I went, in order, Sir, to your command." As they point out, a passage having no parallel in Dryden intervenes, followed by Muley's extended description of the ships.[10]

It is clear enough that the two descriptive passages have much in common; it is not clear to me that the resemblances prove Dryden wrote with Calderón's play before him. The resemblances may rather be the consequence of two dramatists, who were contemporaries and may both be described truly (though not very precisely) as baroque poets, addressing themselves to similar subjects. We know that the prophecy of the foreigners' arrival to which Dryden's high priest alludes just after Guyomar's narration is widely mentioned in the chronicles of discovery; Dryden himself had mentioned it in the prologue to *The Indian Queen*. Should we not regard the preceding passage as an imaginative realization of the prophecy, an elaboration of a situation present at least in embryo in the prophecy? The circumstances of the arrival and the natives' superstitious response to it appear in the voyage literature; [11] only specific descriptive details could constitute evidence of borrowing, and the resemblances may not go beyond what would arise from the common subject. The most striking similarities in the passages are those having to do with

9. Dryden, *Works,* 9 : 35–36.

10. Quoted in Shergold and Ure, "Dryden and Calderón," pp. 373–74.

11. As Dougald MacMillan has pointed out, they appear as well in Davenant's *The Cruelty of the Spaniards in Peru* of 1658: "The Sources of Dryden's *The Indian Emperour," Huntington Library Quarterly* 13 (1950) : 357–59.

the visual illusions—clouds, sea, and ships indistinctly separated from one another, and only gradually emerging to the eye of the beholder. Yet as the experience of sailors will testify, this is precisely the kind of detail that would occur to anyone writing about the sighting of distant ships at sea. Given the shared rhetorical inheritance of Calderón and Dryden, it is not surprising that they employed similar figures of speech.

E. H. Gombrich, concerned with the "Psychology of Pictorial Representation," quotes the passage from *El príncipe constante,* in describing mental processes brought into play in the discrimination of distant objects, as a literary account of the "uncertainties and the activity they provoke in the searching mind." "Relating the appearance of the hostile fleet during a voyage," he writes, "one of Calderón's characters is reminded of the blurred distances of the subtle painter." After quoting the passage, Gombrich adds, emphasizing the universality of the experience Calderón describes, "the poet succeeds where many psychologists have failed in describing the panorama of illusions that may be evoked by the indeterminate." [12] Although he makes no reference to Dryden, I would suggest that his elucidation of the psychological basis of the experience helps to explain how the two poets could write independently in similar veins.

Shergold and Ure call attention to metaphorical similarities in the two passages, and the nature of these is perhaps crucial. If there were indeed close and detailed resemblances in the texture of language, they would constitute convincing evidence of Dryden's borrowing, but I do not think that they exist. It is impossible to consider all the images in question; perhaps the quality of the evidence may best be suggested by quoting Shergold and Ure's first paragraph devoted to the subject:

> The images used to describe the approach of the fleet are similar in both writers, though the Dryden speech is much shorter than the Calderón original, and he only selects some of this material for his own use. As we have seen, he does not adopt, or adapt, any of Calderón's description of the dawn, though structurally this has its equivalent in lines 4–8 of the English passage quoted,

12. E. H. Gombrich, *Art and Illusion: A Study in the Psychology of Pictorial Representation* (New York, 1960), pp. 223–25.

with its "foaming billows," and the clouds, heavy with rain upon the horizon. The next lines, beginning "At last, as far as I could cast my eyes," and the first appearance of the indistinct forms of the ships, may be compared with the "gruessa tropa / de naves," the mighty fleet of ships, in Calderón, but again Dryden handles the passage selectively, and takes over only a few of Calderón's comparisons. Muley at first cannot tell whether he is seeing ships or rocks, and, alluding to the deceptive effect of distance, he draws an image from painting, where subtle brushwork and use of perspective might make the vessels look like hills or cities. Guyomar does not liken his ships to any of these things, for Dryden changes the image and makes their masts suggest "tall straight trees"; but his phrase about the "bluish mists" may have been suggested by the Spanish "paises azules," or "blue landscapes," and the "dreadful shapes" into which the "mists" materialize as they come closer suggests comparison with Calderón's lines about distance forming "Impossible monsters." The line then spoken by Montezuma echoes the Spanish here: "What *form* did these new wonders represent?" There is another reference to their shapes or forms in Calderón, where Muley says that sea, sky, clouds, and waves are confused with one another, so that only the "shapes," "los bultos," can be perceived, and not their actual forms or nature: "la vista . . . / solo apercibiò los bultos / y no distinguiò las formas." [13]

Remembering that Dryden and Calderón were both addressing themselves to the nature of optical illusion in the first sighting of distant ships at sea, a subject which would have been suggested to Dryden by his historical sources, I find nothing here—or in Shergold and Ure's following paragraphs—that cannot more easily be accounted for as independent composition.

The resemblances between the parallel passages in the two plays do not occur in isolation but rather amidst others of theme and plot. Shergold and Ure call attention to the "constancy" of Montezuma and compare him to Calderón's title character. The comparison is just enough, but in this case we can be sure that Dryden drew upon the historians of the conquest: first, because he says so and,

13. Pp. 374–75.

second, because in a crucial passage in the torture scene (act 5, scene 2) he paraphrases López de Gómara. In the "Connexion of the *Indian Emperour,* to the *Indian Queen,*" published with the preliminaries of the play, he writes about the Indians' religion: "that which you find of it in the first and fifth Acts, touching the sufferings and constancy of *Montezuma* in his Opinions, I have only illustrated, not alter'd from those who have written of it." [14] Probably his source for the torture scene was Gómara as paraphrased by Montaigne; [15] Florio's translation of Montaigne includes an account of the fortitude of a king of Mexico (not identified by name) that is strikingly like Dryden's.[16] With Montaigne before him (and his use, with slight modification, of a vivid metaphor spoken by the Mexican king suggests that it was), Dryden had no need to turn to *El príncipe constante* for an example of "constancy."

Shergold and Ure's argument for detailed resemblances of plot in the two plays may best be presented in their own summary:

> In Calderón we have: 1. The offer of a queen's crown to Fénix, which she refuses; 2. Muley and his report of the fleet; 3. The landing, on the North African coast, of Fernando and the Portuguese; 4. The battle scene in which Fernando takes Muley prisoner, and lets him go. This brings us almost to the end of Act I, which finishes with the capture of Fernando by the Moors. In Dryden the pattern of the numbered scenes is the same, but they occur in a different order: 3, 1, 2, 4. Thus, placing in brackets the number of the Calderón equivalents, we have: 1 (3). The landing, in Mexico, of Cortez and the Spaniards. 2 (1). The offer of a queen's crown to Almeria, which she refuses. 3 (2). Guyomar and his report of the fleet. 4 (4). The battle, in which Cortez takes Guyomar prisoner, and then lets him go. Of these four scenes, 1–3 occupy Act I, Scene i and about half Scene ii; and the capture of Guyomar occurs in Act II, Scene iv. In between are the scenes of the battle, treated in other respects rather differently by the two writers, and the conjuration scene in the Magician's Cave, Act II, Scene i. The latter probably owes noth-

14. Dryden, *Works,* 9 : 28.
15. Ibid., pp. 310–11.
16. "Of Coaches," in Montaigne, *Essays,* trans. John Florio (Tudor Translations, 1892–93), 3 : 147–48. Cf. Dryden, *Works,* 9 : 311.

> ing to Calderón, despite a certain parallel with the omens that occur in Act I of *El príncipe,* and Fénix's prophetic dream at the beginning of Act II.[17]

All this, as well as the other resemblances to which they point, is impressive, and yet perhaps finally inconclusive. If Dryden drew on Calderón, he did so selectively, changing and rearranging much of what he borrowed, and intermingling borrowed materials with much that he took from the historians of the conquest. In this, as in all his heroic plays, he used stylized characters and plot situations familiar to him from the French romances. (He took the serious plot of his next play, *Secret Love,* from Madeleine de Scudéry's *Le Grand Cyrus,* as he acknowledged in his preface.) The neatly symmetrical arrangement of characters is a commonplace both of the heroic play and the French romance, and the stylized movement of the love plot derives from literary convention. Such a detail as Cortes's capture and release of a noble enemy and his subsequent experiencing that enemy's generosity when he in turn is a captive—this is the common matter of heroic drama and heroic fiction in the seventeenth century and is not useful as evidence of a literary debt.

Dryden had already written, in collaboration with Sir Robert Howard, *The Indian Queen,* to which *The Indian Emperour* is a sequel, so called in the Stationers' Register. Although the earlier play contains nothing like the conflict of civilizations central to the later one, it anticipates the later one in the nature of its characters and the epic conception of its dramatic action. Much of Dryden's reading in preparation for the one play would have been useful in writing the other. Conceivably, a reading of *El príncipe constante* could have given him the idea of reworking the American materials into a pattern suggested by the Spanish play.

Conceivably, but I do not think so, and in part at least because neither in his long dedicatory epistle to *The Indian Emperour* nor in the "Connexion of the *Indian Emperour,* to the *Indian Queen,*" in both of which he mentions his sources, does Dryden allude to Calderón; nor indeed elsewhere in his critical writings, though he frequently mentions the Spanish dramatist, does he say anything about him that would be compatible with a close knowledge of one

17. P. 379.

of his best tragedies. In the preface to *The Conquest of Granada*, in which Dryden provides an account of the literary antecedents of the heroic play, he does not mention Calderón. Dryden was generous enough in his tributes to Corneille, in this preface as elsewhere; would he have been reluctant to acknowledge a more detailed and extended debt to Calderón than any he owed the French dramatist?

It is perhaps not possible to give a final answer to the question raised by Shergold and Ure. On the one hand, the similarities between the two plays are numerous, extended, and specific; on the other hand, many of them are demonstrably traceable to literary convention and to the fact that each play dramatizes a historical episode about a voyage of conquest and a resulting clash of religions and civilizations. Yet apart from the perhaps unanswerable question, the correspondences provide an opportunity to examine the plays comparatively and to elucidate dramaturgical similarities and differences between them.

I shall discuss the similarities and differences in several related and overlapping categories: the codes of conduct controlling the principal characters; the religious ideas that are a principal determinant of the authorial judgments on characters and action; and the employment in profusion of verbal artifice as ornamentation.[18]

As already noted, both plays celebrate an ideal of constancy, including in central scenes characters who choose to undergo sufferings of an extreme and potentially fatal kind rather than betray an obligation to their nation or religion. The title characters, both of them historical figures, had achieved literary status as exemplars of constancy before the dramatists wrote about them. In both cases the legend surrounding the figure involved distortion of historical fact. Prince Ferdinand, son of King John I of Portugal and younger brother of Prince Henry the Navigator, was captured by the Moors in 1437 when an expedition sent to capture Tangier failed.[19] The

18. Although in this chapter and the next I discuss qualities of seventeenth-century drama that are often called "baroque," I avoid the use of that term. I do so merely from prudence: the term would complicate rather than clarify my comparative examination of English and Spanish drama. For an analysis of difficulties in applying the term to Spanish drama, see A. A. Parker, "Reflections on a New Definition of 'Baroque' Drama," *Bulletin of Hispanic Studies* 30 (1953): 142–51.

19. On the historical background of this play, see Albert E. Sloman, *The Sources of Calderón's 'El Príncipe Constante'* (Oxford, 1950), pp. 13–21.

Portuguese were unwilling to purchase his release with the surrender of the Christian city of Ceuta, and Ferdinand died in captivity in 1443. His posthumous reputation for fortitude and constancy derived from an account of him written by his secretary. Although laudatory of his master, the secretary made it clear that the historical Ferdinand, unlike the hero of legend, was willing that Ceuta be surrendered as a condition of his freedom. Among the later writers who contributed to the legend about him were Camões, in the fourth canto of *Os Lusiadas,* and the author of the play that was Calderón's primary source, *La fortuna adversa del Infante don Fernando de Portugal.* The process of elaboration on historical event is parallel in the case of the "Indian Emperour," whom Dryden calls Montezuma. The literary character is in fact a composite of three Indian sovereigns: the Aztec whose name he bears, Montezuma's successor Quahutimoc, and the Inca Atabalipa.[20] It was about Quahutimoc that López de Gómara wrote in the passage that is the ultimate source of the torture scene.[21]

The two dramatists, then, use and elaborate on semihistorical legends about the heroic endurance of royal persons. Both heroes have an exalted conception of personal honor; they exemplify what the French call *gloire* [22] (the quality that Corneille's Polyeucte demonstrates in a situation ironically parallel to that in which Montezuma finds himself). Both exhibit, more specifically, a willingness to die rather than betray religious convictions—though Fernando's self-abnegation in the service of a religious ideal is much more fully and convincingly developed than Montezuma's.

The magnanimous willingness to sacrifice oneself to a higher cause is not confined, in the two plays, to Montezuma and Fernando. Dryden's Cortes, whose role—and not Montezuma's—is structurally parallel to Fernando's, is, like the Portuguese prince of the first act, a chivalrous knight.[23] Although little is made of his religious beliefs, he too leads a military expedition to enlarge the boundaries of

20. MacMillan, "Sources of *The Indian Emperour,*" pp. 365–67.

21. Dryden, *Works,* 9 : 310–14.

22. Cf. Paul Bénichou, *Morales du grand siècle* (Paris, 1948), pp. 13–76; Arthur C. Kirsch, *Dryden's Heroic Drama* (Princeton, 1965), pp. 51–53.

23. Dryden's Cortes is the protagonist in the sense that he is the character whose decisions determine events: cf. Dryden, *Works,* 9 : 300. See also Jean H. Hagstrum, "Dryden's Grotesque: An Aspect of His Art and Criticism," in Earl Miner, ed., *John Dryden* (London, 1972), p. 101.

Christianity, experiencing captivity and imprisonment; and he too refuses to purchase his freedom with a city, not yet held but closely blockaded by his Christian comrades.[24] His refusal does not receive the emphasis given to Fernando's, and yet it reveals a Christian knight's fortitude. Unlike Fernando, Cortes is later freed, and in victory he is magnanimous. Although he says little about religious faith, he refuses to tolerate the sadistic cruelty practiced by his lieutenant in the name of Catholicism. He is a generous enemy to the Indians. His relationship to Cydaria, the daughter of Montezuma, is not totally unlike Fernando's to Fénix, the daughter of the King of Fez. Cortes loves and ultimately wins Cydaria; Fernando, a knight who becomes a Catholic martyr, shows no such open love for Fénix, who is loved by Muley. But as Leo Spitzer demonstrated, the relationship between Fernando and Fénix is a dynamic one, in which love is not absent on either side.[25]

Cortes and his Indian adversary Guyomar, the brother of Cydaria and the son of Montezuma, have binding conceptions of the point of honor that would do credit to Corneille's heroes.[26] After capturing Guyomar in battle, Cortes releases him upon learning that he is a lover, with an explanation that would not be out of place in a romance of Madeleine de Scudéry (act 2, scene 3). This act of generosity to an enemy in war is repaid when Guyomar later (act 3, scene 4) intercedes with his father on behalf of Cortes, then a captive himself.

This reciprocal generosity to a captured enemy has a parallel in *El príncipe constante* in the changing relationships of Muley and Fernando.[27] The role of Muley, the nephew and general of the King of Fez and lover of the king's daughter Fénix, parallels that of Guyomar. (Muley is an example of the generous Moor of literary tradition,[28] as is Almanzor of *The Conquest of Granada,* who cap-

24. Cf. Shergold and Ure, "Dryden and Calderón," pp. 371, 381–82.

25. Leo Spitzer, "The Figure of Fénix in Calderón's *El príncipe constante,*" in *Critical Essays on the Theatre of Calderón,* ed. Bruce W. Wardropper (New York, 1965), pp. 137–60.

26. On the Spanish contribution to the French conception of chivalric love, see Octave Nadal, *Le Sentiment de l'amour dans l'oeuvre de Pierre Corneille* (Paris, 1948), pp. 62–64.

27. Shergold and Ure, "Dryden and Calderón," pp. 379–80.

28. Bruce W. Wardropper, "Christian and Moor in Calderón's *El príncipe constante,*" *Modern Language Review* 53 (1958): 512–20.

tures and then releases an enemy, the duke of Arcos [part 1, act 2, scene 1].) Before releasing Guyomar on the battlefield, Cortes questions him about his melancholy expression. Guyomar's answer is not the obvious one, that he has been defeated in battle and is held captive, but rather a courtly one, that he has a rival in love whose success he fears (act 2, scene 3). So also Fernando, when in the first skirmish with the Moors he captures Muley, asks him the reason for his melancholy; and again the adversary, disclaiming the obvious reason, attributes it to his misfortune in love. He has a rival, he explains, and he fears that the rival will win the lady during his own captivity (act 1). Fernando's response to the afflicted lover is as great-hearted as Cortes's, and it is more disinterested. Unlike the conquistador, he is not himself a lover.

Apart from their relevance to the problem of Dryden's possible indebtedness, these correspondences testify to shared conventions of behavior in heroic characters of high station. Both dramatists are less concerned with psychological probability than with depicting characters capable of indifference to the extremities of present misfortune by sustaining loyalty to an ideal of chivalric love, as in these parallel instances, or to an ideal of duty or religion elsewhere in the two plays. *"Love and Valour ought to be the Subject"* of a heroic play, Dryden wrote in his preface to *The Conquest of Granada* ("love and honor" in the customary modern paraphrase); and if we make generous allowance for the religious theme of *El príncipe constante* expressed in Fernando's transformation from a knight to a martyr, the phrase is applicable to Calderón's play as well.[29]

As these initial acts of generosity to a captured enemy turn on a magnanimous recognition of the claims of love, so the later reciprocal acts or intended acts turn on and are complicated by an acceptance of a code of behavior involving obligation to one's superior or to one's country. While Fernando, having refused to acquiesce in the surrender of Ceuta as his ransom, languishes in captivity, Muley out of gratitude undertakes his rescue (act 2). He will have a boat waiting at the shore, he explains secretly to Fernando, in which the

29. Fernando is much more consistently portrayed as an exemplar of Christian virtue than is Cortes. See Sloman, *Sources of 'El Principe Constante,'* pp. 72–73: "It would seem that Calderón had in mind, throughout the play, the *Summa Theologica* of St. Thomas Aquinas. At all events, Calderón's conception of Prince Ferdinand corresponds precisely with St. Thomas's treatment of the virtue of fortitude."

prince and his fellow prisoners can return to Portugal after they have broken out of prison with the tools Muley will supply. He acts on a principle of honor, and—ironically—it is that principle which frustrates his plan.

The king of Fez approaches as they converse, and although he does not overhear their conversation he becomes suspicious, the more so since Fernando steps into hiding to avoid meeting him. Knowing the strength of Muley's sense of duty, the king cleverly appoints him personal guard over Fernando, admonishing him to prevent the prince from escaping. After the king has walked on, Muley explains his dilemma to Fernando in an analysis of scruples not unlike the dissection of motive in tragedies by Corneille and even by Racine (act 2). Fernando resolves his dilemma, telling Muley that no obligation to a friend can rival that to one's king. Fernando thus condemns himself to a continuing imprisonment of increasing severity rather than acquiesce in a friend's violation of a courtly code of behavior.

Guyomar encounters a dilemma similar to Muley's. Like the Moor, he finds his adversary, who had earlier released him from captivity, himself a prisoner. After having, with his brother Odmar, captured Cortes, Guyomar moves to protect Cortes when Montezuma, goaded by Almeria, considers killing him.[30] Guyomar restores Cortes's sword, thereby arousing the anger of Montezuma, who tries to kill him, his own son. First Odmar and then Cortes intercedes. Cortes's statement to Odmar and Guyomar is not unlike Fernando's response to Muley's analysis of his dilemma after he has been made Fernando's guard (act 3, scene 4). Cortes, too, chooses continuing captivity rather than accept aid that would constitute a violation of the courtly code, though in his case captivity proves not to be perpetual. He is later rescued by his comrades.

I do not know whether or not these correspondences result from Dryden's borrowing from Calderón. The matter is complicated by the wide diffusion in the seventeenth century, in prose fiction as well as in the drama, of conventions of characterization and plotting; this will become more apparent when we turn to *The Conquest of Granada* and *Don Sebastian*. It would be possible, I think, to find approximate parallels to these instances of self-abnegating observance of a chivalric code in the English heroic play, in French tragedy and

30. Cf. Shergold and Ure, "Dryden and Calderón," pp. 379–81.

prose romance, and in the comedia. As already pointed out, Muley belongs to a well-established literary tradition of the generous and sentimental Moor.[31] Nevertheless, the similarities between *The Indian Emperour* and *El príncipe constante* provide remarkable testimony to Dryden's and Calderón's common preoccupation with the superlatives of human behavior. In the preface to *The Conquest of Granada,* Dryden defended his choice of *"the highest patern of humane life"* as the subject of his heroic plays. Calderón would not have subscribed to all Dryden wrote in that essay. Yet he provided, in Fernando, a Roman Catholic version of an exemplary prince.

In their religious themes, the plays are of course different, and any account of the chivalric code governing the two sets of characters must take the religious differences into account. Calderón's play is systematically and coherently Roman Catholic; Dryden's is periodically anti-Catholic; yet it finally celebrates the spreading of Christianity into a new continent. "The theme of the geographical expansion of Christianity," Anne T. Barbeau writes, referring to this play, *Tyrannic Love,* and *The Conquest of Granada,* "constitutes the larger pattern of the middle three heroic plays." [32] Consistent with a conception of epic movement in the heroic play, *The Indian Emperour* ends in triumph for Cortes, and Cortes's triumph is of course that of the Roman Catholic religion; but the play is far indeed from a celebration of Catholic piety. If Fernando in *El príncipe constante* is, before the extremity of his misfortunes, a chivalric commander like Cortes, his religious faith places on him obligations that transcend those of chivalry; and in the latter part of the play he willingly undergoes humiliation unlike anything in *The Indian Emperour.* Dryden's Cortes may have more in common with Calderón's great-hearted Moor, Muley, than with Fernando.

Bruce W. Wardropper has established an illuminating contrast between "Christian and Moor in . . . *El príncipe constante,*" between Fernando who achieves a Christian disdain for the values of the world in his preoccupation with eternity, and Muley, a good and generous man who is nevertheless bound by time.[33] The transitori-

31. Wardropper, "Christian and Moor."
32. Barbeau, *Dryden's Heroic Plays,* p. 58.
33. Wardropper, "Christian and Moor."

ness of beauty, strikingly represented by the princess Fénix, provides a recurrent theme, emblematically represented in the most famous lines in the play (act 2), the sonnet beginning "Estas, que fueron pompa y alegría" spoken by Fernando to Fénix in a garden. In his renunciation of the world to achieve a martyr's death, Fernando escapes from time. Christian eternity, non-Christian mortality—this thematic contrast has no counterpart in *The Indian Emperour.*

The admiring characterization of Cortes notwithstanding, Dryden's version of the expansion of Roman Catholicism reveals something of what has been called the "black legend" of Spanish atrocity in America.[34] Although the Indians in the play have faults enough of their own, the Spaniards, who possess invincible arms, bring greed and superstition to a people who had earlier been, in their better moments at least, rational primitives. Dryden's depiction of the Spaniards' exploitation of Christianity in conquest and colonization follows a well-established literary tradition, which had been given striking expression on the London stage just two years before in Davenant's *A Playhouse to Be Let,* one of Dryden's sources.[35] Dryden's retention of the ideas present in Davenant's play and other literary treatments of the "black legend" produces tension between his celebration of the Spaniards' victory and his depiction of their methods and motives. For there is no escaping the impact of the torture scene (act 5, scene 2). *The Indian Emperour* was still in repertory when Voltaire visited England in the 1720s; and it tells much about the force of Dryden's arraignment of Catholic hypocrisy and cruelty that Voltaire admired the play and wrote a play of his own resembling Dryden's, *Alzire ou les Américains* (1736), about Spanish atrocity in Peru.[36]

Because there is now difference of opinion [37] concerning Dryden's

34. For a comprehensive treatment of the hostile interpretations of Spanish colonization, and a rebuttal to them, see Julián Juderías y Loyot, *La leyenda negra y la verdad histórica,* 2d ed. (Barcelona, 1917).

35. MacMillan, "Sources of *The Indian Emperour,*" pp. 357–60.

36. Trusten Wheeler Russell, *Voltaire, Dryden and Heroic Tragedy* (New York, 1946), p. 75.

37. For interpretations of Dryden's treatment of the conquest that differ from mine, see Michael W. Alssid, "The Perfect Conquest: A Study of Theme, Structure and Characters in Dryden's *The Indian Emperor,*" *Studies in Philology* 59 (1962): 539–59; Barbeau, *Dryden's Heroic Plays,* pp. 81–94.

authorial judgment in *The Indian Emperour* on the Spanish conquest of Mexico, it may be helpful to look briefly at the literary context in which he wrote.

Before the Restoration, Davenant had turned to the Spaniards' adventures in America for two dramatic entertainments: *The Cruelty of the Spaniards in Peru* and *The History of Sir Francis Drake,* both of 1658. The former is the more relevant here; the latter celebrates the English naval hero who triumphed over the Spaniards. Davenant's motive for writing *The Cruelty of the Spaniards in Peru* is to be sought in Oliver Cromwell's war against Philip IV (the war that forced the exiled Charles II into an alliance with Philip). The little play has the oversimplification and overemphasis of propaganda written in time of war. Its chief source seems to have been Las Casas, and in fact the subject may have been suggested to Davenant by the publication in 1656 of John Phillips's translation of his work under the title *The Tears of the Indians* (with a dedication to Cromwell).[38] This is uncertain; the source may rather be the translation of Las Casas in *Purchas His Pilgrims.*[39] In any event, it was useful to Davenant, in his effort to reestablish drama during the Interregnum, to produce a propagandistic play in support of an English war. Paradoxically, the war that led the exiled royalists into alliance with the Spanish—an alliance that in time resulted in a spate of English adaptations of Spanish plays—led also to a dramatic indictment of Spain.

It is no coincidence that both the translations of Las Casas into English before the Restoration, by "M.M.S." in 1583 (reprinted in *Purchas His Pilgrims*), and by John Phillips in 1656, were made in time of war against Spain. The descriptive title of Phillips's translation will suggest the usefulness of Las Casas to a government attempting to arouse popular support for a war: *The Tears of the Indians, Being an Historical and True account of the Cruel Massacres and Slaughters of Above Twenty Millions of Innocent People;* and in this instance the title is an accurate summary of the work. Although the most influential of the expositors of the "black legend," Las Casas was by no means the only one. Francisco López de Gómara,

38. Cf. MacMillan, "Sources of *The Indian Emperour,*" p. 359.
39. Ibid.

among others, wrote an eloquent condemnation of Spanish atrocity, and, in this case, we know that Dryden, if not Davenant as well, was familiar with his ideas through Montaigne as intermediary (see above, pp. 185–86).

From Shakespeare's time to Dryden's, Montaigne, in Florio's translation, was a widely read book. It was a source of *The Tempest,* a play which, like *The Indian Emperour,* draws on accounts of travel to America. In Montaigne's essays "Of the Cannibales" and "Of Coaches," Englishmen found a condemnation of Spanish bigotry and cruelty taken over from Las Casas, Gómara, and other writers, and they also found ideas suggested by the voyages of discovery assimilated into the older classical culture. Montaigne's conception of the Indians combines notions concerning rational primitives drawn from classical antiquity with materials drawn from the historians of the Spanish conquest.[40] Montaigne's ideas concerning natural religion anticipate the ideas on the subject expressed by Dryden's Montezuma, as well as those of the eighteenth-century deists.[41] It was not the facts of the exploration and discovery of America, if indeed they were or are ascertainable, that mattered to the English men of letters, but rather the organization of the travelers' reports into intelligible patterns having relationship to traditional learning; and for this many of them, including Dryden—and perhaps Davenant—turned to Montaigne.

The Cruelty of the Spaniards in Peru, a masquelike entertainment "Exprest by Instrumentall and Vocall Musick, and by Art of Perspective in Scenes," does not, in its printed form, include dialogue but merely set speeches, songs, and descriptions of what passed on the stage. The sequence of scenes, embodying an interpretation of the conquest, is summarized in an introductory "Argument of the whole Designe." Davenant anticipates Dryden in his conception of the Indians, their earlier innocence having given way with the advance of their civilization, even before the arrival of the Spaniards, to a destructive civil war. Within the framework of a masque, the successive songs and speeches articulate a theory of primitivism expressed amidst fact and legend concerning the Indians, including an

40. Gilbert Chinard, *L'Exotisme américain dans la littérature française au XVIe siècle* (Paris, 1911), pp. 193–218.

41. Cf. Dryden, *Works,* 9 : 316–17.

account of the preconquest prophecy that "a Bearded People . . . should spring out of the Sea, and conquer" them.[42] Such dramatic continuity as the little piece has, reaches its climax in a scene anticipating the torture scene of *The Indian Emperour,* in which "are discern'd Racks, and other Engines of torment, with which the Spaniards are tormenting the Natives and English Marriners"; two Spaniards in particular, "appearing more solemn in Ruffs," "the one turning a Spit, whilst the other is basting an *Indian* Prince." [43] From all this, the Indians expect deliverance by the English, whose victory is prophesied.

Davenant seems to have had a popular success with *The Cruelty of the Spaniards in Peru,* and a few months later he presented the companion piece, *The History of Sir Francis Drake.* The events depicted in the second play, imaginary adventures of Sir Francis Drake and his son in Peru, would have come before the English invasion prophesied in the earlier entertainment; and when in 1663 Davenant, with literary thriftiness, made use of both pieces as "acts" in his dramatic miscellany *A Playhouse to Be Let,* he placed *Sir Francis Drake* earlier, as act 3, and the other as act 4. The date of *A Playhouse to be Let,* 1663, is only about a year before Dryden wrote *The Indian Emperour.* At the least, Davenant's interpretation of the Spanish conquest would have influenced the expectations of Dryden's first audiences. It is scarcely surprising that there should be reservations in Dryden's celebration of the territorial expansion of Christianity.

Dryden's reservations about Roman Catholicism constitute, of course, a major difference from Calderón. Between *The Indian Emperour* and *El príncipe constante,* we encounter the perennial difference in religious structure between English and Spanish drama, and this notwithstanding the resemblances in the central movement of the two plays. Dryden chose to emphasize the chivalry of his protagonist, Cortes, rather than his piety.

The Spaniards conquer Mexico; the Portuguese do not conquer Fez. Yet no less than Cortes, Fernando achieves victory, religious rather than military. The diverse strands of both plays are subordi-

42. Davenant, *The Cruelty of the Spaniards in Peru* (London, 1658), p. 7.
43. Ibid., p. 19.

nated to the celebration of the protagonist's victory. The love intrigue of *The Indian Emperour* is contingent on the military fortunes of the Spaniards, which turn on the will of Cortes since the Spanish possess irresistible weapons; the far less prominent love intrigue of *El príncipe constante* is determined by the decision and resolution of Fernando. In recognition of Muley's friendship for Fernando, King Alfonso, in the symbolical exchange of the dead prince's body for the captured Fénix, specifies that she be awarded to Muley.

Although the love relationships of Dryden's play are schematically subordinate to the theme of conquest, they are developed with a leisurely amplitude that is foreign to the ascetic tone of Calderón's play, and the fact that they are numerous permits a balanced elaboration absent in *El príncipe constante*. Montezuma has one daughter and two sons; the two daughters and one son of the late Indian queen are present at his court. Dramatic conflict results from interruptions of and rearrangements in the potential pairings. Both of Montezuma's sons love one daughter of the Indian queen, whereas their father loves the other; the son of the Indian queen loves Montezuma's daughter. However, she and Cortes, in the first meeting of Spaniards and Mexicans, conceive an instantaneous love for each other that ultimately is consummated in marriage. Cortes and Montezuma, older men and the leaders of the opposing forces, are alike in their love for a younger woman, and their respective success and failure in winning a response parallels their success and failure in war. The symmetry of these relationships, emphasized in the successive focus on them, contributes to the calculated remoteness from the conditions of observed life and to the stately formality of the play. In all this, Dryden's foreign models are perhaps French rather than Spanish. The balanced patterns of his action as well as the courtly code of his characters are anticipated in the French romances.

Yet there are structural resemblances to *El príncipe constante* that are worth examining as clues to rhetorical ideals that Dryden and Calderón shared. Written nearly forty years after Calderón's play and only a few months before a draft of the essay *Of Dramatick Poesie, The Indian Emperour* reveals a preoccupation with neoclassical theory that is foreign to *El príncipe constante*. Unlike Calderón, Dryden observes, at least loosely, the unities of time and place, though they force him to some palpable improbabilities; [44] and again unlike Calderón, he excludes comic characters and prominent characters of inferior social station. Still, these matters are superficial, the result of formal conventions that had as one of their objectives the achievement of clarity and intensity in theme and mood. If we look beyond neoclassical conventions to the objectives they were intended to serve, we may see the results in *El príncipe constante* of similar rhetorical ideals. Writing in a later generation and under the influence of French formalist critics, Dryden extended and made emphatic structural principles observed by Calderón.

The history of Spanish drama in the seventeenth century reveals a movement toward greater orderliness of structure and more clearly established thematic unity,[45] a movement that can be illustrated in the work of Calderón. As a means to the study of "The Dramatic Craftsmanship of Calderón," Albert E. Sloman has examined the use the dramatist made of his sources, in *El príncipe constante* as well as in seven other of his best plays.[46] Calderón appropriated the work of other dramatists freely, concerning himself rather with what he could make of earlier plays than with considerations of originality. What Dryden said of Ben Jonson, that he "invades authors like a monarch," [47] is also applicable to him. Calderón's attitude toward earlier Spanish drama as a source for his own work was not unlike Dryden's attitude toward English Renaissance drama, though with the distinction that Calderón's changes for the sake of orderliness, clarity, and emphasis were in fact improvements whereas Dryden's sometimes were not.

Calderon's source play for *El príncipe constante* was *La fortuna adversa,* a dramatization, apparently written in the last half-dozen years of the sixteenth century, of a biography of Prince Ferdinand, Hieronymo Román's *Historia y vida del religioso Infante don Fernando.*[48] The author of the play followed the biography closely, including most of the historical episodes that appear in *El príncipe constante* and a number of others as well. Unlike Calderón's play, the earlier one opens in Portugal, and it proceeds with rapid transi-

44. Cf. Dryden, *Works,* 9 : 299.
45. A. A. Parker, "New Definition of 'Baroque' Drama," pp. 150–51.
46. Albert E. Sloman, *The Dramatic Craftsmanship of Calderón* (Oxford, 1958).
47. *Of Dramatick Poesie,* in *Essays,* 1 : 82.
48. Sloman, *Dramatic Craftsmanship of Calderón,* p. 189.

tions in time and place not unlike those of contemporary chronicle plays in England. In the number of its characters, thirty-six, it differs from *El príncipe constante,* in which there are only fourteen characters in all, and only nine important ones.[49] The reduction in the number of characters and of episodes is accompanied by more emphatic thematic emphasis, embodied in the moral fortitude of Fernando. The crucial events become moral decisions by Fernando: his rejection of the Portuguese king's offer to surrender Ceuta, his reinforcement of Muley's reluctance to betray his own king, his defiance of the king of Fez and Fénix even as death approaches. Other events and other characters serve to interpret those decisions.

Taking merely as a working hypothesis the assumption that Dryden based his play upon Calderón's, we may attempt briefly the kind of structural comparison of the later play with the earlier that Sloman has provided in more detail for the Spanish. *El príncipe constante* is a better play than *La fortuna adversa; The Indian Emperour* is so different from *El príncipe constante* as scarcely to admit a qualitative comparison, but if one must be made, Dryden's play is inferior, inferior as well as different. It is not a tragedy in the specialized sense of Calderón's play,[50] or even in the usual English seventeenth-century sense, but a heroic play. Yet Dryden, like Calderón before him, subordinates action to moral evaluation. It is in fact arguable that his play suffers in comparison with Calderón's because of the greater emphasis in *The Indian Emperour* on moral tests and moral comparisons.

We have not one embodiment of constancy but two: Montezuma and Cortes, the one, in the fifth act at least, a strong-hearted rationalist, the latter a magnanimous Christian knight. Emphasis shifts in the course of the play from the moral quality of Cortes to that of Montezuma, as the two heroes in turn display their fortitude in adversity.[51] The audacity of Cortes's expedition lends grandeur to his character, and his conduct in love, as in war, reveals his magnanimity. Montezuma's moral force does not become fully apparent until he has been defeated and captured. Great in adversity, the humiliated but courageous leader of a dying empire, he resembles charac-

49. Ibid., p. 211.
50. Cf. Arnold G. Reichenberger, "Calderón's *El príncipe constante,* a Tragedy?" in *Critical Essays on the Theatre of Calderón,* ed. Wardropper, pp. 161–63.
51. Cf. Shergold and Ure, "Dryden and Calderón," p. 381.

ters in several of Dryden's later plays—Boabdelin, the Moorish king in *The Conquest of Granada,* for example, and Cleopatra in *All for Love.*[52] Then he is as steadfast as Calderón's Fernando.

The climactic scenes in which Montezuma and Fernando confront their adversaries reveal similarities of structure and even of moral values amid the abiding English and Spanish differences in religion. Consider the final meeting between Fernando and the king of Fez. Crippled and wasted by illness and hunger, Fernando has been reduced to begging in the streets to sustain himself. He acknowledges the resemblance between himself and the biblical Job, even while he distinguishes between Job's malediction of the day he was born and his own pious acceptance of the will of God. He epitomizes Christian humility as well as constancy, accepting willingly the symbols of his servitude; and with the Christian discrimination between the things that are Caesar's and those that are God's, he acknowledges the mastery of the king of Fez, praising the august rank of kingship. Carefully and defiantly, he differentiates his obligation to his worldly master from his transcendent obligation to God (act 3). Christian humility and Christian defiance constitute his final victory, and his martyr's death soon follows.

Fernando's confrontation with the king of Fez represents a culmination of qualities he had exhibited throughout the play. Not so Montezuma's defiant confrontation, while undergoing torture on the rack, with Pizarro and a Christian priest. Yet the episode represents an emphatic return to the theme of constancy, earlier conveyed by other characters. Montezuma, compelled to sustain, not Job-like misery and humiliation, but the most intense and active pain, responds to his torturers (act 5, scene 2) with an argument not unlike Fernando's reply to the king of Fez:

> *Christian Priest:* Those Pains, O Prince, thou
>   sufferest now are light
> Compar'd to those, which when thy Soul takes flight,
> Immortal, endless, thou must then endure:
> Which Death begins, and Time can never cure.
> *Montezuma:* Thou art deceiv'd: for whensoe're I Dye,

52. R. J. Kaufman, "On the Poetics of Terminal Tragedy: Dryden's *All for Love,*" in *Dryden: A Collection of Critical Essays,* ed. Bernard N. Schilling (Englewood Cliffs, N. J., 1963), p. 89.

The Sun my Father bears my Soul on high:
He lets me down a Beam, and mounted there,
He draws it back, and pulls me through the Air:
I in the Eastern parts, and rising Sky,
You in Heaven's downfal, and the West must lye.

(Could Dryden's use of the image of the personified sun derive from a memory of Fernando's reference to his faith, in his defiance of the king of Fez, as "el sol que me alumbra" and as "la luz que me guía"? Not necessarily, for Dryden would have known of sun-worship as an aspect of the Aztec religion.) In response to further goading by the Christian priest, Montezuma replies with a succinct statement of "natural religion," rejecting the hypocritical Catholicism exemplified by Pizarro. Although the Indian high priest who shares his torture succumbs, Montezuma survives and is soon rescued by Cortes, who after denouncing Pizarro *"kneels by* Montezuma *and weeps."*

All this is likely to seem an abrupt intrusion of conventional anti-Catholic feeling. Yet Montezuma's conduct in this situation in which he is tested to the utmost represents an example of personal fortitude, a quality celebrated throughout the play. Dryden's scene is more emphatic than the parallel one in the Spanish. This is the most extreme case in which he has simplified and clarified an episode beyond the point that Calderón took a corresponding one, but there are other aspects of *The Indian Emperour* that illustrate a similar process of intensification.

Consider Dryden's use of Pizarro in comparison with Calderón's use of Enrique (Henry the Navigator). Both characters, historical figures placed in situations that are not historical, provide contrast for the protagonists. Calderón has reduced the stature of Enrique, who represents time-serving expediency, even as he has amplified that of Fernando, his brother, who represents an other-worldly refusal to compromise. Dryden has heightened the character of Cortes while darkening that of Pizarro, whose name would in any event have called to the minds of audiences, stories of Spanish atrocity in Peru.

Cydaria and Fénix are not historical figures, and their roles differ, and yet there are parallels between them. Each is the daughter of the non-Christian sovereign, and each is a beautiful young woman whose attractions tempt the protagonist to a betrayal of his duty. Dryden is the clearer and more emphatic in handling the relationship. Cortes recognizes that his love is a complication in his military campaign, and so does everyone else. Fernando represses his love and finally, in his last meeting with Fénix, overcomes it, but his love has been an obstacle in his progress toward martyrdom. The garden scene (act 2), Spitzer explained, is an approximation to a love scene. Alluding to the more overt love scene in the source play, he referred to this one as "merely glimpsed on the horizon at the moment when fate has already spoken and the Christian knight must follow his true vocation." [53] The much later meeting between Fernando and Fénix, when she is repelled by his loathesome appearance and stench, acquires a subtle dimension of irony, as does his disdainful rejection of her (act 3). The temptation of her beauty is Fernando's final test.

Dryden's elaboration on themes that have less emphatic parallels in Calderón appears in his treatment of Guyomar, an Indian equivalent of the "sentimental Moor," whose nobility is elucidated by means of a contrasting character, Odmar, his older brother and rival for the love of Alibech. Muley, the parallel character in *El príncipe constante,* acts largely in isolation from other Moorish knights; there are no contrasts to interpret the quality of his chivalry, nor is his relationship with Fénix given prominence comparable to that of Guyomar's with Alibech. Alibech serves not only as the prize to be won for valor but as commentator on and evaluator of the degrees of meritorious service, as when (act 3, scene 1), after the first battle of Mexicans and Spaniards, she is called on to discriminate between the conduct of Guyomar, who fought until captured, and that of Odmar, who fought only until retreat became necessary to escape captivity. She renders tentative judgment in favor of Guyomar but refuses to make a final decision in the midst of an unresolved war. Subsequent events prove that her judgment, which is reinforced by spontaneous preference, is the just one: Guyomar remains resolutely committed to his obligation and Odmar grows progressively more self-serving.

One of the most elusive of the affinities between *The Indian Emperour* and *El príncipe constante* lies in their dramatic verse. In this instance, the affinities could in the nature of things owe little to direct borrowing. Conceivably, Dryden could have taken from the

53. Spitzer, "Figure of Fénix," p. 154.

Spanish play ideas for images and even for the rhetorical strategy of extended passages, as in the description of the first sighting of distant ships at sea; but he plainly wrote in a tradition of English dramatic verse, as Calderón had written earlier in a tradition of Spanish dramatic verse. Yet there are resemblances that repay examination.

The declamatory quality of the dialogue in the heroic play, the semioperatic conception of dramatic language, contributes to the similarity between *The Indian Emperour* and *El príncipe constante.* In the heroic play there is a closer approach to the long Spanish monologue than in any other dramatic form of the Restoration; and the amplitude of statement permitted by the extended speeches encourages an elaboration of metaphor resembling that common in the comedia.

Dryden did not comment on the Spanish conventions of dialogue. But in *Of Dramatick Poesie* he wrote about the French dramatists' fondness for extended declamations, and his remarks have an application, even if not intended, to the comedia. To be sure, the conversational structure of the essay must be taken into account: in offering rebuttal to Lisideius's praise of the French dramatists, Neander is more critical of them than we should assume Dryden himself was. Still, the specifics of Neander's argument merit attention. The verses of the French, he says,

> are to me the coldest I have ever read. Neither, indeed, is it possible for them, in the way they take, so to express passion, as that the effects of it should appear in the concernment of an audience, their speeches being so many declamations, which tire us with the length; so that instead of persuading us to grieve for their imaginary heroes, we are concerned for our own trouble, as we are in the tedious visits of bad company; we are in pain till they are gone.
>
> . . . .
>
> But to speak generally: it cannot be denied that short speeches and replies are more apt to move the passions and beget concernment in us, than the other; for it is unnatural for any one in a gust of passion to speak long together, or for another in the same condition to suffer him, without interruption.[54]

54. *Essays,* 1 : 71–72.

There is more at issue in Dryden's remarks than the relative merits of long and short speeches: specifically, the contrast between concentration on a single tragic mood, on the French side, and a variation of mood, on the English side. In this aspect the Spanish would resemble the English more than the French. But Neander gives two reasons for the English objection to the long speech that apply to the Spanish as well as the French: first, they are tedious and, second, they are "unnatural" because they are unlike conversation. Dryden elsewhere rejected the argument that dramatic dialogue should approximate conversation,[55] but he was consistently pragmatic in his appeal to audience taste. He was no doubt right that English audiences—owing to the conventions of their stage—found long speeches intolerable. As noted in previous chapters, English dramatists, even when writing adaptations of the comedia so close as to be free translations, broke up the speeches of the originals with conversational exchanges.

In *The Indian Emperour* Dryden made perhaps his closest approach to the Spanish—and French—conventions of dialogue. But consistent with the opinion expressed in *Of Dramatick Poesie,* he stopped far short of the length customary in Calderón. Guyomar's extended description of Cortes's landing, for example, is twice interrupted by questions, which help to preserve the illusion of conversational exchange. Muley's corresponding description, although it is much longer than Guyomar's, is not interrupted. Still, Dryden in this instance, like Calderón, foregoes the dynamic interrelationships of characters to develop a detailed rendering of a visual phenomenon; and thus the effect is that of a set speech.

Dryden's willingness to suspend dramatic movement in order to elaborate a description or narration often reminds us of the comedia. The heroic play is not a dramatic form that encourages the depiction of sensitive and subtle interrelationships between characters. Dryden had other objectives in view. This suspension of dramatic movement for the sake of a long speech is not damaging in his heroic plays because of the emphasis on the ornamental and ceremonial. Guyomar's report of the landing of the Spanish ships interrupts a scene the narrative business of which is a succession of proposals of marriage; and

55. Notably, in his debate with Sir Robert Howard about rhyme in serious drama. See Dryden, *Works,* 9 : 303–05.

after the report, and a brief exchange between Montezuma and the high priest about its meaning, the courtships resume.

The rhymed verse, very regular heroic couplets in this play,[56] contributes to a disjunction between successive speeches, to an emphasis on the speeches in isolation rather than in their relationships with what other characters have said. The emotions of characters in heroic plays, though fully analyzed, are more private, less social, than in most other forms of English drama: characters are more self-consciously aware of conflicts within their own minds than intuitive of the thoughts of persons surrounding them. A corollary of their isolation is their ethical intensity. Dryden's Neander in *Of Dramatick Poesie,* defending the use of rhyme, acknowledges that, as in all forms of drama, the objective is the imitation of nature. But he adds the important qualification that in the serious play " 'tis Nature wrought up to an higher pitch. The plot, the characters, the wit, the passions, the descriptions, are all exalted above the level of common converse, as high as the imagination of the poet can carry them, with proportion to verisimility." [57] Rhyme as well as other means of providing intensification and ornamentation, such as extended metaphor, were needed to achieve the objective, and for the resources of rhetoric to be exploited fully, extended speeches were necessary.

Only a short time before Dryden wrote Neander's observation that descriptions, among other aspects of serious drama, are "exalted above the level of common converse," he had written Guyomar's description of the Spanish ships (act 1, scene 2):

> The object I could first distinctly view
> Was tall straight trees which on the waters flew,
> Wings on their sides instead of leaves did grow,
> Which gather'd all the breath the winds could blow.
> And at their roots grew floating Palaces,
> Whose out-bow'd bellies cut the yielding Seas.

This has psychological verisimilitude in that the Indian, never having seen ships before, uses familiar referents in his metaphorical description; and it gains emotional intensity from his understandable awe. Perhaps in writing this Dryden had Calderón's parallel

56. Mark Van Doren, *The Poetry of John Dryden* (New York, 1920), pp. 110–11.
57. *Essays,* 1 : 100–01.

passage before him. He would have removed the mythological allusion as inappropriate to an Indian, adopted as appropriate the image of the sails as wings, and introduced the uncertainty that only an aboriginal would experience. Whether this happened or not, the fact that he could introduce an extended and extravagant, though successful, metaphorical description turned on his theory of the heroic play.

Apart from the descriptive passages about ships at sea, the affinities in the texture of dialogue in *El príncipe constante* and *The Indian Emperour* are scarcely very close. Yet there are generalized resemblances in the stately dramatic poetry of the two plays: for example, in the ceremonial proposals of marriage.[58] In both plays the proposals are preceded by passages that serve lyrical rather than expository functions. In Calderón, a group of captives is asked to sing in order that their sad music may divert Fénix while she dresses; and when she comes on stage with her maids she explains, in a strikingly beautiful passage in which she evokes the rival charms of a garden and the sea, the imperviousness of her melancholy to her surroundings. Then her father comes, bringing a portrait of Prince Tarudante as a symbol of the prince's proposal to her. Only when her father urges Tarudante's claim does she discover, in her love for Muley, the cause of her unhappiness.

Dryden's scene opens in an Aztec temple, with priests describing the morning's worship, which included the sacrifice of five hundred captives. Montezuma enters with his train, as the high priest announces in a chant the emperor's intention to choose a wife. Montezuma makes his choice known symbolically, as after circling the ladies he *"at length stays at* Almeria *and bows."* Then she, in an aside, like Fénix in the other play, expresses displeasure—in Almeria's case because of resentment for injuries her mother had suffered from Montezuma. Immediately after the royal proposal in both plays, the messenger arrives with the alarming news that a foreign military expedition has landed. In Dryden though not in Calderón other proposals follow: Orbellan's to Cydaria and Odmar's and Guyomar's, in competition, to Alibech. The episodic parallels in the two plays are accompanied, it will be noted, by parallels in the sequence of moods, as the sadness evoked by the fate of captives gives way to a ceremonial courtship of an unreceptive princess, which

58. Cf. Shergold and Ure, "Dryden and Calderón," pp. 378–79.

is interrupted by alarming news of military danger. The scenes in both plays exemplify formalized drama of courtly behavior, drawing force from emblematic action and lyrical commentary. Certainly the two dramatists shared a pervasive literary culture, whether or not Dryden borrowed from Calderón in *The Indian Emperour.*

I am aware that I have not solved the enigma presented by the striking resemblances between these two plays, on the one hand, and, on the other hand, the difficulties involved in believing that the later is based on the earlier. I would surmise, in fact, that my detailed discussion of the resemblances between the two plays might seem to have strengthened the argument advanced by Shergold and Ure, to which I have attempted rebuttal. If so, I have no regrets: the subject is too subtle, and if we care about literary history too important, for the scoring of debater's points to have significance. I remain unconvinced of Dryden's specific indebtedness, for the reasons I have stated, as well as for reasons that will emerge in the following chapter. This treats of Dryden's extensive debt to French fiction and drama, much of it based on Spanish sources, which share literary patterns and codes of conduct with Spanish fiction and drama of the Golden Age. Literary culture in the middle years of the seventeenth century was indeed international. And there are few more striking proofs that it was international than the resemblances, however they came about, between Dryden's play celebrating epic achievement in exploration and conquest, and Calderón's play celebrating a Catholic prince's progress toward martyrdom.[59]

59. The resemblances are perhaps analogous to those between Davenant and Dryden's adaptation of *The Tempest* and Calderón's *En esta vida todo es verdad y todo mentira.* Hermann Grimm (*Fünfzehn Essays,* Berlin, 1875, pp. 183–224), who first noted the resemblances—of character, episode, and theme—argued that Davenant and Dryden had borrowed from the Spanish. Although his argument is not now accepted, the qualities common to the plays are indeed impressive. Maximillian E. Novak (Dryden, *Works,* 10 : 331 n.) refers to the plays as providing the subject of "what might be a fascinating exercise in archetypal criticism or the study of the influence of the seventeenth-century *Weltanschauung* on writers in England and Spain." Novak remarks that Calderón's play has all of his "preoccupation with illusion and reality, which finds its best English equivalent in Shakespeare's *The Tempest,* and contains a magician to raise a storm, a prince returned to his throne after being brought up as a wild man, and even a duel between Heraclio and Leonido to parallel that between Hippolito and Ferdinand."

VII: AN INTERNATIONAL LITERARY CULTURE
Dryden's Plays about the Moors and Their Continental Sources and Analogues

FEW subjects to which Dryden turned had such extensive antecedents in Spanish and French literature as the wars of the Hispanic peoples against the Moors. Corneille's *Le Cid* provides a classic illustration of the power of the subject in French drama. *Le Cid* derives from Castro's *Las mocedades del Cid,* based in turn on ballads celebrating the medieval defender of the Spanish Christians. In Spanish and French prose fiction the subject was even more popular than in drama. Ginés Pérez de Hita's historical novel *Guerras civiles de Granada* (1595, 1619) was so widely imitated in seventeenth-century France as to establish a subgenre of the French romance.[1] Dryden had read some of the dramatic and fictional renderings of the subject, and he had a firm grasp of the "*ground work the History afforded.*"[2] *The Conquest of Granada* and *Don Sebastian* are permeated with borrowings from or analogues to the Continental novels and plays, as well as with passages that are dramatizations of history.

Neither of Dryden's plays has a known source in the comedia. Yet both of them bear strong resemblances to Spanish plays: *The Conquest of Granada* to *Las mocedades del Cid,* and *Don Sebastian* to *El príncipe constante.* If Dryden used Calderón's play for *The Indian Emperour,* then it acquires special relevance for his own tragedy

1. For a bibliography of the editions and translations of Pérez de Hita's work, and for a discussion of its popularity in France, see the introductions by Paula Blanchard-Demouge to her edition of part 1 (Madrid, 1913) and of part 2 (Madrid, 1915).

2. The phrase is Dryden's: Preface to *Don Sebastian.*

about a constant Portuguese prince in Moorish captivity in North Africa. This must remain hypothetical. But the existence of common themes, ideals of conduct, and plot situations in the English and Spanish plays about the wars against the Moors is not hypothetical. Dryden drew from a reservoir of literary strategies and episodes that had served the Spanish and French dramatists and novelists. His plays about the Moors provide firm evidence of his participation in an international literary culture.

Dryden's two plays are very different from one another, their similarities of subject notwithstanding. Much more of the exoticism of romance appears in *The Conquest of Granada,* a play in which, as in Pérez de Hita, Moors rather than Christians appear as the principal characters. Almanzor pursues an epic course of heroic adventure like the Cid of Castro's play; but not until the closing scenes, when he learns his true descent from a Christian nobleman, does he ally himself with the Spaniards. The later play celebrates Catholic piety. Don Sebastian proves himself by a devotion to his religion and by a passive fortitude in opposition to the Moors. The somber subject inhibits an expansive depiction of Moorish customs. Don Sebastian is magnanimous in defeat; Almanzor is audacious in success—the one a tragic, the other an epic, hero. The fates of these two protagonists indicate the historical themes of the plays: the failure of the effort to establish Christianity in North Africa; the success of the reconquest of all Spain.

The pattern of organization of both parts of *The Conquest of Granada* resembles that of the medieval epic of the Cid in the prominence given to episodes illustrating the courage, prowess, and magnanimity of the hero. "The most striking resemblance to the epic," B. J. Pendlebury writes, "is the unity given to 'The Conquest of Granada' by the dominating figure of Almanzor. The play is not the study of a tragic conflict, but a representation of a triumphant career." [3] Dryden provides a chronicle of Almanzor's military career, first on the side of the Moors and finally in the service of King Ferdinand. Here is the Moorish Spain of the literary imagination, a setting

3. B. J. Pendlebury, *Dryden's Heroic Plays: A Study of the Origins* (London, 1923), p. 99. Quoted by Cecil V. Deane, *Dramatic Theory and the Rhymed Heroic Play* (London, 1931), p. 7.

that helps to disguise implausibilities of characterization and action.

As in plays of Lope such as *El remedio en la desdicha,* quarrels between rival factions of Moors complicate the plot. Royal pomp, both Moorish and Spanish, provides ceremonial. The first scene includes an account of a bullfight (from horseback, as was customary in the Spain of Dryden's day) [4] in which Almanzor, then of unknown origin, distinguished himself; and subsequent scenes show him winning spectacular victories. Yet there is more dramatized history in *The Conquest of Granada* than may at first appear (see below, pp. 221–26); accurate accounts of Ferdinand and Isabella's campaign provide a framework for the narrative line, which is fictional.

Dryden himself described the resemblance between Almanzor and the heroes of epic. I have referred more specifically to the resemblance between Almanzor and the legendary Cid. It will be useful to look for possible connections between *The Conquest of Granada* and the body of literature surrounding the Cid.

Describing in his preface the origins of the heroic play, Dryden refers to Davenant's *The Siege of Rhodes* as the first exemplar of the form; and reviewing the literary background of that play, he writes that Davenant "heightened his characters (as I may probably imagine) from the example of Corneille and some French Poets." [5] Probably he had in mind Corneille's most famous play, *Le Cid.* In *Of Dramatick Poesie* he had referred to it and *Cinna* as "the two best of Corneille's plays." [6]

How much did Dryden know about the Cid, or rather about the literature surrounding him, apart from Corneille's play? He seems not to have known the medieval epic. Yet presumably he knew, at the least, what Corneille said in his *examen* of his own play, including Corneille's liberal acknowledgment of his debt to Guillén de Castro's *Las mocedades del Cid.* In the examen Dryden would have encountered references to Castro's treatment of historical details and an account of the political circumstances responsible for the king of Castile's reluctance to act decisively when confronted with disrespectful or even insubordinate behavior among his feudal barons.

4. Clarendon provides a detailed account of bullfighting in the mid-seventeenth century. *History of the Rebellion,* 12 : 90.

5. *Essays,* 1 : 149.

6. Ibid., p. 83.

In other words, Dryden would have learned from Corneille's collected edition of 1660 that *Le Cid* was closely based on the Spanish play of Guillén de Castro, itself a historical play to some extent limited by historical event.

In earlier editions of *Le Cid,* published between 1648 and 1656, Corneille had provided an extended guide to his Spanish sources. His purpose was defensive—to circumvent the charges of plagiarism that had been directed against him in the *Querelle du Cid* by making a full acknowledgment of his extensive borrowings. He quoted, in the preliminaries to his play, a passage from Mariana's *Historia general de España* summarizing the events dramatized, and he discussed the literary implications of the historical material. "Voilà ce qu'a prêté l'histoire à D. Guillen de Castro," he writes after the quotation in Spanish, "qui a mis ce fameux événement sur le théâtre avant moi." [7] Corneille indicated the passages in his own play which he regarded as closely imitated from Castro by printing them in italics and placing the Spanish passages from which they were taken at the bottom of the page.[8]

Dryden knew the collected edition of Corneille's works published in 1660,[9] which included the examen of *Le Cid* but not the detailed notes to the borrowings from Castro. We do not know that he had seen one of the earlier editions of the play, with the extensive quotations from the Spanish. Yet in view of the great reputation of *Le Cid,* this is not improbable. In any event he knew the French play, which, though more compactly constructed than the Spanish, follows the first of the two parts of Castro's play closely and, like it, dramatizes the historical legend surrounding the youth of the hero.

All this has relevance to *The Conquest of Granada,* I think, a play about the youthful exploits of Almanzor. It is attractive to speculate (and we can merely speculate) that Dryden might have known *Las mocedades del Cid* directly and not merely through *Le Cid.* Like his own play, Castro's is in two parts, loosely and even episodically organized; however, Castro's separate parts, unlike Dryden's, are complete in themselves. Neither the Spanish nor the

7. *Oeuvres,* ed. Ch. Marty-Laveaux, 3 (Paris, 1862) : 80.

8. The Spanish passages are reprinted in the edition of Marty-Laveaux, 3 : 199–207.

9. Lawrence E. Padgett, "Dryden's Edition of Corneille," *Modern Language Notes,* 71 (1956) : 173–74.

English play possesses the structural neatness and emotional intensity of the French. The resemblances between *The Conquest of Granada* and *Las mocedades del Cid* are intensified by their common depiction of Spanish and Moorish hostilities, Dryden focusing on the Moors and Castro on the Spanish. The plays have both dramaturgical and thematic similarities of detail.

Leaving aside the insoluble problems concerning Dryden's reading in preparation for *The Conquest of Granada,* it is profitable to look at the similarities between his play, and Corneille's and Castro's. More than the French, the Spanish and the English plays rely rather on the exploits of the hero than on a single, sustained conflict of emotion and will as organizing principle. Corneille is defensive with good reason, in his examen, about his introduction late in the play, without adequate preparation, of the conflict with the Moors.[10] The Spanish and English plays approximate more closely the movement of epic than does the French. "Where epic and tragedy essentially differ, apart from the fact of performance," Clifford Leech has written, "is that in epic we have 'tragic moments' in a context which is characterized by amplitude and variety rather than concentration and crisis."[11] Corneille has "concentration and crisis"; Castro and Dryden "amplitude and variety." Castro was writing about the medieval hero of his own country, basing his episodes on folk ballads celebrating the Cid. His obligation to the revered memory of a legendary figure required the inclusion of episodes having little relevance to the central relationship between the Cid and Ximena.

An extended passage in the third act of part 1, for example, dramatizes the Cid's compassionate treatment of an abandoned leper—who miraculously turns out to be St. Lazarus.[12] Although it does not advance the action, the episode is functional in illustrating an aspect of the hero's character that is neglected by Corneille: his Christian piety, humility, and charity. The Cid's relationship with Ximena provides an organizing framework for the first of the two parts of the play, to be sure, and in act 1 the complexities of the relationship are presented swiftly and with little interruption;[13] but not so in acts 2

10. Marty-Laveaux, ed., *Oeuvres,* 3 : 98.
11. Clifford Leech, *Tragedy* (London, 1969), p. 30.
12. J. B. Segall, *Corneille and the Spanish Drama* (New York, 1902), pp. 45–50.
13. Ibid., pp. 38–39.

and 3, as dynastic problems to be treated in the second part of the play are introduced, some of them having little apparent relevance to the fortunes of the Cid, whose triumphant course, culminating in his winning of Ximena, remains the center of interest.

Dryden's preface to *The Conquest of Granada* offers justification for the episodic structure of his play as well as for the extraordinary prowess of his hero Almanzor. Although Dryden does not refer to the Cid in the preface, the conception of dramatic epic he elaborates has appropriateness to *Las mocedades del Cid* as well as to *The Conquest of Granada,* both of them plays depicting dynastic rivalries and acts of insubordination in plots primarily concerned with the military career of the hero and his troubled fortunes in love. The similarity in the literary strategies of the plays, extending to such details as admiring descriptions of the strength and courage of the two heroes, can be referred to the similarity in the author's conceptions of their task—to the obvious if unstated fact that Castro was dramatizing epic matter and the acknowledged fact that Dryden followed epic models.

In both plays inhibitions arising from a sense of duty impede the hero's courtship of his beloved. Ximena will not accept the Cid, although she loves him, because he killed her father; Almahide will not accept Almanzor, although she loves him, because she is first the betrothed and later the wife of the king of Granada. The Cid achieves success at the expiration of a year; Almanzor is promised success at the expiration of a year of mourning following the death of the king. The "amplitude and variety" of their actions notwithstanding, the Spanish and English plays are controlled by a code of honor resembling that of Corneille.

Corneille's *Le Cid,* much more tightly constructed than either *Las mocedades del Cid* or *The Conquest of Granada,* focuses on the single tragic conflict deriving from the Cid's obligation to kill the father of his beloved in order to avenge an insult to his own father. Although it follows the Spanish play closely, *Le Cid,* as Corneille justly claimed, is altogether his own. It is not a chronicle play or a celebration of a national hero but a love tragedy (or *tragi-comédie,* as he first called it), intense and poignant, distinct from *Las mocedades del Cid* in its emotional quality as in its avoidance of digression. And yet, as Octave Nadal has explained in a passage that merits quotation, the French play retains the ethos of the Spanish. Nadal makes no reference to Dryden or to English drama, but much of what he says about *Le Cid* could be extended, with minor modification, to *The Conquest of Granada.* "A demi-plongée dans l'épopée de la Castille médiévale," Nadal writes about *Le Cid,*

> elle en rapelle les coutumes, les modes de penser, de sentir et même de s'exprimer. Le soin qu'apporta Corneille à adoucir l'âpreté des modèles espagnols ne suffit pas, fort heureusement, à retirer tout à fait du *Cid* certaines couleurs naïves et brutales. Il y a plus: Corneille et toute son époque si sensible à l'honneur ne pouvaient que se reconnaître dans l'oeuvre exemplaire de Castro. En particulier ils devaient ensaisir la solidité harmonieuse de toutes les parties en ce qui concern les rapports entre personnes fondés sur les notions de générosité, d'honneur et de gloire. Ils s'appuyaient eux aussi sur les mêmes valeurs.[14]

If it would be hazardous to say that the court society of the Restoration also accepted "les mêmes valeurs," we can at least say that Dryden based his heroic plays on an approximation to them.

Corneille's abridgment of Castro's title is appropriate to the French play, in which the Cid appears less as a newly dubbed knight who must prove himself than as a mature man. If his exploits against the Moors, described in the French rather than depicted, remain an important determinant of the king's esteem for him, they receive far less attention than in Castro. On the other hand, the dialectic of love and honor, the analysis of the emotional conflict precipitated by the Cid's revenge of his father and the intellectual effort to resolve the conflict, receive more emphasis. Dryden shares with Castro the attention to warfare and with Corneille the emphasis on analysis of conflicting obligations.

Apart from the common background of warfare between Spaniards and Moors, it is the thematic preoccupation with the emotional consequences of sharply conflicting affections and obligations that represents the most important quality common to the Spanish, French, and English plays. Already in *Las mocedades del Cid* the tragic dilemma, first of Rodrigo and later of Ximena, is developed—not with unremitting concentration as in the French play, and not with-

14. Octave Nadal, *Le Sentiment de l'amour dans l'oeuvre de Pierre Corneille,* p. 163.

out attention to subsidiary conflicts that are only tangentially relevant to it, but still emphatically developed. The Spaniards of the comedia are famous for punctilious observance of points of honor, and the courtly Spaniards of Castro's play are classic examples of this national preoccupation. Just after Rodrigo learns from his father the terrible obligation that is his, he cries out to a personified "Fortuna" in an agonized soliloquy (act 1). His "santo honor" prevails, of course, and after the duel the same dilemma passes to Ximena, who is as sensitive as he to the code of chivalric honor. When he comes to see her, after having killed her father, and offers her his own dagger so that she in turn may be revenged on him, she absolves him from blame for the duel even while she upbraids him for the impropriety of his visit to her (act 2). Her recognition of the justice of his action notwithstanding, she is impelled by her sense of obligation to her dead father to wreak vengeance on him. The latter part of the play is devoted, not without digression, to her successive stratagems. Castro, unconcerned with the unity of time, could allow the passage of a year to reconcile the conflict between Ximena's love and her duty. Ximena promises herself and her fortune to a knight of suitable rank who can survive a duel with Rodrigo and bring her his head as a trophy. Rodrigo kills her champion and brings *his* head to her on the point of his lance—as well as his own head firmly attached to his body.

Even this brief account of the emotional tensions in *Las mocedades del Cid* will suggest how closely the theme of "love and valour" in *Le Cid* is fashioned after the Spanish. The passages in which first Rodrigo and later Ximena describe their dilemmas have parallels in the French play, and so has, in less sanguinary form, the final turn by which Rodrigue, victorious in a duel, appeases Chimène's demand for revenge. If, as is not unlikely, Dryden knew the Spanish play only through the French intermediary, he would nevertheless have been aware of the dramatic potential of the Spanish point of honor as a blocking force to the natural expression of young love.

The breadth of Dryden's literary culture and the originality of his mind provide sufficient cautions against assuming that any aspect of *The Conquest of Granada,* thematic or stylistic, is closely imitated from *Le Cid,* much less from *Las mocedades del Cid.* Yet it is apparent that he shared with Corneille and Castro an interest in the dialectic of love and honor. Passages from the Spanish play reveal Ximena and Rodrigo expressing, with a logician's concern for distinctions, the nature of their emotional conflicts, and comparable passages in *Le Cid* are well known. Because the pace of the French play is more leisurely than that of the Spanish—the result of the omission of episodes not relevant to the love of Rodrigue and Chimène—there can be more deliberative passages exploring the meaning of decisive events. The English play includes many comparable passages of analysis and interpretation, in Ozmyn's wooing of Benzayda as well as in Almanzor's wooing of Almahide.

The verse of *The Conquest of Granada* recalls that of *Le Cid* in passages of dialectic devoted to the proprieties of courtly behavior. The heroic couplet, like the French alexandrine, encourages by its balanced and antithetical nature the expansive development of paradox and argument. "I bring a claim which does his right remove," Almanzor tells Almahide in trying to win her from Boabdelin by what must appear a specious argument (part 1, act 3), and the strategy of his rhetoric is conditioned by the ease with which the heroic couplet lends itself to antithesis:

> You're his by promise, but you're mine by Love.
> 'Tis all but Ceremony which is past:
> The knots to tie which is to make you fast.
> Fate gave not to *Boabdelin* that pow'r:
> He woo'd you, but as my Ambassadour.

Almahide's analytical response states more justly the relationship between present infatuation and prior obligation:

> Your passion, like a fright suspends my pain:
> It meets, 'ore-powr's, and bears mine back again.
> But, as when tydes against the Current flow,
> The Native stream runs its own course below:
> So, though your griefs possess the upper part,
> My own have deeper Channels in my heart.

—an expansive metaphor in which each of the three couplets turns on an aspect of the opposition between love and duty, the first line describing the claims of passion and the second responding with a reminder of obligation.

Dryden disavowed, in his preface, the French scrupulosity with the point of honor, and yet he did so in a passage which reveals that he had studied French precedent closely, and furthermore had qualified admiration for it. "You see how little these great authors," he wrote, after describing the impetuosity of Homer's Achilles and Tasso's Rinaldo, "did esteem the *point of honour,* so much magnified by the French, and so ridiculously aped by us. They made their heroes men of honour; but so as not to divest them quite of human passions and frailties." He prefers, he insists, the impetuous heroes to those of the French romances: "I shall never subject my characters to the French standard, where love and honour are to be weighed by drachms and scruples." But he adds a major qualification that almost reverses the thrust of his argument: "Yet, where I have designed the patterns of exact virtues, such as in this play are the parts of Almahide, of Ozmyn, and Benzayda, I may safely challenge the best of theirs." [15] In the paragraphs that follow, he offers extenuation for Almanzor's seeming inconstancy in action and extravagance in speech, qualities for which, the argument goes, there is precedent in Homer and Tasso. His care to defend Almanzor from the critics notwithstanding, Dryden's reference to the exemplary nature of Almahide, Ozmyn, and Benzayda reveals that he was far from indifferent to the demands imposed by the chivalric code observed by Corneille—and by Castro.

The latter paragraphs of the preface, after the account of the literary ancestry and development of the heroic play, are a defense of Almanzor—more precisely, a self-defense of Dryden himself against the imputation of having violated decorum in portraying his hero in revolt against a king. More was involved here than literary theory. Just as there had been political overtones in the *Querelle du Cid,*[16] there are political overtones in Dryden's extended justification of Almanzor's conduct. If we recall that the play was first presented only a decade after the Restoration and that the king himself was known to have objected to a minor infringement of the courtesy due a stage monarch,[17] we can understand why Dryden is defensive about the portrayal of a hero who declares independence from a king, even one to whom he does not owe allegiance by birth. "But whence hast thou

15. *Essays,* 1 : 156–57.
16. Paul Bénichou, *Morales du grand siècle,* pp. 83–87.
17. Dryden's preface to *Secret Love* (1668), in *Works,* 9 : 117, 335.

the right to give me death?" Almanzor replies to Boabdelin's order for his execution (part 1, act 1):

> Obey'd as Soveraign by thy Subjects be,
> But know, that I alone am King of me.
> I am as free as Nature first made man
> 'Ere the base Laws of Servitude began
> When wild in woods the noble Savage ran.

Although this is not an expression of authorial judgment, it is the opinion of a hero who, in the distributive justice of the final act, is rewarded with a promise of marriage to the king's widow—all this in a play performed little more than twenty years after Charles II's father had been executed by his rebellious subjects.

The Moorish king of the play is an indecisive figure, in striking contrast with the aggressive Almanzor, on whom the king shows himself dependent. "Boabdelin is represented as an almost psychopathically inept king," Eugene M. Waith has pointed out, ". . . whose weakness encourages not only foreign attack but civil strife."[18] There are parallels, less emphatic to be sure, not only in *Le Cid* but also in *Las mocedades del Cid,* ones that Dryden would have known about through Corneille's comments on the Spanish play. Corneille had described the historical circumstances of royal power during Ferdinand I's reign as an explanation for the king's failure in his own play to have the count arrested; and he had cited the precedent of *Las mocedades del Cid,* referring to Castro's knowledge of the history of his own country. Corneille expresses concern with a problem of decorum similar to that posed in *The Conquest of Granada* by the relationship between Almanzor and Boabdelin. Corneille writes that the king in *Le Cid*

> ne paroît pas assez vigoureuse, en ce qu'il ne fait pas arrêter le Comte après le soufflet donné; et n'envoie pas des gardes à don Diègue et à son fils. Sur quoi on peut considérer que don Fernand étant le premier roi de Castille, et ceux qui en avoient été maîtres auparavant lui n'ayant eu titre que de comtes, il n'étoit peut-être pas assez absolu sur les grand seigneurs de son royaume pour le pouvoir faire. Chez don Guillen de Castro, qui a traité

18. Eugene M. Waith, *The Herculean Hero* (New York, 1962), p. 158.

ce sujet avant moi, et qui devoit mieux connoître que moi quelle etoit l'autorité de ce premier monarque de son pays, le soufflet se donne en sa présence et en celle de deux ministres d'État, qui lui conseillent, après que le Comte s'est retiré fièrement et avec bravade, et que don Diègue a fait la même chose en soupirant, de ne le pousser point à bout, parce qu'il a quantité d'amis dans les Asturies, qui se pourroient révolter, et prendre parti avec les Maures dont son État est environné. Ainsi il se résout d'accommoder l'affaire sans bruit, et recommande le secret à ces deux ministres, qui ont été seuls témoins de l'action. C'est sur cet exemple que je me suis cru bien fondé à le faire agir plus mollement qu'on ne feroit en ce temps-ci, où l'autorité royale est plus absolue.[19]

Corneille's strategy of self-defense turns on two considerations: the historical basis of his play and literary precedent, here *Las mocedades del Cid,* in which the affront to the king's dignity and the seeming indecisiveness of the king's response were more extreme than in *Le Cid.* Dryden's strategy in his preface turns on the same considerations, history and literary precedent: the precedent of Homer's and Tasso's heroes and the history of Granada. Dryden writes that his critics have accused Almanzor of performing impossibilities: "They say, that being a stranger, he appeases two fighting factions, when the authority of their lawful sovereign could not. This is indeed the most improbable of all his actions, but 'tis far from being impossible. Their king had made himself contemptible to his people, as the history of Granada tells us." [20] He does not cite Corneille in this passage, and there is no reason to think he had *Le Cid* in mind when writing it; but he faced a problem not unlike that which Corneille had encountered in the reign of Louis XIII (the uncle of Charles II), and he employed a similar strategy of defense.

Given the complexity of the literary background of *The Conquest of Granada,* emphasized by Dryden in his preface and in a different way twenty years later by Gerard Langbaine in his effort to convict Dryden of plagiarism, we may not profitably look for borrowings from *Las mocedades del Cid* or even from *Le Cid.* Dryden's sources seem in the main to have been prose romances and, to a lesser extent,

19. Marty-Laveaux, ed., *Oeuvres,* 3 : 95–96.
20. *Essays,* 1 : 158.

history, probably Mariana's *Historia general de España.* Yet there are many similarities of detail among the three plays that suggest indebtedness to a common literary tradition. All three, for example, include in a penultimate position what is in effect a trial by combat: specifically, a trial in *The Conquest of Granada* as Almanzor and Ozmyn fight to clear Almahide of false charges of infidelity, and an approximation to a trial in the Spanish and French plays as the Cid faces his final test in a duel with the champion of Ximena-Chimène. It is typical of the greater restraint of the French that, whereas the opponent of Corneille's Cid emerges with his life though he has been defeated, the opponents of Castro's Cid and Dryden's Almanzor are killed.

Again in all three plays the hero, in despair at the seeming loss of his beloved, demands death in her presence: in the French and the Spanish, the Cid in an agonized interview with her after having killed her father, demands death by her own hand; in the English, Almanzor calls on his guards to kill him when Almahide explains that she has purchased his life, after his assault on the king, by promising to marry the king. Dryden also uses the motif in the secondary action (part 1, act 4, scene 2), in which Ozmyn, after having killed the brother of Benzayda, begs for death at her hand. In all three plays the hero wins forgiveness from the king for impetuous acts that infringe on the royal prerogative by valor in battle against the king's enemies. One episode in *The Conquest of Granada,* though it does not have a parallel in the two plays about the Cid, does have one in Calderón's *El príncipe constante*—as well as in Dryden's earlier *The Indian Queen* and *The Indian Emperour*—that in which Almanzor captures and then releases the duke of Arcos. We recall Don Fernando's capture and release of Muley as well as Cortes's of Guyomar, and the reciprocal acts of Muley and Guyomar when positions are reversed (see above). The young Montezuma in *The Indian Queen* (act 1, scene 1) offers freedom to his prisoner Acacis, who a moment later offers to protect Montezuma with his life. The duke of Arcos's expression of admiration for Almanzor (part 2, act 3, scene 3) articulates the generous admiration for magnanimous valor shared by the heroic characters in the dramas of all three countries.

Because *The Conquest of Granada* dramatizes a great event in Spanish history, the climactic event of the seven-century effort to free the country from the Moors, we may profitably look at its Spanish texture. There are more frequent, and more precise, historical allusions than are apparent in a casual reading. Dryden drew extensively on prose fiction for characters and episodes (for what George Saintsbury called "canvass"),[21] but he nevertheless informed himself of the historical events of the conquest.

As always, we must approach an assessment of Dryden's sources with humility, remembering that he had read much more widely in the history and literature of the several preceding centuries than we have and that, furthermore, he had the creative power of genius. Yet if we cannot trace his reading in history, we can look for correspondences between his account of the conquest and that in the most popular history of Spain of his time, Mariana's *Historia general de España*.[22] It is this history, we recall, that Corneille cites in the preliminaries to *Le Cid*. Dryden refers to Mariana a decade after *The Conquest of Granada,* in his preface to *Religio Laici* (1682) and again in his *Vindication of the Duke of Guise* (1683),[23] implying his familiarity with the history. Certainly the work was well known in England at the time. The Restoration sale-catalogs reveal that many private libraries included Mariana in Latin or Spanish. (The first translation into English, by John Stevens, did not come until 1699.) Pepys mentions in his diary, April 28, 1669, that he received a gift of Mariana, specifying that it was in Spanish. The history had the status of a standard work of reference.

Mariana devotes a full book of his history, the twenty-fifth, to an account of the war of ten years' duration that culminated in the capture of Granada. (It will suggest the amplitude of scale in his narration to point out that he devoted only a single chapter of the following book to an acount of the voyages of discovery in America.) Dry-

21. Saintsbury, ed., *John Dryden* (Mermaid Series, 1904), 1 : 22.

22. Dryden could have read Mariana's account of the campaign against Granada in either Latin or Spanish. See footnote 55 below.

23. Scott-Saintsbury, ed. *Works,* 10 : 19. Ibid., 7 : 182–84: "It is Mariana, I think, (but am not certain,) that makes the following relation; and let the noble family of Trimmers read their own fortune in it: 'Don Pedro, King of Castile, surnamed the Cruel, . . .'" (and Dryden continues with an anecdote illustrating the point that neutralists are abominable).

"I have only a dark remembrance of this story, and have not the Spanish author by me, but I think I am not much mistaken in the main of it; and, whether true or false, the counsel given, I am sure, is such, as ought, in common prudence, to be practised against Trimmers, whether the lawful or unlawful cause prevail."

den begins *The Conquest of Granada* not long before the capitulation of the city; but early in the play he introduces, by way of a retrospective conversation, detailed references to early events in the war. The duke of Arcos appears at the Moorish court as an ambassador to urge upon Boabdelin the claims of Ferdinand and Isabel. Boabdelin rejects those claims, arguing that he holds title to his kingdom by force: "from force the noblest title springs". Arcos counters with reference to the humiliating fact that Boabdelin had been captured by the Spaniards (part 1, act 1):

> Since then by force you prove your title true,
> Ours must be just; because we claim from you.
> When with your Father you did joyntly reign,
> Invading with your Moores the South of *Spain*,
> I, who that day the Christians did command,
> Then took; and brought you bound to *Ferdinand*.

In these few lines Dryden alludes to a sequence of events that Mariana describes at length in the early chapters devoted to the war. In chapter 2, "Cómo el rey Albohacen fué echado de Granada," [24] he describes civil turmoil in Granada, arising from resentment of injuries suffered in the war and from discord produced by factions that resulted in the expulsion of King Albohacen and his replacement by his son "Boabdil." Though expelled from Granada, Albohacen retained control of several other cities in the kingdom, and father and son thereafter vied with one another in their attacks on the Spaniards surrounding them. It is this state of affairs to which Dryden refers as Boabdelin's joint rule with his father. In chapter 4, "Que el rey Mahomed Boabdil fué preso," Mariana describes a raid led by Boabdelin that failed. He was captured by the Spaniards and taken to Ferdinand. The duke of Arcos's allusion to all this troubles Boabdelin:

> Ile hear no more; defer what you would say:
> In private wee'l discourse some other day.

But the duke of Arcos continues, describing the conditions under which Boabdelin regained his freedom:

24. My quotations from Mariana are taken from the edition in Biblioteca de Autores Españoles, ed. D. Francisco Pí y Margall (Madrid, 1854; reprinted 1950).

> Sir, you shall hear, however you are loath,
> That, like a perjur'd Prince, you broke your oath.
> To gain your freedom you a Contract sign'd,
> By which your Crown you to my King resign'd.
> From thenceforth as his Vassail holding it,
> And paying tribute, such as he thought fit:
> Contracting, when your Father came to dye,
> To lay aside all marks of Royalty:
> And at *Purchena* privately to live;
> Which, in exchange, King *Ferdinand* did give.

Again, most of the details are found in Mariana. On Ferdinand's order, the historian writes, the captive king was taken to the castle of "Porcuna" (presumably Dryden's "Purchena"), and there in Ferdinand's presence agreed to conditions that made him a subordinate monarch: he promised to pay twelve thousand *escudos* annually in tribute and to attend the Spanish *Cortes* when he was summoned.[25] Mariana, however, does not allude to Boabdil's promise to live privately at Porcuna without the emblems of royalty when his father should die.

When Boabdelin replies to the duke of Arcos that the contract he had made with Ferdinand under duress is void, Arcos recalls the benefits Boabdelin had received from the Spaniards and refers to his rivalry with his uncle for sovereignty in Granada. By the treaty with Ferdinand, Arcos explains, Boabdelin

> had not only freedome then,
> But since had ayd of mony and of men.
> And, when *Granada* for your Uncle held,
> You were by us restor'd, and he expel'd.

Again, the sequence of events is recounted by Mariana. Chapter 6, "Que Abohardil se alzó con el reino de Granada," describes the deposition and murder of King Albohacen by his more vigorous brother. Subsequent chapters refer to the hostilities between uncle and nephew, rival kings of Granada, the nephew having an alliance of sorts with Ferdinand. Early in chapter 15, Mariana describes the

25. Ed. cit., chap. 4, pp. 217–18.

moral problem this alliance presented to the Spanish king in his effort to terminate the war: "Una dificultad muy grande impedía sus intentos; esta era que demás de la fortaleza de la ciudad de Granada guarnecida, municionada y bastecida asaz, tenía empeñada su palabra en que prometió los años pasados al rey Boabdil que él y todos los suyos no recibirían agravio ni daño alguno." [26] It was civil war in Granada, Mariana explains, which enabled Ferdinand to enter Granada without violation of his treaty obligations. The Moors of the city, disregarding the danger from the Spaniards, took up arms against Boabdil and surrounded him in the Albaicin, threatening to kill him. "No era razón," Mariana writes, "desamparar en aquel peligro aquel Príncipe confederado, mayormente que él mismo pedía le socorriesen." [27] Presumably, it was this request for aid from Boabdil, and Ferdinand's response to it, to which the duke of Arcos referred in charging the Moorish king with ingratitude.

At approximately this point in the sequence of historical events, as Mariana narrates them, Dryden's play begins, in a first act devoted, apart from the fictional exploits of Almanzor, to the depiction first of civil discord and then of the embassy of the duke of Arcos. Mariana refers to just such an embassy: "Junto con esto el rey don Fernando envió á avisar los ciudadanos de Granada que si, dejadas las armas, quisiesen entregarse, serían tratados de la misma manera que los demás que se le habían rendido." [28] The result of the proposal, in the history as in the play, was defiant rejection of the Spanish king's claims and a suspension of the factional disputes within Granada in consequence of the now recognized danger from the Spaniards. The leading people of Granada, Mariana writes, explained to their fellow citizens that "un solo reparo les quedaba, que era tener ellos paz entre sí; si la discordia iba adelante, los unos y los otros se perderían. Con esta diligencia se tomó cierto acuerdo y se hizo cierto asiento entre los moros." [29] Just so, we find Dryden's second act opening with a group of Moorish leaders rejoicing in their newfound unity against the Spaniards. Abdalla, King Boabdelin's brother, speaks (part 1, act 2):

26. Ibid., p. 234.
27. Ibid.
28. Ibid., pp. 234–35.
29. Ibid., p. 235.

This happy day does to *Granada* bring
A lasting peace; and triumphs to the King:
The two fierce factions will no longer jarr,
Since they have now been brothers in the war:
Those, who apart in Emulation fought,
The common danger to one body brought;

Abdalla refers to skirmishes with the Spaniards outside the walls of Granada, and again Mariana provides the historical background, with his account, in chapter 15, of raids conducted by the Spaniards on the plain of Granada after the rejection of Ferdinand's proposal for peace. With the renewal of hostilities, the Moors, again under the leadership of King Boabdil (in Mariana's phrase "ya declarado por enemigo de cristianos"),[30] won a minor victory.

Dryden refers to *"the History of* Granada" in his preface, remarking that *"Their King had made himself contemptible to his people";* and indeed Mariana's narrative provides abundant support for the observation. In chapter 17 Boabdil, in order to induce his subjects to accept a surrender already agreed to by representatives of both sides, makes a humiliating confession of his past errors: "Bien confieso haber en muchas cosas errado, en fiarme del enemigo y en alzarme con el reino contra mi padre, pecados que los tengo bien pagados"; [31] and his final humiliation comes in presiding at the capitulation of the city. The sustained impression of him conveyed by the historian is that of a weak opportunist, vulnerable to determined conspirators among his subjects—notably, to a Moor whose mutiny, described at length by Mariana in chapter 17, threatens to prevent compliance with the terms of surrender by arousing the people to new fear of and hostility toward the Spaniards. Dryden's King Boabdelin, himself weak, capricious, and vulnerable to powerful and determined conspirators, follows—at a distance appropriate to the qualified accuracy of poetry—the historical record of the last king of Granada.

The correspondences between Mariana's account of the conquest of Granada and the play testify to Dryden's care for historical detail,

30. Ibid.
31. Ibid., p. 238.

though not beyond doubt to his knowledge of Mariana's history. Probably he had read it, and perhaps he had read other histories.[32] But he could have found many of the details to which I have referred in one or more of the historical novels on the subject. Two of them are of especial importance, Pérez de Hita's *Guerras civiles de Granada,* part 1 (1595), and Georges de Scudéry's *Almahide ou l'esclave reine,* the latter partially based on the former.[33] These two novels would seem to be among Dryden's principal sources for exotic detail, characters' names, episodes, as well as perhaps for some of the history. *Almahide* opens briskly in a manner that will remind us of *The Conquest of Granada:*

> L'on entendoit crier *aux armes* par toute la grande et superbe ville de Grenade: et tout le Peuple sortant en foule des Maisons, excitoit un tumulte si horrible et si confus, qu'il auroit donné de la terreur à l'âme la plus assurrée. . . . Cent Drapeaux flottoient au gré du vent, sur le haut des Murailles du fort et magnifique Chasteau de l'Halambre, Palais des derniers Rois de Grenade.

This is a calculated evocation of mood that is fully, if more subtly, anticipated in the long romance of Pérez de Hita, which is a detailed account of the fall of Granada, "vista por dentro," as the modern editor of the work explains, "en medio de las querellas y discordias de los moros entre sí." [34] In its internal view of the doomed city and focus on the rivalries of the hostile factions that led to its destruction, the Spanish novel anticipates *The Conquest of Granada.*

It would not be profitable, if it were possible, to trace in detail Dryden's borrowings from prose fiction. Langbaine tried to do it in the seventeenth century, Montague Summers in the twentieth.[35] Both men, their querulous tones notwithstanding, provide valuable

32. Langbaine, *Account,* p. 161, includes a list of the relevant general histories.

33. Jerome W. Schweitzer, who believes *Almahide* to have been written by Georges de Scudéry rather than by his sister Madeleine, asserts that "All internal evidence in *Almahide* indicates that Scudéry used *Las Guerras Civiles,* not only as a source for the framework of his own novel and for a few of the romanesque details, but as the pseudo-historical source for the central action as well." *Georges de Scudéry's 'Almahide': Authorship, Analysis, Sources and Structure* (Baltimore, 1939), p. 65.

34. Paula Blanchard-Demouge, ed., *Guerras Civiles de Granada,* pt. 1, p. xxviii.

35. Langbaine, *Account,* pp. 158–61. Dryden, *Dramatic Works,* ed. Montague Summers (London, 1932), 3 : 3–13.

guides to the subject. Langbaine's catalog of Dryden's borrowings in the play is even more extensive than usual for that most diligent of source hunters, and if we make allowance for exaggeration and oversimplification, we find a near contemporary guide to the literary background of the play, supplementary to that provided by Dryden himself in his preface: "I have already hinted, that not only the *Episodes,* and main Plot, but even the Characters are all borrow'd from *French* and *Spanish* Romances, as *Almahide, Grand Cyrus, Ibrahim,* and *Gusman.*" [36]

Langbaine continues with several paragraphs of specifics, tracing Dryden's principal characters and many of his episodes to sources, most of them at least plausible sources, in the romances.[37] His list could be extended by the inclusion of *Guerras civiles de Granada,* which Dryden could have read in Spanish, in editions published in Paris in 1606 and 1660, both of which include many French glosses of Spanish words in the margins, or in a literal French translation of 1608.[38] Summers, if he is needlessly severe in his criticism of Langbaine's account of Dryden's sources, would seem to be correct in a central point: that by failing to cite Pérez de Hita, an inclusive source, Langbaine complicated the source problem with unnecessary references to scattered romances. Yet because the *Guerras civiles* was widely imitated, it is difficult to determine what Dryden drew from it directly and what through intermediaries.[39]

Even more perhaps than the characters and episodes, the tone and texture of *The Conquest of Granada* resemble those of the Spanish and French romances: the emotional heightening and simplification of responses to events, the preoccupation with the ennobling effect of love, the narrowing of awareness to a courtly perception of life. The play, like the romances, is aristocratic and royalist in social and political assumptions—intensely, self-consciously so. For all this there

36. Langbaine, *Account,* p. 158. On Dryden's borrowings, see also Aloys Tüchert, *John Dryden als Dramatiker in seinen Beziehungen zu Madeleine de Scudéry's Romandichtung* (Zweibrücken, 1885), pp. 26–34.

37. Eugene M. Waith traces "several of the circumstances of Almanzor's first appearance" and the primitivism inherent in Dryden's portrayal of him to La Calprenède's *Cléopâtre: The Herculean Hero,* pp. 156–57.

38. Pérez de Hita, *Guerras civiles,* Introduction to pt. 1.

39. Jerome W. Schweitzer, "Dryden's Use of Scudéry's *Almahide,*" *Modern Language Notes* 54 (1939) : 190–92; and Schweitzer, "Another Note on Dryden's use of Georges de Scudéry's *Almahide,*" *Modern Language Notes,* 62 (1947) : 262–63.

is precedent in earlier English drama—in Fletcher, and even more in what has been called the "Pre-Restoration Platonic drama."[40] Dryden knew Fletcher well, and probably he knew many of the Caroline plays. To differentiate in detail what—apart from episodes, characters, and local color—he took from English drama and what from the French and Spanish dramas and romances is an impossible task, one that would probably have been too difficult even for Dryden himself.

He drew on some of the romances, he knew Corneille and acknowledged a debt to him, he knew a good deal of Spanish history, probably from a reading of Mariana. Whether he knew more about Castro's *Las mocedades del Cid* than he would have learned through *Le Cid* and the critical apparatus printed with it cannot be determined. And yet a parallel examination of *The Conquest of Granada* and the Spanish play reveals that in the moral and chivalric values celebrated, in dramatic structure, in the organization of set speeches devoted to the analysis of emotion in conflict with duty, as well as in subjects, they have similarities that are more than casual. Dryden's play is perhaps the finest rendering in English of the famous matter of romance provided by the wars of the Reconquest; and if it is not an imitation of *Las mocedades*—even an imitation at one remove thorugh Corneille—it nevertheless approximates much that is distinctive in Castro's play.

The Conquest of Granada has often seemed a critical enigma.[41] Dryden's first audiences were ambivalent. They laughed at the parody of it in *The Rehearsal,* and yet they continued to attend performances of it. Downes lists it among the most "taking plays" of the King's Company; Langbaine refers to the "great Applause" it attracted.[42] If the rhymed verse cannot now be heard in the theater,

40. Kathleen Lynch, "Conventions of Platonic Drama in the Heroic Plays of Orrery and Dryden," *PMLA* 44 (1929) : 456–71. See also Waith, *The Herculean Hero,* pp. 144–51.

41. Cf. Bruce King: "There is what might be described as the question of *The Conquest of Granada* (1670). The problem that has hung over Dryden criticism for the past century has been: what are we to make of a play in which almost every character, whether admirable, heroic or villainous, speaks in an extravagant fashion? How can we defend a sensibility that produced ten acts of romantic adventures dressed up in rant and bombast?" *Dryden's Major Plays* (Edinburgh and London, 1966), p. 59.

42. Downes, *Roscius Anglicanus,* pp. 14–15. Langbaine, *Account,* p. 157.

a reading of it by skilled actors remains possible; and an experience of such a reading will suggest that Dryden's first audiences had good reason for their applause. Far too considerable to be quietly forgotten, the play simultaneously attracts and repels. It attracts by the virtuosity displayed in heroic tirades and alternately in scenes of tender emotion, as well as by its strong plot line, carefully and even symmetrically organized; and it repels by its bombast and its violation of probability in motive and even possibility in military prowess. Yet much of our uneasiness with the play arises from our failure to perceive Dryden's emphasis on "design": his employment of characters as representatives of emotions and ideas, his construction of a plot that embodies a kind of historical dialectic. Anne T. Barbeau's discussion of the play as a "drama of ideas" would suggest that modern students have projected upon the play critical standards of other eras that are inappropriate to the elucidation of Dryden's intention.[43] Certainly Dryden's contemporary, the wife of John Evelyn, praised the play as "so full of ideas that the most refined romance I ever read is not to compare with it." [44]

Miss Barbeau's study represents a new approach; to some extent it attempts to approximate the original attitudes of Dryden's audiences. Still another approach lies in an insistence on complexity of tone in the play, an insistence in particular on the wit and even calculated self-parody on Dryden's part, in some of the more extravagant passages. This subject has been canvassed by D. W. Jefferson and, more recently and insistently, by Bruce King.[45] It received passing attention a generation after Dryden from Colley Cibber, whose remarks on the character Morat in *Aureng-Zebe* would seem to be applicable to Almanzor in *The Conquest of Granada.* "There are in this fierce Character," Cibber wrote, in criticizing Barton Booth's subdued performance of the role, "so many Sentiments of avow'd Barbarity, Insolence, and Vainglory, that they blaze even to a ludicrous Lustre, and doubtless the Poet intended those to make his

43. Barbeau, *Dryden's Heroic Plays.*

44. Quoted from *British Dramatists from Dryden to Sheridan,* ed. G. H. Nettleton, A. E. Case, and G. W. Stone (Boston, 1969), p. 7.

45. D. W. Jefferson, "The Significance of Dryden's Heroic Plays," *Proceedings of the Leeds Philosophical and Literary Society,* 5 (1940) : 125–39. King, *Dryden's Major Plays.*

Spectators laugh, while they admir'd them."[46] It is attractive to assume that Dryden, in writing the more extravagant tirades of *The Conquest of Granada,* intended to evoke laughter as well as admiration; and within narrow limits the assumption would seem to me to be justified. Yet the preliminaries to the play, Dryden's dedication to the duke of York and his preface, provide a caution, I think, against assuming that Dryden intended a sustained satire on the heroic ideals held by his characters. Dryden calls attention to the appropriateness of dedicating the play to the duke, recalling the duke's own military triumphs when as a young man he fought against an army of Cromwell's in the Netherlands; and this Dryden could scarcely have done had his play been intended and recognized as satire directed against heroic ideals. (Whatever the duke of York's limitations as a politician, he seems to have followed the current plays, and town gossip about them, with some care.)[47] *The Conquest of Granada* would not have been so vulnerable to the criticism in *The Rehearsal* had it included an insistent strain of self-parody.

Still, the fact that the existence of parody or satire can be argued suggests a major difference from *Le Cid* and *Las mocedades del Cid,* a less harmonious assimilation of the ideals of heroic and chivalric

46. Cibber, *Apology,* ed. Robert W. Lowe (London, 1889), 1 : 122–24 (cited by King, *Dryden's Major Plays,* p. 10). Yet Cibber's comments on Addison and Shakespeare in the same paragraph soften the impact of his reference to Dryden: "In Mr. *Addison*'s *Cato, Syphax* has some Sentiments of near the same nature, which I ventur'd to speak as I imagin'd *Kynaston* would have done had he been then living to have stood in the same Character. Mr. *Addison,* who had something of Mr. Booth's Diffidence at the Rehearsal of his Play, after it was acted came into my Opinion, and own'd that even Tragedy on such particular Occasions might admit of a *Laugh* of *Approbation.* In *Shakespear* Instances of them are frequent, as in *Mackbeth, Hotspur, Richard the Third,* and *Harry the Eighth,* all which Characters, tho' of a tragical Cast, have sometimes familiar Strokes in them so highly natural to each particular Disposition, that it is impossible not to be transported into an honest Laughter at them: And these are those happy Liberties which, tho' few Authors are qualify'd to take, yet, when justly taken, may challenge a Place among their greatest Beauties. Now, whether *Dryden,* in his *Morat, feliciter Audet,*—or may be allow'd the Happiness of having hit this Mark, seems not necessary to be determin'd by the Actor, whose Business, sure, is to make the best of his Author's Intention, as in this Part *Kynaston* did, doubtless not without *Dryden*'s Approbation."

This seems to be the only near-contemporary discussion of tone in a heroic play of Dryden's, and it would seem to me, in its entirety, to argue against assuming that Dryden intended a pervasive irony.

47. Pepys describes the duke, for example, as joining in the laughter at Sir Robert Howard when he was caricatured as "Sir Positive At-all" in Shadwell's *The Sullen Lovers* (Diary, May 8, 1668).

conduct than in the Continental plays. It lacks the strength the Spanish play gains from its folk origins—the strength that comes from a dramatization of a nation's ideals of piety as well as of magnanimity, chivalry, and courage.[48] It lacks the intensity and near faultless control of language the French play has. Yet it remains a remarkable English dramatization of medieval Spanish themes similar to those that animate the other two plays.

I have already alluded to the resemblances between *The Indian Emperour* and *Don Sebastian.* Both of them have protagonists who, like Fernando of *El príncipe constante,* are Catholic crusaders, and both of them, again like Calderón's protagonist, endure captivity with fortitude and magnanimity. *Don Sebastian* differs from the earlier English and the Spanish play in departing, after an opening situation, from the pattern of known historical events. Even so, it includes much that can be traced to the historical narratives of the Portuguese king, Don Sebastian, who in 1578 led an army into North Africa to its destruction at the Battle of Alcazar-Kebir.

Dryden's play turns on the assumption that Don Sebastian survived the fatal battle and became a captive of the Moors. In his idealized rendering of the monarch's character, Dryden departs from modern (though not necessarily sixteenth- and seventeenth-century) judgments of him; for the man as revealed by recent historians lacked maturity and discretion and in fact, in his limitations, was a major cause of Portugal's subsequent loss of political independence. Yet in the play—as in Camões's dedication to him of *Os Lusiadas*—he is a Renaissance hero and magnanimous sovereign, embodying the neoclassical principle that a character's personal qualities should be commensurate with his rank.

The historical inaccuracies are, after all, irrelevant to Dryden's accomplishment in the play. Portuguese in its subject, it has an expansiveness and exoticism of episode that are nevertheless compatible with a coherent plot. The setting in North Africa allows him to exploit the picturesque qualities of Moorish civilization, but he does so with more restraint than in *The Conquest of Granada,* and with-

48. For an authoritative discussion of the drama of the Golden Age as an expression of the beliefs of the Spanish nation, see Arnold G. Reichenberger, "The Uniqueness of the *Comedia,*" *Hispanic Review* 27 (1959): 303–16.

out damage to the integrity of his theme—or "moral," to use his own word.[49] Though it is an eventful and very long play, it is, to judge by the standards of *The Conquest of Granada* though not of *All for Love,* unencumbered with extraneous detail. It includes a comic subplot, to be sure, but one brought into functional relationship with the main plot. The play is longer than usual, so long that it required abridgment to be suitable for performance in the theater; [50] and yet it has a clear focus in the fortunes of the captive Portuguese king, who, contrary to historical record, retires finally to a life of religious contemplation in a monastery, as had the historical Emperor Charles V.

Don Sebastian is in important ways different in tone, characterization, and structure, from Dryden's earlier serious plays, the tragedies as well as the heroic plays; and often it is different in a manner reminiscent of Calderón's *El príncipe constante.* If we could assume that he borrowed from Calderón for *The Indian Emperour,* we could plausibly assume that *El príncipe constante* contributed to a distinctive quality of *Don Sebastian:* that is, the severity of it, the reverence shown for self-denial and asceticism. I can find no other direct connection between this play and the comedia. In his preface, although he writes at length and with familiarity of Portuguese history and legend, Dryden does not allude to Spanish drama even when Spanish dramatic practice has relevance to his subject, as in his discussion of the comic scenes. We must, I think, regard the qualities of *Don Sebastian* which seem to be reminiscent of *El príncipe constante* as parallels rather than as generalized borrowings.

Certain of the parallels are apparent. An invading force of Portuguese meets adversity (of differing magnitude in the two plays) in an African campaign against the Moors, and a royal leader is captured. Calderón, not concerned as Dryden is with the unity of time, opens his play before the opposing forces meet, Dryden, after, presenting an account of the calamitous battle retrospectively. In both plays, the focus of dramatic interest is the royal captive, in each in-

49. Cf. the preface: "*This is not a Play that was huddled up in hast; and to shew it was not, I will own, that beside the general Moral of it, which is given in the four last lines, there is also another Moral, couch'd under every one of the principal Parts and Characters, which a judicious Critick will observe, though I point not to it in this Preface.*"

50. The preface to *Don Sebastian.*

stance a dignified and devout Catholic who in the face of Moorish cruelty shows constancy to his faith and a stoical regard for the personal obligation entailed by his rank. In each instance the royal captive is generous to his fellow captives of lesser rank; and in each instance the Moorish sovereign places the royal captive in the custody of a nobleman who has strong obligations to the captive. The subjects of the two plays, both of them impinging on history, enforce a muting of the love relationships and an emphasis on duty.

Before looking more closely at the similarities between *Don Sebastian* and *El príncipe constante,* it will be useful to consider what Dryden tells us and what we can infer about his sources. He is unusually full and circumstantial on the subject in his preface, and for a reason we can surmise. About two years before the play was acted, Gerard Langbaine, in *A New Catalogue of English Plays* (*Momus Triumphans*), had listed at length and with bitterness Dryden's alleged borrowings for his earlier plays. The remarks on sources in the preface to *Don Sebastian* as well as the reasoned distinction between legitimate borrowing and plagiarism would seem to have been written in response to Langbaine. At any rate, Langbaine so interpreted them: in his expanded work, *An Account of the English Dramatick Poets* of 1691, he quotes from Dryden's remarks and offers rebuttal to them.[51] Dryden had reason to be circumspect and accurate in writing his preface just after Langbaine's first assault on him.

"As for the story or plot of the Tragedy, 'tis purely fiction," Dryden writes, "for I take it up where the History has laid it down." And he continues with an exposition of the historical events leading to the battle and its fatal outcome, alluding to the widely circulated reports of the subsequent appearance in Venice of a man resembling Don Sebastian.[52] No doubt Dryden had many sources in history and legend for this summary account. In speculating about his interest in and knowledge of Portuguese history, we must remember that during much of his adult life the queen of England had been a Portuguese princess of the same royal house of Braganza as Don Sebastian, and that she had brought to England a Portuguese retinue.

51. Langbaine, *Account,* pp. 161–63.

52. Several persons claimed to be the lost Don Sebastian. See Miguel Martins D'Antas, *Les Faux Don Sébastien: étude sur l'histoire de Portugal* (Paris, 1866).

Portuguese history had a timely interest, to which Fanshawe's translation of *Os Lusiadas,* with which Dryden was familiar,[53] would have contributed.

If Dryden's sources of historical information were various, the single history of Spain (and Portugal) with which he seems to have been most familiar was, as I have said, Mariana's. If he had not read a substantial part of it by the time he wrote *Don Sebastian,* then he was guilty of deception, and needless deception, in his reference to it in *The Vindication of the Duke of Guise* (1683).[54] In any event, Mariana provides a brief summary of the "ground-work the history afforded" Dryden that will repay quotation.[55] The year 1578 was very unfortunate for Portugal and for all Europe, Mariana writes,

> porque el rey don Sebastian, llevado del fervor de su mocedad y del deseo encendido que tenía de extender en Africa el nombre cristiano, recibió debajo de su amparo al rey Muley. Para la empresa juntó con las fuerzas de su reino gentes de Alemaña, de Italia y de Castilla. Apercibió una gruesa armada, en que con toda su gente, por el mes de julio, se hizo á la vela, y llegó á Arcilla, ciudad sujeta á los portugueses en Africa. Lo primero que pretendía era acometer el castillo de Alarache, que está á la boca del río que hoy se llama Luco, y antiguamente se dijo Liso. Comenzaron los portugueses á marchar por la tierra adentro; salióles el Moluco al encuentro con muy mayor número de gente. Dióse la batalla á 4 de agosto; fueron vencidos los portugueses; la matanza fué grande, los cautivos sin cuento, y entre ellos muchos de los mas nobles que allí iban. Ninguna pelea de muchos años acá se ha visto tan desgraciada; en particular perecieron aquel día tres reyes, el Moluco de enfermedad de que andaba trabajado de días atrás; dejó por sucesor un su hermano, llamado Hamet; el rey de Portugal pereció en la pelea; Muley se ahogó al pasar del río huyendo de los enemigos.[56]

53. Dryden refers to the poem in *The Author's Apology for Heroic Poetry and Poetic Licence* prefixed to *The State of Innocence* (1677). In *Essays,* 1 : 190.

54. *Works,* ed. Scott-Saintsbury, 7 : 182–84.

55. Mariana's work, published in Latin (1592–1605) and in Spanish (1601), includes thirty books, which take the history of Spain and Portugal to the death of King Ferdinand (1516). To subsequent editions there are appended brief recapitulations of the great events of succeeding years, including 1578. These seem to have been published only in Spanish prior to the date of *Don Sebastian.*

56. Mariana, *Historia general de España,* 31 : 401.

Here Dryden could have found an account of Sebastian's fatal expedition, including reference to the rivalry between two claimants to the Moorish throne and Sebastian's alliance with one of them (King Muley, the Muley-Mahomet to whom he refers in his preface). As Mariana explains, both of the Moorish kings perished. Dryden acknowledges in the preface his poetic license in his portrayal of the reigning king as killed in a revolt: *"I have somewhat deviated from the known History, in the death of* Muley-Moluch, *who, by all relations dyed of a feaver in the Battel, before his Army had wholly won the Field."* That Dryden should concern himself to explain such a detail suggests a closer attention to historical sources than we have commonly assumed. His version of the death of the rival king is notably similar to Mariana's, whose account of Muley's drowning as he crossed a river while fleeing from his enemies could have been the source of Benducar's lines in the opening scene of the play (act 1, scene 1):

> The Rival of our threatned Empire, Mahumet,
> Was hot pursued; and in the general rout,
> Mistook a swelling Current for a Foord,

in which, having been thrown from his horse, he was drowned.[57]

Langbaine would seem to have been mistaken in the importance he attributed to Dryden's borrowings from a French novel about Don Sebastian. Dryden mentions the novel in his preface, and in doing so makes passing allusion to Charles II's widow:

> *For what relates to* Almeyda, *her part is wholly fictitious: I know it is the surname of a noble Family in* Portugal, *which was very*

57. Langbaine (*Account,* pp. 162–63) mentions as a historical source for the play, Antonio Vasconcellos's *Anacephalæoses: Id Est, Summa Capita Actorum Regum Lusitaniæ,* a Latin history of the kings of Portugal published in Antwerp in 1621, and Dryden could indeed have found in the twentieth chapter of the work a comprehensive biography of Don Sebastian, including a brief account of the fatal expedition into North Africa. Perhaps he read it, but we may note, if only to point out the limited accuracy of Langbaine, that Vasconcellos's report of the death of one of the Moorish kings differs from what Dryden said on the subject in his preface, and that Vasconcellos omits a detail pertaining to the death of the other Moorish king which Dryden includes. About the reigning king, the Portuguese historian writes, making no allusion to an illness: "Moleimum Abdelmelechum (ut funesta Barbaris esset victoria) pila ferrea deturbavit [p. 322]." About the other king he writes simply that "Mahometum fluminis in trajectu vortex rapidus abripuit [p. 322]," making no reference to the circumstance that he was fleeing from his enemies. These are small details, but they demonstrate that the version of the battle Dryden knew, corresponded to Mariana's rather than to Vasconcellos's.

> *instrumental in the Restoration of* Don John de Braganza, *Father to the most Illustrious and most Pious Princess our Queen* Dowager. *The* French *Author of a Novel, call'd* Don Sebastian, *has given that name to an* Affrican *Lady of his own invention, and makes her Sister to* Muley-Mahumet. *But I have wholly chang'd the accidents, and borrow'd nothing but the supposition, that she was belov'd by the King of* Portugal.

Langbaine rose to the subject, a year after the play was printed, in *An Account of the English Dramatick Poets;* and he predictably implied that Dryden's debt was greater than he had acknowledged: "The Foundation of it [the play] is built upon a French Novel call'd *Don Sebastian.* How far our Author has followed the *French-man,* I leave to the Readers of both to judge." [58] We may indeed judge for ourselves. The French work, "An Historical Novel," had appeared in English translation "by Mr. Ferrand Spence" in 1683,[59] and, as Dryden wrote, the plot of it is very different from his own.

Yet Dryden may have been attracted to the subject by the novel, which, as he acknowledged, provided the name for his character Almeyda and the relationship between her and Don Sebastian's Moorish ally, the deposed King Muley. In the retrospective conversation in the final act of the play (act 5, scene 1), we learn that Almeyda had accompanied her brother Muley to Portugal when Muley, defeated by his kinsman, sought Sebastian's aid in regaining his kingdom. Moved by a desire to assist the exiles as well as by religious fervor, Sebastian undertook the expedition that led to his own and Almeyda's capture and Muley's death. For this action antecedent to the opening of his play, Dryden drew on the French novel, making alterations of detail. However, he did not find precedent in the novel for the kinship between Don Sebastian and Almeyda that leads to catastrophe in the play. In the novel Don Sebastian, after his capture, is sent first to the galleys and then, by the Spaniards, to a prison where he is poisoned. If Dryden, as Langbaine charged, built upon the "Foundation" of the novel, he nevertheless constructed most of the play himself.

He took suggestions for episodes and situations from a number of sources, some of which we can never know. It would seem, as

58. Langbaine, *Account,* pp. 161–62.
59. *Don Sebastian, King of Portugal* (London, 1683).

N. B. Allen has argued, that he borrowed for his comical subplot from *Le Pelerin,* a French novel by Gabriel de Bremond, on which he had earlier drawn for *The Spanish Friar.*[60] And he would perhaps have been aware of resemblances between his subplot and situations in Shakespeare's *The Merchant of Venice* and Middleton and Rowley's *The Changeling.* Like Shylock, the hypocritical Mufti loves both his daughter and his wealth, and his experience with Antonio is not unlike Shylock's with Lorenzo. The subplot also resembles that of Middleton and Rowley in several details, including the use of the same name, Antonio, for characters in parallel roles.[61] Dryden would have known *The Merchant of Venice* and probably *The Changeling* as well, for it was revived on the Restoration stage.[62] On the other hand, there is no reason to believe that he would have known the late sixteenth-century play about Don Sebastian's African campaign, *The Battle of Alcazar,* attributed to George Peele, or that he would have known the brief but striking appearance of Don Sebastian introduced late in Calderón's *A secreto agravio, secreta venganza,* in which the king, full of hope, looks forward to the expedition that was to bring his own and his army's destruction.

The complexity of the literary background of *Don Sebastian*—in earlier English drama, in French fiction, in Portuguese history and legend—provides sufficient caution against an emphasis on what Dryden might have derived from the comedia, even if he had earlier in his career read *El príncipe constante.* Apart from the unprovable possibility that his depiction of Don Sebastian's fortitude and piety in adversity owed something to a recollection of Calderón's Fernando, Dryden's play has no resemblances to *El príncipe constante* that cannot be referred to seventeenth-century literary tradition. Yet the resemblances merit attention for what they reveal about the literary tradition the English and the Spanish shared.

As I have already explained, Dryden's evaluation of the comedia was prejudiced by his application to it of neoclassical criteria, de-

60. Allen, *Sources of Dryden's Comedies,* pp. 125–36; 144–48. Brémond's *Le Pèlerin* was translated into English in 1680, after *The Spanish Friar* but before *Don Sebastian.*

61. I am indebted to David M. Vieth for pointing out to me the resemblances to *The Merchant of Venice,* and to Mrs. Linda Brownrigg for those to *The Changeling.*

62. On the performances of *The Changeling* after the Restoration, see the edition of the play by N. W. Bawcutt (London, 1961), pp. xxviii–xxx.

rived in part from the writings of French formalist critics (see above, pp. 3–16). His earlier tentative and incomplete acceptance of neoclassical doctrines, evident at once in *Of Dramatick Poesie* and his plays, gave way to a more comprehensive though never complete acceptance of them after Thomas Rymer in the 1670s began to publish his critical writings. A consideration of *Don Sebastian* in comparison with *El príncipe constante* must take into account Dryden's neoclassicism —and the opinions of Rymer, to which, in the criticism Dryden published, he was deferential.[63] The fact that *Don Sebastian* bears formal similarities to *El príncipe constante,* Dryden's neoclassicism notwithstanding, reinforces the opinion, expressed by Sloman among others, that despite departures in certain conventions Calderón himself was not uninfluenced by neoclassical theory.[64]

The impact made by Rymer on his contemporaries may be gauged by Dryden's response to him. In a letter written to a nobleman about September 1677, Dryden refers to Rymer's having sent him a copy of the recently published *The Tragedies of the Last Age:* "which has been my best entertainment hitherto: 'tis certainly very learned, and the best piece of criticism in the English tongue; perhaps in any other of the modern." [65] This is curiously high praise of a critic who has seemed to later readers opinionated, imperceptive, and even obtuse; and that Dryden's admiration was sincere, though strongly qualified, is demonstrated by his subsequent critical and dramatic writings.[66] If he was never as censorious as Rymer of English infringement of French conceptions of decorum and the dramatic unities, he nevertheless, in *All for Love* (performed late in 1677 and published early in the following year), produced one of the closest—and finest—approximations in English to the kind of tragedy that Racine had made his own, and this notwithstanding a petulant

63. His important rebuttal, *Heads of an Answer to Rymer,* written in 1677, was not published during his lifetime.

64. Cf. Sloman, *Dramatic Craftsmanship of Calderón,* p. 12.

65. John Dryden, *Of Dramatic Poesy and Other Critical Essays,* ed. George Watson (London, 1962), 1 : 208–09.

66. Dryden may have been prejudiced in Rymer's favor by a high compliment paid to him in the preface to Rymer's translation of Rapin's *Reflections on Aristotle's Treatise of Poesie* (1674). In an extended passage Rymer compares, to Dryden's advantage, a description of the night in *The Indian Emperour* with passages on similar subjects in ancient and modern languages. Curt A. Zimansky, ed., *The Critical Works of Thomas Rymer* (New Haven, 1956), pp. 10–16.

reference in his preface to the excessive "nicety of manners" in French tragedy, with an illustrative allusion to *Phèdre*.

All for Love came about seven years after *The Conquest of Granada* and about two years after *Aureng-Zebe,* the last of Dryden's rhymed heroic plays. Between *All for Love* and *Don Sebastian,* confining attention to the serious plays, Dryden reworked Shakespeare's *Troilus and Cressida* and collaborated with Nathaniel Lee on *Oedipus* and *The Duke of Guise. Don Sebastian* was his first major effort in tragedy for a dozen years. He had written the play carefully, he insists in his preface, with attention to neoclassical theory as formulated by Rymer, whose opinion on poetic justice he cites. Yet he also reveals in the preface, in his defense of his comic underplot, a limited emancipation from French precept.

The most obvious formal difference in the practices of Dryden and Calderón lies in the former's loose adherence to "the three *Mechanick rules of unity*" and the latter's departure from two of them. Dryden has interpreted them, he explains, with latitude: *"I knew them and had them in my eye, but follow'd them only at a distance."* He keeps throughout the same *"General Scene"*—the Moorish castle; and he has *"taken the time of two days, because the variety of accidents, which are . . . represented, cou'd not naturally be suppos'd to arrive in one."* He defends the underplot with a prudential appeal to the taste of English audiences, who *"will not bear a thorough tragedy"* but insist on an intermingling of comic scenes. Yet he affirms the close relationship between the underplot and the main action, citing instances in which they are brought into functional relationship. His attitude toward the unities reveals a certain ambiguity the more conspicuous if we think of *Don Sebastian* in contrast with *All for Love.* In the earlier tragedy the unities demanded compression and intensity and conditioned the interpretation of the protagonist.[67] In this later tragedy, they serve no such decisive function and are likely to seem mere *"Mechanick rules,"* evident only to an analytical critic who bothers to look for them amid diversity of episode and tone.

Calderón accepted, of course, the convention of fluidity in time

67. Cf. R. J. Kaufmann, "On the Poetics of Terminal Tragedy," in *Dryden: A Collection of Critical Essays,* ed. Bernard N. Schilling (Englewood Cliffs, N. J., 1963), pp. 86–94.

and space firmly established by Lope de Vega: years of imagined time pass in *El príncipe constante,* and locales, in and around Fez and Tangier, are frequently changed. There is more compression, to be sure, than in the source play, *La fortuna adversa,* but the changes Calderón made were determined by a desire to gain focus and coherence.[68] Yet if we turn from the unities of time and place to that of action, we find a firmer conception in *El príncipe constante* than in *Don Sebastian.* Calderón's play reveals a singleness of preoccupation with the successive phases of Fernando's ordeal as he undergoes transformation from chivalrous knight to Christian martyr that is unlike the dramatic movement in the English play. The apparent divergence in plot line represented by Muley's courtship of Fénix does not constitute a turning away from the central preoccupation because the two characters function, the one as generous friend and the other as symbol of earthly love and beauty, as agents for the elucidation of Fernando's constancy to chivalric and Christian ideals.

El príncipe constante is more uniform in tone than *Don Sebastian;* it is consistently somber, the occasional interjections of the gracioso Brito notwithstanding. The role of the gracioso is muted: his appearances are rare, and some of his remarks reveal more pity than humor, as when on the street of Fez the dying Fernando meets the king for the last time. Even a clown could be moved to compassion by Fernando's plight. Only in the battle scene of the latter part of the first act, when with a Falstaffian conception of courage he escapes by feigning death, is his dramatic function the conventional contrasting one. He responds with the instincts of common humanity to the danger so eagerly sought by the contending knights. The incongruity of a gracioso's chatter with the religious burden of the play would account for the minimal use of the character.

Comic characters are far more prominent in *Don Sebastian,* as prominent as in some of the English tragedies of the Renaissance and as important in the elucidation of theme and tone. Dryden's underplot functions like that in Middleton and Rowley's *The Changeling* by providing comment on the main action by indirection and contrast. The Antonios of both plays carry on intrigues with the wives of their keepers, Dryden's character unwillingly since his primary

68. Sloman, *Dramatic Craftsmanship of Calderón,* pp. 188–216.

objective is the keeper's daughter; and both Antonios, in their exuberance and ingenuity in the pursuit of wanton love, provide parallels to lustful intrigue in the main plots. All this is only tangential to our subject. What is relevant is Dryden's return, neoclassical precept notwithstanding, to an organizational pattern with a long history in English tragic drama—a pattern for which there is a parallel, if not in *El príncipe constante,* then in many other Spanish plays. Dryden's Mustapha, who is "Captain of the Rabble," sometimes speaks in the calculating and cynical tones of the Spanish gracioso. It would be attractive to assume that Dryden was encouraged by Lope's critical pronouncements in introducing contrasting comic scenes, and as noted in an earlier chapter there is some evidence that he was so encouraged.[69] But he could not have found significant precedent in *El príncipe constante.*

In his preface Dryden insists, with an emphasis that is petulant and would seem boastful were it not for the circumstances of his career, on his observance of decorum in characterization: *"And there may be also some secret Beauties in the decorum of parts, and uniformity of design, which my puny judges will not easily find out; let them consider in the last Scene of the fourth Act, whether I have not preserved the rule of decency, in giving all the advantage to the Royal Character; and in making* Dorax *first submit."* It was not poverty of creative imagination, he explains, that led him to make Don Sebastian and Almeyda alike in all respects except their sex, but rather a desire to provide foreshadowing, in depicting *"the greatness of their Souls,"* for the final revelation that they are brother and sister.

The point may seem oversubtle to a modern reader who does not share Dryden's monarchical convictions. It derives from his belief that personal attributes of dramatic characters should be commensurate with their social ranks—in this instance, supreme rank. Dryden was at one with Rymer, René Rapin, and many others on the important principle that drama should embody patterns of behavior that are ideal, in the Platonic sense of representative of types of persons. The Portuguese of his play conduct themselves appropriately to their rank—the two principal characters obviously so, and even

69. See above, pp. 8–9. Dryden's remark about the Spanish critics, reported by Lord Bolingbroke to Joseph Spence, must have been made late in Dryden's life: Bolingbroke was not born until 1678.

Dorax, in his ultimate recognition of the inalienable claim of his sovereign on his loyalty, and Antonio, if allowance is made for his youth and amorous disposition. Dryden would have assumed, as we may conclude from a passage about a usurping sovereign in *The Grounds of Criticism in Tragedy*,[70] that the dynastic conflicts among the Moors gave him freedom in depicting their royal persons. Even so, the emperor Muley-Moluch is the noblest of them, capable of a generous recognition of Don Sebastian's dignity and courage. As elsewhere in his plays, Dryden characterizes a courtier harshly, here the deceitful and rebellious Benducar, "Chief Minister and favourite to the Emperour"; but severity with a traitor does not constitute a breach of decorum. A more difficult case is the sanctimonious and ridiculous Mufti, the self-serving interpreter of the Moslem religion. Yet he is not a Christian clergyman (though his hypocritical quibblings with Moslem law [act 1, scene 1] sound like calculated parodies of the easy accommodation to expediency of some seventeenth-century English clerics) and hence is not immune from Dryden's malignant wit.

El príncipe constante was written sixty years before *Don Sebastian,* before the *Querelle du Cid* and before the appearance of the treatises of Corneille, François Hédelin, René Rapin, and Thomas Rymer that contributed to Dryden's opinions on dramatic characterization and "the decorum of parts." Calderón wrote in an earlier and Spanish context, free from the neat, almost schematic formulations that followed in mid-century France. Yet little in *El príncipe constante* is inconsistent with decorum as Dryden understood the concept. The Portuguese king and princes are admirable; and by the weaker lights of their false religion, the Moorish king and his nephew Muley are but slightly less so. Muley, as already noted, is the generous and chivalrous friend of Fernando. The king of Fez changes from an indulgent captor of Fernando to an oppressive one, whose severity causes Fernando's death from malnutrition and disease. Yet the king's mounting severity is calculated policy, defensible with respect to his own political and religious objectives; it is not the capricious cruelty of a tyrant but the studied and reluctant cruelty of a monarch

70. Dryden writes that Sophocles in *Antigone,* "though he represent in Creon a bloody prince, yet he makes him not a lawful king, but an usurper, and Antigona herself is the heroine of the tragedy." In *Essays,* 1 : 218.

committed to the interests of his country. Nor are the amenities of courtly life violated—those same amenities emphasized by the French later in the century. Even the captive Fernando is deferential to the king. The gracioso speaks in the king's presence, but briefly and without cynical wit. The Spanish dramatist had no need of French theorists to teach him "the decorum of parts."

Like *El príncipe constante* and many other of Calderón's plays, *Don Sebastian* has a concept of "moral" as an organizing principle. Dryden states his "general moral" (whether he knew it or not, in the manner of many Spanish dramatists who interpreted the generalized meaning of their plays in a final speech), *"which is,"* he explains in the preface, *"given in the four last lines."* The lines are spoken by Dorax just after Sebastian and Almeyda have separated:

> And let *Sebastian* and *Almeyda*'s Fate,
> This dreadfull Sentence to the World relate,
> That unrepented Crimes of Parents dead,
> Are justly punish'd on their Childrens head.[71]

That is to say, the moral is the biblical admonition that the sins of the fathers are visited on the children even unto the third and fourth generations. This has seemed harsh to many men, and it apparently seemed harsh to Dryden. In his preface he refers to the inadvertent nature of Don Sebastian's crime: *"for the Learned Mr.* Rymer *has well observ'd, that in all punishments we are to regulate our selves by poetical justice; and according to those measures an involuntary sin deserves not death."* An involuntary sin, but nevertheless a sin, so much is implied by the adverb *justly* in the final line of the play: parents' crimes "Are justly punish'd on their Childrens head."

This was a difficult moral on which to shape a play. In his fortitude and constancy in the humiliating circumstances of captivity, Don Sebastian is scarcely the good but imperfect man described by Aristotle as the most suitable protagonist of tragedy. The contrast with Antony in *All for Love* is marked. Antony's imperfections so overshadow his goodness that the disaster which overwhelms him, a consequence of an inability to free himself from a love that by

71. For a perceptive commentary on the theme summarized in these lines, see Bruce King, *"Don Sebastian:* Dryden's Moral Fable," *Sewanee Review* 70 (1962): 651–70.

Roman standards is reprehensible, may provoke pity but scarcely fear or admiration. *All for Love* may be read, as the title (but not the subtitle, *The World Well Lost*) implies that it should be read, as a study in the choice of a lesser over a greater good; but not so the later play, in which the protagonist lacks the knowledge prerequisite for moral choice.

Yet a remark of Dryden's in the preface of the earlier play reveals that he saw advantages in the kind of situation he later devised in *Don Sebastian*. "That which is wanting to work up the pity to a greater heighth," he writes about the classical sources for the history of Antony and Cleopatra, "was not afforded me by the story: for the crimes of love which they both committed, were not occasion'd by any necessity, or fatal ignorance, but were wholly voluntary; since our passions are, or ought to be, within our power." The comment sounds almost as though Dryden had his plan for *Don Sebastian* in mind, so accurately does he describe "the crimes of love" committed in the play out of "necessity, or fatal ignorance." The title character compels admiration by his manly acceptance of disaster. The traumatic interruption of his marriage evokes pity. His involuntary commission of a terrible sin, which is a consequence of a sin committed in the first instance by his parents, evokes fear because we recognize his experience as a parable of our common experience. We are all, in the Christian interpretation of our condition, the victims of the original sin of Adam and Eve, and thus limited in our understanding of the results of our actions and vulnerable to the gravest kind of error. It follows from the nature of the parable that, because Don Sebastian is primarily a victim rather than an agent of his unfortunate destiny, Dryden can depict only within narrow limits an interrelationship between character and event.

The play is a coherent study in the consequences of sin—of inherited, unexpiated sin producing a later involuntary sin. This is one of the few English tragedies to explore systematically and coherently a legacy of guilt from a preceding generation, already deceased. The subject is somber, and the play is somber, the subplot notwithstanding. Even in the passionate meeting in the second act (scene 1), Don Sebastian and Almeyda are more troubled by the memory of dark warnings than by the present threat of their imprisonment and the emperor's infatuation with Almeyda. Just after Sebastian's proposal, Almeyda avows her own love, not so much in joy as in fear, recalling her mother's admonition:

> . . . Wed not *Almeyda!*
> Forewarn'd *Almeyda,* Marriage is thy Crime.

Sebastian acknowledges that he too has been warned of a horrible marriage:

> Fam'd *Nostradamus,* when he took my Horoscope,
> Foretold my Father I shou'd wed with Incest:

Like Oedipus before him, he lacks the knowledge that could lead him to understand the prognostication.[72] "Ere this unhappy War my Mother dy'd," Don Sebastian explains as much to reassure himself as Almeyda, "And Sisters I had none."

Because *Don Sebastian* is a play with a virtuous protagonist that unfolds the delayed consequences of a sin committed by persons who are not characters in the play, it presents a distinctive problem in tragic theory. The problem resembles, though it is not identical with, that presented by *El príncipe constante,* which has seemed to some critics not to be a tragedy at all. Arnold G. Reichenberger's analysis of Calderón's play will suggest analogies with Dryden's:

> *El príncipe constante* lacks the one essential quality for tragedy, catastrophe at the end. Fernando is a flawless character who lives unflinchingly by a code of hierarchically arranged values, both secular and religious. His death, chosen by himself in the exercise of his *libre albedrío,* is the logical conclusion of his Christian constancy. His re-appearance as a spirit after death brings on the triumph of right. Fernando is a martyr and a saint, but not a tragic hero.

Reichenberger concludes that, rather than a tragedy, *El príncipe constante* "is an exemplary Christian martyr play." [73]

This description cannot apply in detail to *Don Sebastian.* Dryden's

72. On the parallel between Don Sebastian and Oedipus, see King, *Dryden's Major Plays,* p. 166.

73. Reichenberger, "Calderón's *El príncipe constante,* A Tragedy?" in *Critical Essays on the Theatre of Calderón,* ed. Wardropper, p. 163. See also Reichenberger, "The Uniqueness of the *Comedia,*" p. 312.

hero does indeed live "unflinchingly by a code of hierarchically arranged values, both secular and religious." He is constant in his faith, as Dryden explains in the preface: *"In the drawing of his character I forgot not piety which any one may observe to be one principal ingredient of it; even so far as to be a habit in him"*; but he is not flawless, again as Dryden remarks, citing an instance of his deviation from piety *"by the violence of a sudden passion, to endeavour a self-murder."* Yet this is a momentary transport, which is never acted upon; the catastrophe can be related to a flaw of Don Sebastian only if one assumes that he should have heeded the dark warnings both Almeyda and he had received, or his father's injunction against marriage to her, which he considered no longer applicable when she became a Christian. Just as in *El príncipe constante,* emphasis falls, not on interplay of moral choice and consequence, but on the heroic endurance and piety of a near-perfect protagonist.

The piety determines Don Sebastian's and Almeyda's decision to pass the remainder of their lives in secluded religious contemplation. Dorax describes the retreat to which Sebastian is destined to repair (act 5, scene 1):

> Under the ledge of *Atlas,* lyes a Cave,
> Cut in the living Rock, by Natures hands:
> The Venerable Seat of holy Hermites.
> Who there, secure in separated Cells,
> Sacred ev'n to the Moors, enjoy Devotion:
> And from the purling Streams and savage fruits,
> Have wholesome bev'rage, and unbloudy feasts.

Sebastian's brief reply, " 'Tis pennance too Voluptuous, for my crime," testifies to a self-abnegation not unlike Fernando's.

The treatment of Catholic asceticism, so markedly different in its import from the harsh depiction of Catholic hypocrisy and intolerance in *The Indian Emperour,* presumably owes something to Dryden's conversion in 1685. *The Hind and the Panther,* his verse essay in Roman Catholic apologetics, had come in 1687; and just the year before *Don Sebastian* was produced the Revolution had deprived him of his court employments and had placed him in a difficult role as member of a distrusted religious minority—reasons enough for a more appreciative treatment of Catholicism. To be sure, there are jibes, half-disguised in the Mufti's self-serving interpretations of Moslem law, at clerical hypocrisy, but these need not be interpreted as being directed at the Catholics. Dryden retained his acerbity of temper. Neither in *Don Sebastian* nor in any of his other plays did he approximate the intensity of religious devotion that animates *El príncipe constante;* but he could now treat a Catholic theme with fervor. His Don Sebastian is consistently, to use Calderón's closing words about his own Fernando, "príncipe en la fe constante."

VIII: CONCLUSION

Dryden, the Spanish Plays, and Dramatic Tradition

IF Spenser is the poets' poet, Dryden may reasonably be considered the scholars' poet—the one of our classic authors who aids scholars most in mastering their craft. For Dryden was a scholar as well as a poet—not the greatest among the English poets, but the one who first consistently used learning in critical essays to evaluate and interpret literature. He was a theorist of a speculative turn of mind and was concerned with the status of literature as a branch of knowledge; and he was a comparatist, interested in the relative accomplishments of English and foreign literatures, including the Spanish. He watched and wrote about the progress of English literature from his young manhood until his old age, and for many years he did so from a position of eminence as the leading English man of letters. "The life of Dryden," wrote his nineteenth-century biographer and editor Sir Walter Scott, "may be said to comprehend a history of the literature of England, and its changes, during nearly half a century." [1] Because Dryden made frequent use of Spanish history and literature in his plays, sometimes referring in his critical writings to problems he encountered in doing so, his work provides a focus for a study of the Spanish component in the drama at the same time that it represents one of the most important expressions of the Hispanic interests of the Restoration.

The Spanish is just one of many strains in Dryden's dramatic work, and it is as thoroughly assimilated into his distinctive styles in comedy and tragedy as are other influences that can be traced to earlier

1. Scott, *The Life of John Dryden,* ed. Bernard Kreissman (Lincoln, Neb., 1963), p. 1.

drama: Greek, Roman, Italian, French, and Renaissance English. Himself a late Renaissance figure, Dryden was acutely aware of literary tradition, of his dependence on those who had preceded him. He shared with Calderón, Moreto, and many others the classical conception of literary property. *"'Tis the contrivance, the new turn, and new characters, which alter the property and make it ours,"* he wrote in the preface of *Don Sebastian: "The* Materia Poetica *is as common to all Writers, as the* Materia Medica *to all Physicians."*

As if to illustrate the point, which had become controversial by reason of Langbaine's attack on him, Dryden took for his next play, *Amphitryon,* a story that can be traced to Plautus and beyond and that had recently served Molière well. Earlier he had, with Nathaniel Lee, written *Oedipus,* transforming Sophocles's famous story into an English neoclassical tragedy. He had turned, through French intermediaries, to the Italian commedia dell'arte, when early in his career he had, with the Duke of Newcastle, written *Sir Martin Mar-all,* one of the most successful of the English approximations to that form of Italian farcical comedy. He turned to French prose fiction as well as drama, in *Secret Love* and *Marriage à la Mode,* for example, both of which include borrowings from the romances. He used Corneille as one of his principal models for the heroic play. In elaborating his theory of the heroic play, he ranged among classical and Renaissance epics as well as French and English drama. He turned three times to Shakespeare: for *The Tempest* (written with Davenant), *All for Love,* and *Troilus and Cressida.* Not the least of the claims of Dryden's plays on our attention is their summation of late Renaissance themes and literary attitudes.

Although I have concentrated on his Spanish subjects and borrowings, I must not convey what would be a mistaken impression that they are more consequential than well-defined components of his inheritance from other dramas, notably the French and English. His "Spanish plays"—if I may thus for convenience designate his plays based on Spanish or Portuguese history and those that are, at a considerable distance, modeled on the comedia—should be seen within the total range of accomplishment in drama of this prolific and learned man. He chose not to follow his contemporaries, the Cavalier dramatists of the 1660s, in imitating closely the pattern of the cape and sword play. He did approach that pattern in *The Rival Ladies,* written at the height of the vogue of the Spanish plot; but even in that experimental play he revealed his independence by anticipating the wit dialogue and deflationary astringency for which he was soon to become famous. Unlike Tuke, Bristol, Sydserf, and even Davenant, Dryden did not consistently follow a single source, in *The Rival Ladies* or any other of his Spanish plays, showing rather an eclecticism in his use of foreign and English dramatic models. In his work, Spanish materials are assimilated into the mainstream of the Restoration dramatic tradition.

Dryden's limited appreciation for the comedia will by now be apparent and so will some of the reasons why it was limited. The principal reasons were his lack of knowledge of the best Spanish plays and the incompatibility between his own and the Spaniards' assumptions in critical theory.

Dryden's narrow range of knowledge of the comedia was typical of the Restoration dramatists. So far as is known, none of them borrowed from Lope, though two, Sydserf and Crowne, wrote adaptations of Moreto's *No puede ser,* which is in turn based on Lope's *El mayor imposible.* Lope's name was familiar; in fact, he was, so far as I have been able to determine, the only Spanish critic referred to by Dryden or any other English writer in the late seventeenth century. Yet not until Lewis Theobald's preface to *The Fatal Secret* in 1735 do we encounter a detailed assessment of one of his plays.

No one, with the doubtful exception of Colley Cibber in *She Would and She Would Not,* borrowed directly from Tirso. Cibber's play includes borrowings from *Don Gil de las calzas verdes,* and no intermediary story or play is known, but it would seem to me unlikely that Cibber read the Spanish original. We know much about Cibber, who wrote his autobiography, and we find no indication that he had a special knowledge of or interest in Spanish drama. John Leanerd drew from Tirso at second hand when he based his *The Counterfeits* on Moreto's *La ocasión hace al ladrón,* itself an adaptation of Tirso's *La villana de Vallecas.* So also Shadwell in a much more important play, *The Libertine,* drew from Tirso's *El Burlador de Sevilla* through French plays as intermediaries. The English, again, seem to have known Rojas Zorrilla only through the French. In the 1660s Davenant based his *The Man's the Master* on Scarron's rendering of *Donde hay agravios no hay celos;* and in the first decade of the eighteenth century Vanbrugh, in *The False Friend,* followed Le Sage's rendering of *La traición busca el castigo.*

The English dramatists turned frequently to Calderón, but except for *La vida es sueño* and the doubtful case of *El príncipe constante,* only to his intrigue comedies. The predilection for Calderón can partly be explained by the fact that Lord Bristol, who alone among the dramatists had known Spanish from childhood, wrote adaptations of three of his cape and sword plays. The frequency with which borrowings from those three plays, *No siempre lo peor es cierto, Mejor está que estaba,* and *Peor está que estaba,* continue to appear can scarcely be coincidental. If the later dramatists Aphra Behn, perhaps Durfey, and the eighteenth century Richard Savage, did not draw on Bristol's work, they must have been influenced by Bristol's precedent in their choices of sources.

The English credited Calderón, we now believe erroneously, with *Los empeños de seis horas,* the source of Tuke's *Five Hours.* Tuke's adaptation and the three by Bristol were the decisive ones in establishing the Restoration conception of the comedia. Dryden and Wycherley, too, turned to Calderón's intrigue comedies, though they reworked their borrowings thoroughly, producing independent and distinctively English plays that are fundamentally different from the close adaptations of the Cavaliers. Only Aphra Behn, in *The Young King,* provides an unambiguous example of borrowing from one of Calderón's serious plays. Whether she worked directly from the Spanish text of *La vida es sueño* or used some Dutch or French version of it cannot, I think, be determined; in any event, she retained little of the philosophical subtlety of Calderón's masterpiece.

A critical remark of Wildblood in *An Evening's Love* bears repetition, so succinctly does it convey Dryden's own response to an important characteristic of the cape and sword plays (act 5, scene 1): "I hate your *Spanish* honor ever since it spoyl'd our *English* Playes." The history of the Spanish plots in England would be very different if Wildblood's—and Dryden's—opinion on the subject had been shared by all the dramatists. Yet increasingly as the years passed, it was shared by the abler dramatists who borrowed from the comedia —Wycherley, Aphra Behn, Crowne, Vanbrugh, and Cibber, among others—who treated the *pundonor* with casualness or contempt. So central is "Spanish honor" to the comedia that a modification in the treatment of it on the English stage resulted in plays with very different moral structures. Few of the better dramatists cared to approximate, without satirical comment, the Spanish gravity of manner and sensitivity to affront. Hence the paradox that the best renderings of Spanish plots, by Dryden and his younger contemporaries, are those most thoroughly anglicized—sometimes, as in Wycherley and Crowne, anglicized in characters and settings as well as in evaluations of codes of conduct.

Except for the one uncertain case in *The Indian Emperour,* Dryden made no attempt to imitate the long Spanish monologue, that convention of the comedia least reconcilable to the English stage—a convention which helped the Spaniards make their characters' devotion to the point of honor credible. Of those differences in the dramatic traditions of the two nations that inhibited the English in their borrowings from the comedia, one of the most important is the English avoidance and the Spanish acceptance of the long speech, expository or lyrical, by which the Spaniards could quickly explain a complex sequence of events or provide an analysis of a state of mind. When the English wrote adaptations of Spanish plays, they were compelled by the custom of their stage to abridge the speeches or to break them up into conversational exchanges, and neither alternative permitted the expository speed or psychological subtlety of the originals.

Despite their complexity, the plots of the comedia seldom seem hurried or confused, partly because characters were permitted by convention to speak at length and without interruption, explaining in detail their motives for action. Characters on the English stage were not so privileged, and the loss is considerable in terms of speed and clarity, and even more, perhaps, in emotional nuance. The long speech is a principal vehicle for the poetry of the comedia, and no matter how gifted an English poet-translator might have been, that vehicle was not available to him if he wished to have his play performed.

The better Restoration dramatists who borrowed from the comedia followed English convention in dialogue, and in doing so they lessened interest in the suspense provided by an intrigue plot. In Dryden, and still more in Wycherley, intrigue is subordinated to or obscured by wit dialogue with a satirical edge. Even in one of the early and close adaptations of the Cavaliers, Sydserf's *Tarugo's Wiles,* the shift in balance from intrigue to conversational review of manners is discernible; and the shift is emphatic in Crowne's reworking in *Sir Courtly Nice* of Sydserf's source play, Moreto's *No puede ser*. The approximation to comedy of manners in Sydserf and the achievement of it in Crowne is at least partially attributable to the nature of Moreto's play, in which aberrations in behavior are satirically rebuked and the code of honor is examined humorously—not repudiated but still subjected to clear-eyed scrutiny. Moreto comes closer to comedy of manners as Restoration Englishmen understood the form than Calderón did, and yet Calderón could raise a laugh at absurd behavior. If conventions of Spanish dialogue compelled the English in their borrowings from him to invent their own repartee, they nevertheless found situations in his plays that served their comic purposes. Even from the period of the 1660s the Spanish plots include qualities that can be associated with the comedy of manners.

Except perhaps in Wycherley, the plays with borrowings from Calderón retain his emphasis on a strong narrative line. As we try to define the nebulous quality of the "influence" of the Spanish plots on Restoration comic tradition, we find a trace of it in the reinforcement of the English fondness for a good story. There was nothing new in England about drama of action as differentiated from drama of character. More of Shakespeare's plays than we sometimes remember subordinate character to story, and even more of Fletcher's do so. Both Shakespeare and Fletcher were popular on the Restoration stage. But Ben Jonson's comedies, with their emphasis on vivid character and disjunctive episode, also enjoyed high reputation, and the example they provided was reinforced by that of Molière, from whose plays the English dramatists frequently borrowed. We have only to think of the comedies of Shadwell and the two later comedies of Wycherley to understand the power of the Jonson-Molière example in forcing attention to character and episode at the expense of plot line.

The comedia provided a countercurrent of indeterminate effectiveness. Its results can be illustrated in Mrs. Behn's plays, none of them close adaptations from the comedia though there are occasional borrowings—plays with multiple and emphatic plot lines, some of which look as though they are Spanish in origin even when they are not. Her plays are definitely English, in moral assumptions as in conversational convention; and yet they are plays of action in the Spanish manner, some of them with situations deriving from the comedia or from Spanish prose fiction. We can assume, I think, that one of the reasons why the force of the Jonsonian example was not stronger on the Restoration stage was an enduring affection, encouraged by the Spanish plots, for a good story.

Mrs. Behn, like Dryden and other English dramatists, used Spanish narrative materials even while dispensing with the severity of moral judgment portrayed in the originals. Her transformation of *La vida es sueño* into a romantic story subordinated to a plot drawn from French prose fiction is an extreme example of the modification of moral and emotional structure that occurred when the English took over Spanish materials. Sometimes the modification had been initiated in a French intermediary: Rojas Zorrilla's tragedy of divine retribution, *La traición busca el castigo,* had already become a comedy in Le Sage's refashioning of it before it became, in Vanbrugh's *The False Friend,* a cynical Restoration comedy of sexual intrigue. Only Shadwell, in *The Libertine,* wrote an important play that approaches the tragic force of a Spanish original. Yet he worked through French intermediaries, producing a play that, however remarkable, is notably different from *El Burlador de Sevilla.* In the unlikely event that Dryden borrowed from *El príncipe constante* for *The Indian Emperour,* he departed from the dramatic movement and religious theme of the source play.

In tragedy the relations of English to Spanish drama command interest, not so much because of borrowings, direct or indirect, as because of parallels in literary strategy and heroic ideals. The affinities between the tragic dramas of the two countries illustrate the pervasiveness of an international literary culture. French tragedy served as a bridge between them, but of more consequence than any links that can be traced through Corneille and his contemporaries is the acceptance by the English and Spanish, as well as the French, of similar chivalric and heroic ideals of conduct. Strategies for celebrating magnanimous heroism are to some extent common to the work of Dryden, Corneille, and Calderón, each in his time his country's leading dramatist. Parallels in rhetorical patterns exist amid differences arising from attitudes toward neoclassical theory. Calderón was not ignorant of or indifferent to that theory, but he chose to follow conventions of Spanish drama that were incompatible with it, whereas Corneille and Dryden—both of them at times grudgingly—shaped their plays to conform to it.

The English of the Restoration period held a more restrictive conception of dramatic genre than did the Spanish—or for that matter the English—of the Renaissance, a conception in which notions of propriety and decorum were strong. Dryden's disdain for the gracioso is symptomatic of his own and his fellow dramatists' lack of sympathy for the Spaniards' use of contrasting, often incongruously contrasting, characters and emotional attitudes. The English plays are not without broadly comic characters, some of whom approximate the qualities and the function of the gracioso; but apart from Sancho Panza in Durfey's rendering of *Don Quijote,* there are few faithful and successful naturalizations of the dramatic type. Dryden felt uncomfortable in the presence of the drolling Diegos, and we may plausibly attribute his discomfort to his neoclassicism. His attitude is a corollary of the preference for decorum, tidiness, and clarity in dramatic structure that led him to rework Shakespeare's *Troilus and Cressida.*

Dryden was ambivalent about the Spanish Renaissance accomplishment. Spain was to him and his fellow dramatists a reservoir of literary material, of intrigue plots set in exotic places. With its neighbor Portugal it was a country of heroic endeavor—of the discovery and conquest of the New World, of the reconquest of the Peninsula from the Moors, of the gallant if foolhardy expedition of Don Sebastian into Africa. But it was also a country of fanatical Catholicism, the perpetrator of atrocities practiced in the name of religion. And the drama of Spain seemed to Dryden and his literary contemporaries at once attractive and faulty, entertaining and yet presenting critical problems not unlike those they encountered in the Renaissance drama of England.

INDEX